Outward Foreign Direct Investment in ASEAN

The **ISEAS – Yusof Ishak Institute** (formerly Institute of Southeast Asian Studies) was established as an autonomous organization in 1968. It is a regional centre dedicated to the study of socio-political, security and economic trends and developments in Southeast Asia and its wider geostrategic and economic environment. The Institute's research programmes are the Regional Economic Studies (RES, including ASEAN and APEC), Regional Strategic and Political Studies (RSPS), and Regional Social and Cultural Studies (RSCS).

ISEAS Publishing, an established academic press, has issued more than 2,000 books and journals. It is the largest scholarly publisher of research about Southeast Asia from within the region. ISEAS Publishing works with many other academic and trade publishers and distributors to disseminate important research and analyses from and about Southeast Asia to the rest of the world.

Outward Foreign Direct Investment in ASEAN

EDITED BY

CASSEY LEE
SINEENAT SERMCHEEP

ISEAS YUSOF ISHAK
INSTITUTE

First published in Singapore in 2017 by
ISEAS Publishing
30 Heng Mui Keng Terrace
Singapore 119614

E-mail: publish@iseas.edu.sg
Website: <http://bookshop.iseas.edu.sg>

The responsibility for facts and opinions in this publication rests exclusively with the author and his interpretations do not necessarily reflect the views or the policy of the publisher or its supporters.

ISEAS Library Cataloguing-in-Publication Data

Outward Foreign Direct Investment in ASEAN / edited by Cassey Lee and Sineenat Sermcheep.
1.   Investments, Foreign—Southeast Asia.
2.   Investments, Southeast Asian.
I.   Lee, Cassey.
II. Sineenat Sermcheep.
HG5740.8 O93   2017

ISBN 978-981-47-6240-3 (soft cover)
ISBN 978-981-47-6241-0 (e-book, PDF)

Typeset by Superskill Graphics Pte Ltd
Printed in Singapore by Markono Print Media Pte Ltd

CONTENTS

LIST OF TABLES

LIST OF FIGURES

FOREWORD

Outward foreign direct investment (OFDI) from developing countries has been growing significantly since the turn of the century. According to a recent study by UNCTAD, the share of developing country's outward FDI to global outflows has increased from 11.79 per cent in 2000 to 33.79 per cent in 2014. These growing outflows are driven by an increase in capital and trade openness from globalization and economic integration, and an increase in participation in international production networks.

ASEAN, a group of mostly developing countries in Southeast Asia, has, in between times, played an active role in international investment. Many ASEAN countries are already destinations of FDI from the developed economies. More recently, some of these countries have adjusted their own positions from being net capital inflow countries to become net capital outflow countries. Today, the obvious major investors from ASEAN are Singapore, Malaysia, and Thailand — collectively generating 79.54 per cent of outward FDI from ASEAN in 2014. With the advent of the ASEAN Economic Community (AEC) in 2016 and beyond, these net capital outflows from ASEAN to other destinations will continue to expand.

As a matter of fact, outward FDI from ASEAN countries is only at the beginning stage, so there is no wonder why literature on the topic is still very limited. To understand the integrated picture of outward FDI and to foresee the potential future of outward FDI in ASEAN, an overview of outward FDI in the region as well as the role of AEC should be examined. By bringing in the experiences from each country, as major investors or as major recipients of FDI, and the new players in the region will help to contribute to a more complete and integrated picture of international investment in ASEAN.

For this reason, ASEAN Studies Center and the Faculty of Economics, Chulalongkorn University and ISEAS – Yusof Ishak Institute jointly cooperated in this book project. The objectives of this book are to: (1) discuss the development of outward FDI in ASEAN; (2) examine the potential impact of AEC on outward FDI in ASEAN; and (3) discuss the experiences of the major investors from ASEAN (Singapore, Malaysia, Thailand), potential investors (Vietnam and Indonesia) and a major recipient of FDI (Myanmar). The seminar for the book project was organized with the cooperation of all parties concerned. Finally, we would like to thank the editors, chapter writers and the secretariat support staff from both institutions.

Suthiphand Chirathivat
Executive Director, ASEAN Studies Center, Chulalongkorn University

ABOUT THE CONTRIBUTORS

Kornkarun Cheewatrakoolpong is an Associate Professor at the Faculty of Economics, Chulalongkorn University, Bangkok. She is a coordinator of "The study of Thailand's outward FDI", sponsored by Thailand Research Fund (TRF). She publishes "Trade Diversification and Crisis Transmission: A Case Study of Thailand" in Asian Economic Journal and "Trade linkages and crisis spillovers" in Asian Economic Papers. She also has several published papers, chapters of edited volumes and journal articles. Her current work concentrates on trade facilitation, production networks, and FDI.

Aekapol Chongvilaivan is a Country Economist for the Philippines at Asian Development Bank (ADB). He undertakes economic analysis and assessments of ADB's operations in the Philippines and provides technical advice to the Government on its macroeconomic management and structural reforms, and helps facilitate necessary capacity development. Prior to joining ADB, he was Fellow at the Institute of Southeast Asian Studies in Singapore (now known as the ISEAS – Yusof Ishak Institute). He holds a PhD in Economics from the National University of Singapore. He has published in several academic journals such as *Economic Inquiry*, *Labour Economics*, *British Journal of Industrial Relations*, and *Social Indicators Research*.

Cassey Lee is a Senior Fellow at the ISEAS – Yusof Ishak Institute, Singapore. Dr Lee has held academic appointments at the University of Wollongong, Australia, University of Nottingham Malaysia Campus and University of Malaya. Dr Lee received his PhD from University of California, Irvine. He is currently the managing editor for the *Journal of Southeast Asian Economies*.

Lee Chew Ging is the Dean and Professor of Quantitative Methods at Faculty of Social Sciences, University of Nottingham Malaysia Campus. His research papers have been published in peer reviewed journals such as *Applied Economics*, *Journal of Sport Economics*, *Journal of International Development*, *International Journal of Tourism Research*, *Tourism Management* and *International Journal of Hospitality Management*.

Jayant Menon, PhD is Lead Economist in the Economic Research Department at the Asian Development Bank in Manila, Philippines. He holds adjunct appointments with the Australian National University and the University of Nottingham. He is the author or co-author of more than one hundred academic publications, mostly on trade and development, and particularly as they relate to Asia.

Tin Htoo Naing is a researcher at the Center for Economy, Environment and Society (CEES Myanmar) and a visiting lecturer in development economics at Yangon Institute of Economics. He holds a PhD in Economic Policy, Growth and Inequality from University of Malaya, Malaysia. He was an International Research Associate at Asia-Europe Institute, University of Malaya, Malaysia, a Senior Policy Advisor for the Garman Agency for International Cooperation, Myanmar, and a Research Fellow at University of Turin in Italy. As an economist, he possesses sound knowledge and broad experience of providing advisory services for economic policy-making, law-drafting and evaluating projects in Myanmar and works as an Economic Policy Advisor to international institutions. He was also deeply involved in many research areas related to macroeconomic policy, economic integration, inequality and poverty alleviation, agricultural and industrial development and published papers in journals, project reports and international conferences.

Teo Yen Nee is a PhD candidate at the Institute of Malaysian and International Studies, the National University of Malaysia. She graduated with a Bachelor of Arts double majored in Economics and History at the National University of Malaysia, and Msc. Economics from the same university.

Maxensius Tri Sambodo is a Senior Researcher at the Indonesian Institute of Sciences (LIPI) — Economic Research Center. He is also a visiting fellow alumni from the Institute of Southeast Asian Studies (ISEAS), Singapore.

His research interests are on economic development, energy, environment, and natural resources. He obtained a bachelor degree in Economics from Padjadjaran University, Indonesia; masters in International and Development Economic from the Australian National University; and PhD in Public Policy from the National Graduate Institute for Policy Studies (GRIPS), Japan. His latest articles appeared in *ASEAN Energy Market Integration (AEMI): From Coordination to Integration* (2013) and *Government and Communities: Sharing Indonesia's Common Goals* (2014), and his latest book *From Darkness to Light: Energy Security Assessment in Indonesia's Power Sector* is published by ISEAS – Yusof Ishak Institute in 2016.

Panutat Satchachai is an Assistant Professor in Economics, and currently is the Associate Dean taking care of research affairs at the Faculty of Economics at Chulalongkorn University. His research interests are in econometrics and international finance, especially the modelling for foreign direct investments. His other research projects include the economic issues on border trade and investment in the CLMV countries.

Sineenat Sermcheep is an Associate Dean at the Faculty of Economics and the Director of Research Affairs at ASEAN Studies Center, Chulalongkorn University, Thailand. She has a PhD in Economics from the University of Utah and is currently an Assistant Professor in Economics. She mainly undertakes research related to foreign direct investment, economic integration and ASEAN. Her other areas of interest include trade in services and economic development.

Pitchaya Sirivunnabood, PhD in Economics, is an Assistant Director of Financial Integration Division, ASEAN Economic Community Department, ASEAN Secretariat. Her expertise is in the areas of international economics and finance, specializing in regional economic integration and financial cooperation as well as bilateral and multilateral free trade agreements, development of financial markets, and international/transnational investments. Previously, as the Senior Economist at the ASEAN Integration Monitoring Office, ASEAN Secretariat, she was also in charge of monitoring the progress of the ASEAN Economic Community (AEC), including other related regional economic surveillance mechanisms.

Hoang Thi Thu is Associate Professor in Economics and Dean of the Faculty of Banking and Finance at the Thainguyen University of Economics and

Business Administration in Vietnam. She holds an MA in Economics from University of Hawaii at Manoa and received her PhD in Economics from Chulalongkorn University, Bangkok. Her research interests include foreign direct investment, economic growth and financial management in Vietnam.

Jean-Pierre A. Verbiest is a senior economist based in Southeast Asia since over thirty years. He holds a BA in economics and finance from FUCAM in Mons (Belgium), an MSc in Econometrics from the Universite Libre de Bruxelles (ULB, Belgium) and a doctorate in economics from Oxford University (UK). He joined the United Nations Commission for Asia and the Pacific (UNESCAP) in Bangkok, Thailand in 1981 as a research economist, moving to the Economic Research Department of the Asian Development Bank (ADB) in Manila, the Philippines, in 1989. He held several senior positions in the ADB including Manager, Strategy and Policy Department, Assistant Chief Economist (Macro-economics and Finance) and Country Director in Viet Nam (1996–2000) and Thailand (2005–10). In 2011–12, he was principal consultant (ASEAN 2030 study) for the Asian Development Bank Institute (ADBI, Tokyo) and in 2013–14 he was lead consultant/team leader for the ADB's Economic Research Department diagnostic study on Myanmar. He is Policy Advisor, Mekong Institute, and a partner in West Indochina Inc. His principal research interests are macroeconomic policies in East and Southeast Asian countries, economic reforms in Myanmar and regional economic and financial cooperation and integration in Asia.

Tham Siew Yean is a Senior Fellow at the ISEAS – Yusof Ishak Institute, Singapore and Adjunct Professor at Institute of Malaysian and International Studies (IKMAS), Universiti Kebangsaan Malaysia. She was formerly Director and Professor at IKMAS, Universiti Kebangsaan Malaysia. She has served as a consultant to national agencies in Malaysia and international agencies, including the World Bank, Asian Development Bank, and Asian Development Bank Institute. She has also published extensively on foreign direct investment, international trade in goods and services, trade policies, and industrial development in Malaysia and ASEAN. She has a PhD in Economics from the University of Rochester, USA.

Michael Yeo is a Research Associate at the ISEAS – Yusof Ishak Institute, Singapore. Michael was educated at the SOAS University of London and the London School of Economics. An economic historian, Michael is currently pursuing his doctoral studies at the University of Oxford.

Andrew Kam Jia Yi is a Research Fellow at the Institute of Malaysian and International Studies, the National University of Malaysia. He graduated First Class in BSc Economics specializing in Econometrics at the National University of Malaysia, MSc Economics from Warwick University, UK and PhD from the Australian National University (ANU). He was the recipient of the Chevening Scholarship in 2005, Australian Endeavour Postgraduate in 2008 and the 2014–15 Malaysian Fulbright Scholarship programme. His research interests include international trade, industrialization and economic growth.

INTRODUCTION

Cassey Lee and Sineenat Sermcheep

Southeast Asian countries have historically engaged in international trade long before the arrival of European colonial powers in the sixteenth century. The prospects and potential gains from trade and the control of the sources of natural commodities attracted these powers and eventually led to the colonization of much of Southeast Asia. With the exception of Thailand, which was never colonized by any European power, much of Southeast Asia became further integrated with the global economy as foreign colonies. In the aftermath of the Second World War, countries in the region gained independence and with it, sought to develop their economies via export-oriented industrialization. This did not take place simultaneously and concurrently amongst countries in the region. Political and institutional differences meant that some countries (such as Malaysia, Singapore, Thailand and Indonesia) had an earlier headstart than others (such as Cambodia, Laos, Myanmar and Vietnam). As a result, there are still large differences in the level of development amongst countries in the region. This continues to be a significant challenge for member countries of the Association of Southeast Asian Nations (ASEAN) as they seek to achieve higher levels of regional economic integration.

One important manifestation of the differences in the level of development amongst ASEAN member countries is the difference in the patterns of foreign direct investment (FDI). At the initial stage of development, most ASEAN countries have abundant labour but lacked capital and technology. For ASEAN countries that adopted the export-oriented industrialization strategy early, the inflow of foreign direct investment (inward FDI) into the export-oriented industries in the manufacturing sector helped overcome these limitations. Over time, as higher levels of development and income per capita were attained, the factor composition in these more developed ASEAN countries began to tilt towards greater capital intensity and higher technology. At this juncture, enterprises in these countries, both local and foreign-owned, began seeking countries abroad to invest in — with the hope of establishing production facilities and/or accessing the final markets in these countries. The result is the emergence of outward FDI (OFDI) from the more developed ASEAN countries. The above transformation has been observed amongst ASEAN countries. Singapore, Malaysia and more recently Thailand has become net-investors in which outward FDI exceeded inward FDI.

Despite the increasing importance of OFDI in ASEAN countries, relatively little research has been published on the topic. The goal of this book is to rectify this research and literature gap. This is achieved by examining and assessing the current state of OFDI in ASEAN countries. This is undertaken using two approaches. The first approach seeks to analyse OFDI from a cross-country and regional (ASEAN) perspective. The second approach looks at outward FDI from country perspectives.

BOOK COVERAGE

Cross-country and regional analyses of OFDI in the ASEAN region are covered in the first three chapters of this volume. Sineenat Sermcheep (Chapter 1) provides a review of the literature on OFDI as well as the recent trends in the patterns of OFDI in ASEAN countries. The chapter also examines the experiences of East Asian countries and draw some important lessons for ASEAN countries. The issue of intra-ASEAN OFDI is examined by Aekapol Chongvilaivan and Jayant Menon (Chapter 2). The authors also identify and discuss some of the key OFDI players in the region. The ASEAN framework and agreements for regional investment integration is discussed in the chapter by Pitchaya Sirivunnabood (Chapter 3). The author also discusses future challenges facing ASEAN member countries and ASEAN (as an institution) in promoting greater regional economic integration via intra-regional direct investments.

The country case studies on OFDI in this volume covers Singapore, Malaysia, Indonesia, Thailand, Vietnam and Myanmar. The case of Singapore is examined by Cassey Lee, Chew Ging Lee and Michael Yeo (Chapter 4).

The authors provide a review of the Singaporean government's policy on OFDI and analyse the country's OFDI trends. This is supplemented by an econometric analysis of the drivers of the country's OFDI. Malaysia OFDI patterns and drivers are examined by Tham Siew Yean, Teo Yen Nee and Andrew Kam Jia Yi (Chapter 5). Indonesia's OFDI trends are analysed by Maxensius Tri Sambodo (Chapter 6). In addition, the chapter reviews the country's OFDI in Singapore (as a country destination) and MNE's involvement in OFDI. Kornkarun Cheewatrakoolpong and Panutat Satchachai (Chapter 7) review OFDI trends in Thailand and provide an econometric analysis of the determinants of OFDI in Thailand in two groups of ASEAN countries, namely, the ASEAN-5 and CLMV countries. The case of Vietnam is examined by Hoang Thi Thu (Chapter 8). In her chapter, the author traces the evolution of OFDI-related policies, regulations and laws in Vietnam as well as OFDI trends during different periods. Myanmar as a country destination for ASEAN OFDI is discussed by Jean-Pierre A. Verbiest and Tin Htoo Naing (Chapter 9).

MAIN FINDINGS

The level of outward FDI flows from ASEAN countries has increased rapidly in the past two decades despite reversals during periods of economic crises in 1997/98 and 2008. There has been an increase in intra-ASEAN OFDI flows particularly since 2009. As expected, there is significant diversity in terms of the size of OFDI flows across ASEAN countries. Singapore has been a major investor for some time. Malaysia, Thailand and Indonesia are relatively newcomers to OFDI. More recently, OFDI from Vietnam has also increased rapidly. OFDI flows from ASEAN countries have focused primarily in three sectors, namely, manufacturing, financial services and real estate.

What are the drivers of the OFDI flows in ASEAN countries? The theoretical explanations for OFDI ranges from macro-level theories incorporating elements from the Product Life Cycle theory to the more micro-oriented approach by Dunning. The former charts the evolution of production for domestic markets to production from foreign base driven by changes in domestic input and output markets as countries become more developed. Dunning's theory emphasizes on ownership, locational and internalization advantages that accrue to firms from investing abroad. The list of OFDI drivers have also been mapped to different types of

FDI — market-seeking, efficiency-seeking, resource-seeking and strategic asset-seeking. The empirical evidence documented in this volume suggest that the drivers of OFDI differ across different industries and sectors. Key drivers include market size, tax rates, trade cost, transport cost and trade agreements. These results and the qualitative evidence from country case studies point to the importance of trade and domestic policies as well as regulations that can enhance OFDI. Finally, the prospects of OFDI in ASEAN countries are promising, especially OFDI from more developed ASEAN countries to less developed ASEAN countries. The rising importance of intra-ASEAN OFDI supports this view.

1

THE RISE OF OUTWARD FOREIGN DIRECT INVESTMENT FROM ASEAN

Sineenat Sermcheep

1. INTRODUCTION

Over the past decade, developing economies have been actively investing abroad. This is reflected in their share of the world foreign direct investment (FDI) outflows which increased significantly from 11.87 per cent in 2000 to a record of 35 per cent in 2014 (Table 1.1). In particular, due to the surge in outward foreign direct investment (OFDI) from Asian developing economies since 2005, developing Asia became the world's largest investor region for the first time in 2014, accounting for approximately one-third of the global FDI outflows (UNCTAD 2015).

A number of countries from the Association of Southeast Asian Nations (ASEAN) have become major players in the investment arena. Even though ASEAN countries have been major recipients of FDI, they have evolved into an emerging source of investment for many developing economies, especially in the ASEAN region (ASEAN Secretariat 2013). The overall FDI outflow from ASEAN rose rapidly from US$8.97 billion in 2000 to US$56.36 billion in 2013 (Table 1.1).

TABLE 1.1
ASEAN FDI Outflows, 1980–2013 (in US$ million and per cent)

	1980	1990	2000	2010	2012	2013
World	51,252	241,614	1,241,223	1,467,580	1,346,671	1,410,810
Developing economies	2,855	11,317	147,372	420,919	440,164	454,067
ASEAN	394	2,328	8,972	57,546	53,834	56,361
% of World	0.77	0.96	0.72	3.92	4.00	3.99
% of Developing	13.79	20.57	6.09	13.67	12.23	12.41

Source: UNCTAD.

TABLE 1.2
Selected Top 20 Sources of OFDI in Asia, 2014

Rank in 2014		FDI Outflows (US$ billion)		Growth Rate (%)
		2014	2013	2014/2013
2	Hong Kong	143	81	76.54
3	China	116	101	14.85
10	Singapore	41	29	41.38
13	Korea	31	28	10.71
17	Malaysia	16	14	14.29
20	Taiwan	13	14	−7.14

Source: UNCTAD (2015).

Among the top source countries for OFDI, two leading investors from ASEAN — Singapore and Malaysia — made it to the 10th and the 17th rank respectively in 2014 (Table 1.2). Other major investors from East Asia are Hong Kong, Korea, Taiwan and China. The first three have long been leading global investors since the past few decades while China has become the major source of OFDI recently, with a rapid rise in overseas investment. Aside from Singapore, Malaysia and Thailand have emerged as net investors in 2007 and 2011, respectively.

This new FDI landscape in ASEAN has been shaped by many factors including the increase in mergers and acquisitions (M&As) and the rising importance of the region as a key player in the global value chain. In addition, ASEAN's outward investment has been enhanced by regional economic integration. The ASEAN Economic Community (AEC) aims to

FIGURE 1.1
Outward FDI Flows from Selected ASEAN Countries, 2010–13

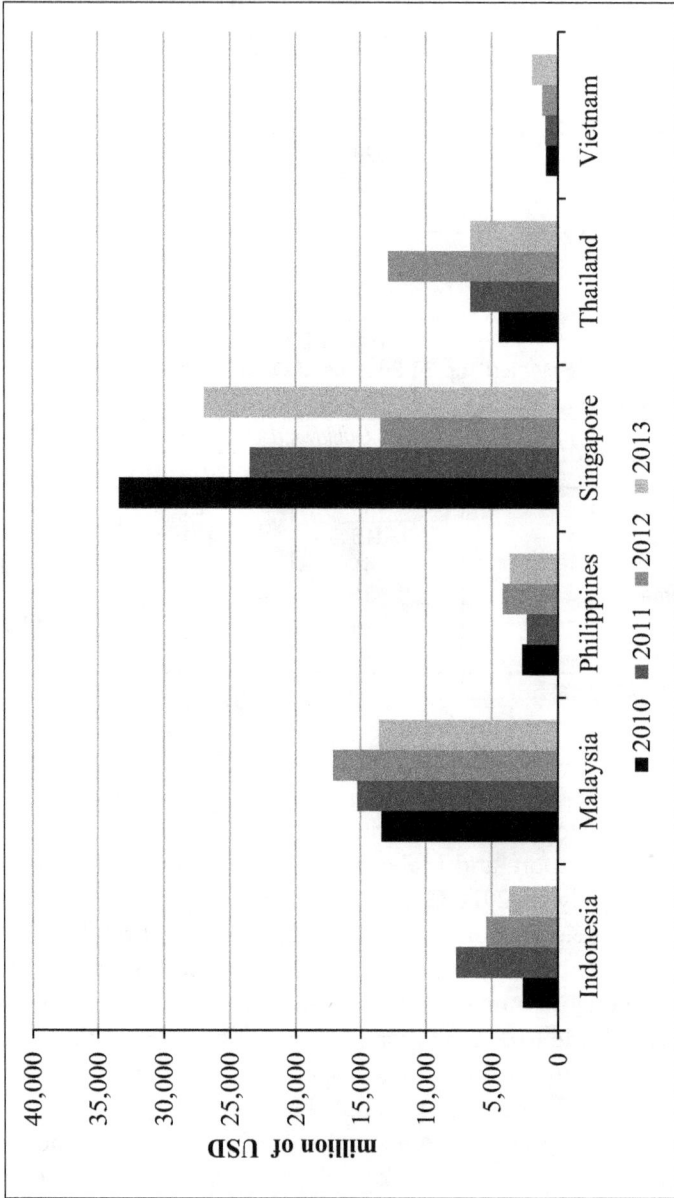

Source: UNCTAD.

achieve a single market and production base in the region. Governments of ASEAN member states have been actively encouraging their national companies to invest abroad to take advantage of the benefits of the AEC (ASEAN Secretariat 2013).

This chapter aims to examine the development of outward FDI in ASEAN countries, its characteristics and motives, as well as prospects for the future. The rest of this chapter is organized as follows: Section 2 provides a brief review of literature on outward FDI from developing countries; Section 3 presents the development, characteristics and motives of ASEAN's FDI outflow; Section 4 examines lessons for ASEAN countries that can be drawn from the experiences of major East Asian investors — China, Hong Kong, Korea and Taiwan. The conclusion is presented in Section 5.

2. OUTWARD FDI FROM DEVELOPING ECONOMIES

It is imperative to review the theories on outward FDI from developing countries in order to develop a theoretical framework where the case of FDI from ASEAN can be examined.

2.1 Ownership Advantages

According to Dunning (1993), ownership (O), location (L) and internalization (I) advantages are the reasons why firms invest abroad. A firm would engage in FDI when it has ownership advantage — technology and know-how, managerial skills and organization capabilities — over other firms in foreign markets. When firms decide to invest abroad, they select host countries based on location-specific advantages which benefit them in terms of access to natural resources, larger markets and cheaper inputs including labour. Thus, firms exploit ownership and location advantages by investing abroad rather than through other options such as exporting or licensing arrangements.

For firms in developing countries, ownership advantages take the form of (i) suitable technologies in which foreign technology can be modified to suit the tastes and preferences in developing markets, and (ii) lower overhead and expatriate costs. The familiarity with local markets is another advantage possessed by MNEs from developing world. Thus, it can be argued that developing economies may have some commonalities in terms of socio-economic root, ethnic and cultural environment, infrastructural conditions and bureaucratic inefficiency. Lastly, investments from the MNEs based in the developing economies may be more welcome in the developing world since they are often perceived to be less threatening compared to their counterparts from developed countries (Nayak and Choudhury 2014).

2.2 Emergence and Development of Outward FDI

The Product Life Cycle (PLC) theory developed by Vernon (1966) can offer an explanation for the emergence of outward FDI from developing economies. Instead of creating new products themselves, firms from developing world generally import technology from developed countries. Such technology is more suitable for large markets. Thus these firms produce to serve the domestic market first and then export to other countries. Once the products become popular and established in foreign markets, the firms tend to set up production facilities abroad rather than export from the present base (Nayak and Choudhury 2014).

The dynamic pattern of FDI from developing countries can also be explained by the revised Investment Development Path (IDP) which is a dynamic approach of the OLI theory. The IDP provides a framework to understand the interactions between economic development, FDI and governments, and the emerging role of strategic asset-seeking investment as a determinant of outward FDI. As countries achieve higher level of development, they participate more in international investment and evolve through several stages of investment-development, starting from FDI inflow, to outward FDI and the balanced inward and outward FDI in the last stage (Dunning and Narula 1996; Dunning et al. 1997; Narula and Dunning 2000).

2.3 Drivers and Motivations of Investment Abroad

Recent work by Banga (2007) demonstrates that trade-related drivers, capability-related drivers and domestic factors are the important determinants of FDI outflow from developing countries to the developed world. First, in terms of trade-related drivers, an increase in export can provide some assurance of the potential business in foreign markets. This results in lower uncertainty and risks from investing abroad. At the same time, imports may displace domestic production which signals to domestic firms to relocate their production to countries with lower production costs and larger markets.

Second, the necessary requirements, in terms of capability, for firms to invest abroad include skills, technology, information and capital. Third, in terms of domestic factors, firms from developing economies may be faced with poor infrastructure, expensive capital, costly skilled labour and small market in the home country. Another domestic constraint is market integration and competition where firms may decide to relocate their production to other countries in order to be more competitive.

Beside the factors mentioned above, home country policies on FDI obviously are major factors that affect FDI outflows. In many developing countries, restrictions on FDI have been relaxed or eliminated as part of liberalization policies that foster the internationalization process (Hill and Jongwanich 2014; Nayak and Choudhury 2014). The government can also introduce new measures to support outward FDI including financial support, taxation, investment insurance, fiscal measures, overseas investment services and institutional services such as administration, information and technical assistance (Kim and Rhe 2009; Sauvant et al. 2014).

It is widely accepted that there are four major types of outward FDI, clustered according to motives underlying investment decisions: market-seeking FDI, efficiency-seeking FDI, resource-seeking FDI and strategic asset-seeking FDI (Kim and Rhe 2009; ASEAN Secretariat 2013).

First, market-seeking FDI happens when firms want to secure markets abroad, to diversify their revenue base, to follow their customers or to establish new markets. In this case, firms tend to invest in markets which are large enough to compensate for the costs of investing in those markets.

Second, firms with efficiency-seeking motives will invest in countries with low production costs in order to increase their cost competitiveness. Kim and Rhe (2009) argue that once the original host country faces intense competition, investors undertake efficiency-seeking investment in other low-wage countries to reduce costs and this investment is likely to recur in the future.

Third, resource-seeking FDI is mainly aimed at securing supplies of natural resources, particularly in the oil and gas industry, other mining industries and agricultural industries.

Fourth, for strategic asset-seeking FDI, firms seek to acquire new advantages in the form of brand names, reputation, business networks and advanced technology. In the real world, firms from developing countries invest in developed countries to strengthen their non-price competitiveness. This type of FDI has grown rapidly during the past two decades (Kim and Rhe 2009).

3. OUTWARD FDI FROM ASEAN

In order to gain some perspectives on the outward FDI from ASEAN, this section begins with a discussion of the development, characteristics as well as drivers and motivation of ASEAN's outward investment. Trends and prospects of ASEAN's outward FDI are also presented.

3.1 Development of FDI Outflow from ASEAN

Overall, even though outward FDI in the ASEAN region has been on an upward trend during the past three decades, countries in the region remain important host countries for inward FDI from the global market (Figure 1.2). Before the late 1970s, the size of outward FDI from ASEAN countries was quite small, lower than US$50 million, and this was driven mainly by investments from Singapore. In 1980, the OFDI flow reached US$394 billion, equivalent to 13.79 per cent of the flow from developing world. This increase was mainly due to the increasing role of Malaysia as an international investor.

During the 1980s, Singapore and Malaysia dominated the outward FDI from ASEAN with more active FDI outflows from Philippines and Thailand. This resulted in a rise in outward investment from US$326 million in 1981 to US$2,328 million in 1990. In the late 1990s, Malaysia had contributed significantly to a big leap of FDI outflows from ASEAN. The upward trend of OFDI from ASEAN has continued until the Asian Financial Crisis (AFC) in 1997–98, which caused a huge drop in FDI from this region.

Entering into the 2000s, ASEAN's outward FDI started rising again. An upward trend in FDI outflows can be observed after 2003 during which firms in the region recovered from the AFC. This rapid rise in FDI outflows was a reflection of the strong interest shown by firms in ASEAN countries to participate in the international market (ASEAN Secretariat, 2013). The new wave of outward FDI from ASEAN countries during the past decade is an important phenomenon. From 2000 to 2010, the outward

FIGURE 1.2
ASEAN Inward and Outward FDI Flows, 1980–2013 (US$ million)

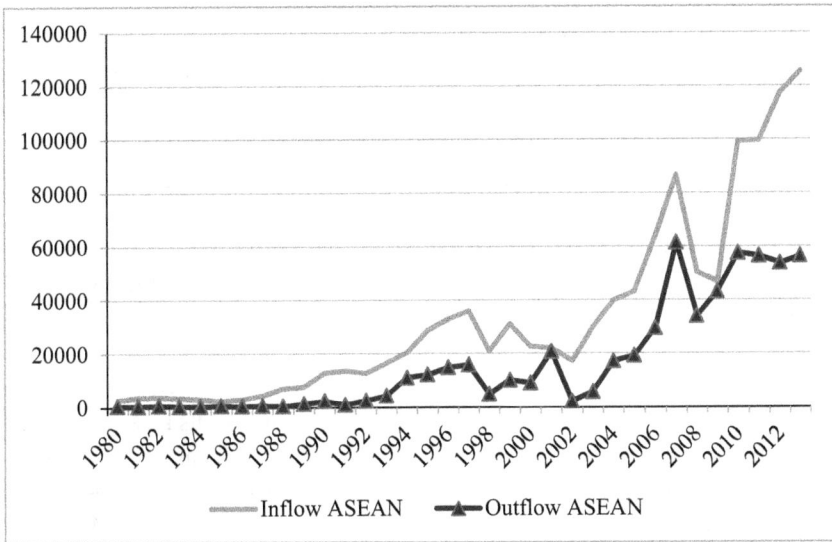

Source: UNCTAD.

investment from ASEAN countries have increased dramatically from US$8,972 million to US$57,546 million, mainly contributed by a jump in intra-regional investment. This rapid development of ASEAN's outward FDI is a reflection of the ASEAN economy becoming increasingly integrated with the regional and global economy.

Since ASEAN countries do not participate equally in outward FDI, it is necessary to examine the pattern of each country's outward and inward FDI. According to the level of outward FDI, countries in ASEAN are divided into three groups: (1) the traditional largest investors abroad — Singapore and Malaysia, (2) the emerging investors abroad — Thailand, Indonesia, Philippines and Vietnam, and (3) the recipients of FDI — Brunei, Lao PDR, Cambodia and Myanmar.

Traditional Largest Investors from ASEAN

Singapore and Malaysia have invested in the international market since the 1980s. Even though Singapore is the largest source of OFDI in ASEAN, with their OFDI having increased significantly from US$97.61 million in 1980 to US$26,966.59 million in 2013, the country remains a net recipient of FDI during most of the past three decades (Figure 1.3).

Malaysia, like other ASEAN counties, started out as a net capital recipient country. FDI inflows into Malaysia increased significantly after the launch of the Promotion of Investment Act in 1986. Even though outward FDI has been observed since the 1980s, a significant upsurge of overseas investment happened only after 2006. The value of Malaysia's OFDI has increased dramatically from US$6,021.02 million in 2006 to US$11,313.89 million in 2007. As a result, Malaysia has transformed itself into the net international investor in 2007. Even the country was hit by the AFC which resulted in a decline in outward FDI, Malaysia has continued to play the role of a major global investor.

Singapore and Malaysia's FDI patterns are not consistent with the revised IDP model because both inward and outward FDIs have increased together since the beginning. This may be explained, in case of Singapore, by the unique characteristics of its trade and investment policies which have always been very open (Hill and Jongwanich 2014). For Malaysia, the constraints of domestic market and the support from government have pushed outward investments since the 1980s.

Emerging Investors from ASEAN

For Thailand, inward FDI has continued to be the country's engine of growth. As one of the major FDI destinations in ASEAN, the FDI inflow to Thailand rose rapidly from US$188.99 million in 1980 to US$12,945.60 million in 2013. FDI outflow from Thailand has grown at a modest rate and only reached US$529.49 million in 2005. Recently, the country's FDI policy has been liberalized and outward investment jumped drastically to US$6,620.47 million in 2011, almost 50 per cent growth from the previous year. With this momentum, Thailand became a country with net FDI outflow during 2011–12.

Another emerging investor is Indonesia. As the largest economy in ASEAN with a vast reserve of natural resources, Indonesia has received a large number of FDI inflows, especially prior to the AFC in 1997–98. Despite a drop in FDI inflow during AFC, it increased again after 2002 and reached a peak of US$19,241.25 million in 2011. Compared to the inflow, Indonesian outward FDI was relatively small and fluctuated around the

FIGURE 1.3
ASEAN Countries' Inward and Outward FDI Flows, 1980–2013
(US$ million)

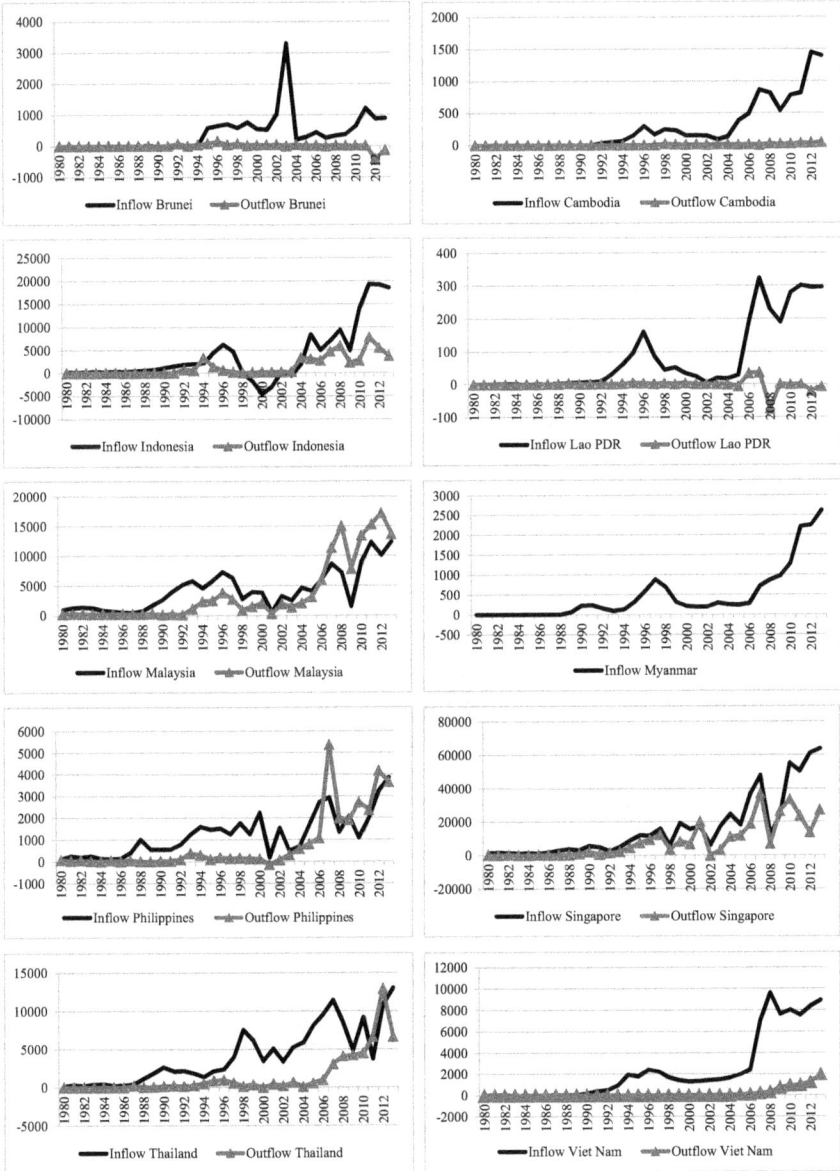

Source: UNCTAD.

AFC period. However, the outward investment had reemerged and jumped to US$3,408 million in 2004. This was caused by the decline in investment climate and higher investment risk in Indonesia during this time. In 2011, the trend in investing abroad has continued and FDI outflow reached the peak of US$7,713 million.

In the case of Philippines, the size of inward and outward FDI has been relatively small. During the 1990s, FDI inflow increased and reached US$2,240 million in 2000 as a result of the effective reforms in Philippines (Hill and Jongwanich 2014). OFDI reached a peak of US$5,372.67 million in 2007. As a result, Philippines became a net capital outflow country, even though this happened at a low level of FDI.

For Vietnam, the value of foreign investment flowing into Vietnam has skyrocketed from approximately US$1,500 million at the beginning of the 2000s to hit a record high of US$9,579 million in 2008. This huge inflow has confirmed the competitive advantage of Vietnam as a host country. For the FDI outflow, even though it has taken place since the mid-2000s, the amount has been insignificant. OFDI only became more visible in 2013 with the surge in outward FDI to almost US$2,000 million.

FDI Recipients

Brunei, Lao PDR, Cambodia and Myanmar have mainly played role as recipients of FDI. Even though the size of inflows were relatively small, they signalled an increasing trend for inward FDI. Outward FDI is limited or negligible in these countries. This situation may be due to the fact that these countries are still at the early stage of the internationalization process and in most cases do not possess the competitive advantage which would enable them to invest abroad. The lack of a strong private sector in these countries is also part of the reason (ASEAN Secretariat 2013).

3.2 Characteristics of Outward FDI from ASEAN Countries

ASEAN's outward FDI has expanded to a greater degree than in the past. To understand the characteristics of ASEAN's OFDI outflows further, questions pertaining to who the investors are, where capital flows have gone and which sectors have received the capital should be examined.

Types of Investors from ASEAN

The players of outward FDI from ASEAN involve a wide range of firms by types and sizes. These firms are mostly large public-listed companies, state-owned enterprises (SOEs) and government-linked companies (GLCs). In ASEAN, GLCs have played a significant role in contributing to the internationalization process of the region (ASEAN Secretariat 2013). These include for Singapore — DBS, Temasek Holdings, Singapore Telecommunications — and for Malaysia — PETRONAS, Sime Darby and CIMB. Moreover, part of the FDI outflow from Singapore has been made by foreign-invested companies based in Singapore.

Governments of Indonesia and Vietnam also encourage their SOEs to expand the business abroad. For Indonesia, those investors are Aneka Tambang, Semen Indonesia and Bank Negara Indonesia (ASEAN Secretariat 2014). The ethnic Chinese Indonesians, who are dominant in the country's modern business sector, are also the major source of outward FDI (Hill and Jongwanich, 2014). For Vietnam, the recent surge of OFDI was mostly conducted by SOEs including Song Da, Petrovietnam and Viettel. In case of Thailand, OFDI flows are led by large private firms such as Siam Cement Group, CP Group and Thai Beverage as well as GLCs such as PTT, Thai Airways International, and the Electricity Generating Authority of Thailand (EGAT) (ASEAN Secretariat 2014).

Aside from large companies, SMEs from ASEAN have also increased their presence abroad especially in the ASEAN region. The key driver of this trend is the goal to be more competitive by expanding their revenue and market base through gaining access to low-cost labour and production inputs. ASEAN Secretariat (2014) also mentioned that SMEs from Malaysia, Singapore and Thailand have been actively expanding their investments within ASEAN and become stronger regional players.

Geographical Distribution

The overall distribution of ASEAN outflow covers all regions. As of 2012, the majority (25%) of ASEAN outward FDI stock was located within ASEAN, followed by the concentration in China (14%), Europe (12%), Latin America and Caribbean (12%) and other East Asia (10%). The rest of the outward FDI stocks from ASEAN were in Australia and New Zealand (7%), Africa (6%), North America (4%) and South Asia (2%) in 2012 (see Figure 1.4).

FIGURE 1.4
Geographical Distribution of Outward FDI Stock, as of 2012

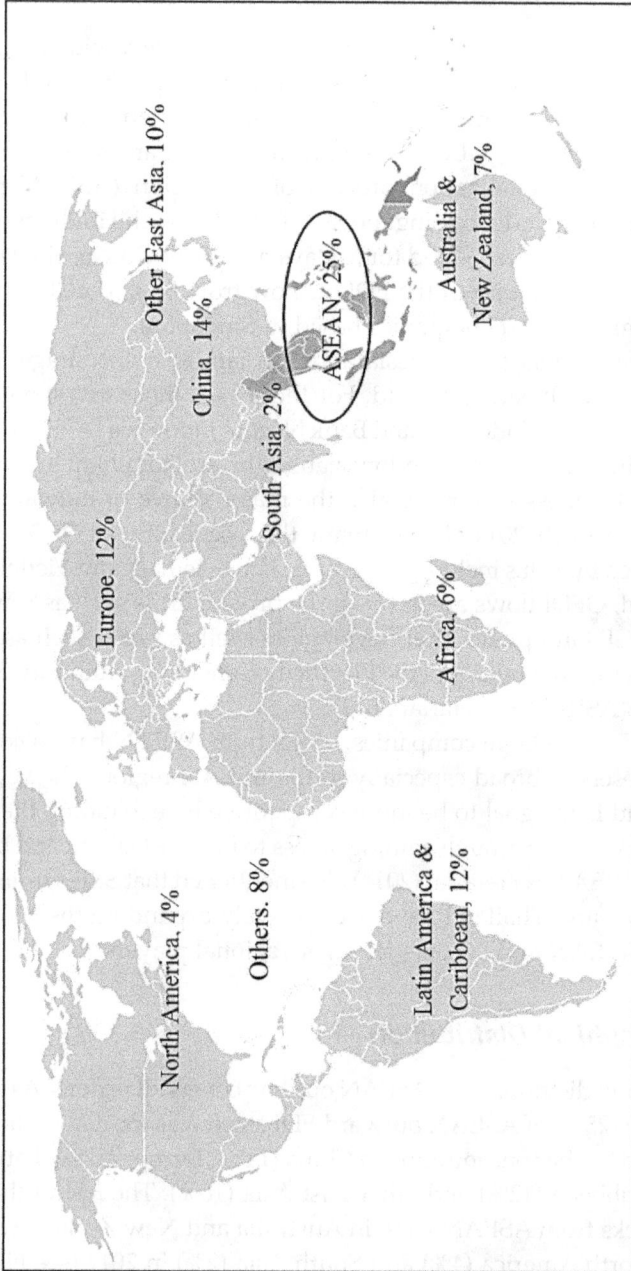

North America, 4%

Others. 8%

Latin America &
Caribbean, 12%

Europe. 12%

Other East Asia. 10%

China. 14%

South Asia, 2%

ASEAN. 25%

Africa, 6%

Australia &
New Zealand, 7%

Source: UNCTAD.

Like other developing countries, ASEAN countries' outward stocks tend to be located in their neighbouring countries with a similar or lower level of development than their home countries (Aykut and Goldstein 2006). For Thailand, more than 35 per cent of outward FDI during 2006–11 flowed to ASEAN whereas 40 per cent of Malaysian outward FDI between 2008 and 2011 were intra-ASEAN investment. In 2010, about 25 per cent of Singapore's outward FDI stocks were in ASEAN (ASEAN Secretariat 2013). Reasons for a surge in intra-ASEAN investment during 2010–11 are (i) the realization of the ASEAN Free Trade Area (AFTA) in 2010, (ii) the closed geo-cultural proximity, and (iii) the spreading of regional value chains and production networks.

Beside intra-regional investment, ASEAN has become a more important source of investment in non-ASEAN countries. FDI from ASEAN countries have spread to African countries in the plantation or agri-based businesses. In Europe, in particular in the United Kingdom and Germany, the focus has been on technology seeking (ASEAN Secretariat 2013). In the 1990s, neighbouring Asian countries and China were the primary destinations for Singapore's investments. Later on in the 2000s, Singapore diversified their outward FDI and become a global investor with more focus on the developed countries and other regions. Unlike Singapore, other ASEAN countries such as Thailand, Malaysia and Vietnam have concentrated their investments in the region.

Sectoral Distribution

Outward investment from ASEAN involves a wide range of sectors. In the case of intra-ASEAN investment, the 2013 data indicates that the highest share (27.67%) was in manufacturing industry, followed by financial and insurance (22.17%), real estate (20.99%), agriculture, forestry and fishing (7.50%) and trade and commerce (4.04%) (see Figure 1.5). This has been partly driven by the expansion of ASEAN production network in manufacturing industry. For Singapore, Malaysia and Thailand, in particular, most of the outflows have gone to mining, manufacturing and services sectors.

The manufacturing investments from ASEAN include those from food and beverage, electronics and automotive industries. In the case of OFDI in the extractive industries, companies from Malaysia (PETRONAS), Thailand (PTT, Banpu, Lanna Resources) and Vietnam (Petrovietnam) are significant

FIGURE 1.5
Sectoral Distribution of Intra-ASEAN Investment in 2013

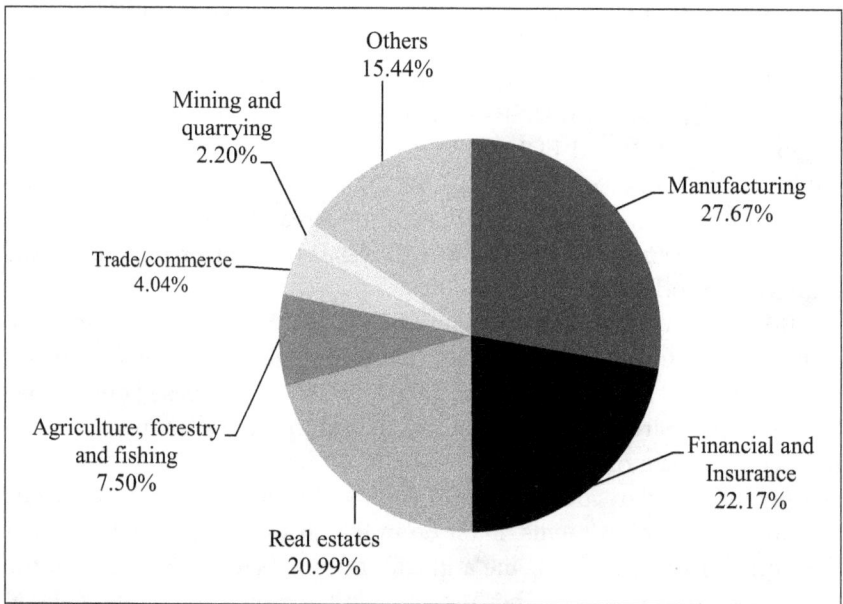

Others
15.44%

Mining and
quarrying
2.20%

Trade/commerce
4.04%

Manufacturing
27.67%

Agriculture, forestry
and fishing
7.50%

Financial and
Insurance
22.17%

Real estates
20.99%

Source: ASEAN Secretariat (2014).

players. In the case of finance and real estate in ASEAN, Singapore and Malaysia dominate in market.

3.3 Drivers and Motivations for ASEAN's Outward FDI

In general, a key driver of outward FDI from ASEAN countries is the competitive pressures from globalization. Companies seek competitive advantage through investing abroad. Regional integration is also a driver for FDI outflow from ASEAN (ASEAN Secretariat 2013).

For ASEAN countries, there are a wide variety of drivers and motives for FDI outflow, depending on the size of firms, countries and industries. First, compared to the large firms, SMEs from ASEAN tend to invest less in countries outside the region and this is driven by a closer geo-cultural proximity and affinity. Second, for countries like Singapore and Malaysia, firms have strong desire to invest abroad because of their domestic constraints: a relatively small home market size, saturated markets, limited opportunities for growth and the need to secure resources including land and labour force. Third, firms from different industries have different reasons for outward FDI. For oil, gas and mining of other natural resources industries, ASEAN's firms invest abroad to access or secure natural resources while agriculture companies go abroad to access agricultural land and utilize low-cost labour. Outward FDI from healthcare industry intend to exploit their brand reputation and some firms acquire existing medical facilities in host countries. In case of infrastructure, real estate and construction industries, investing abroad is to diversify their markets and revenue bases (ASEAN Secretariat 2013).

Beside the firms' motivation, the government has also played an important role in promoting the internationalization process of firms in ASEAN countries. The government of Singapore, for example, has played a very active and direct role in promoting outward FDI through (i) GLCs which used to push regionalization activities either on their own or in partnerships with other firms and (ii) generous incentives and other programmes such as tax incentives, finance schemes or training to foster the development of local firms.

3.4 Trends and Prospects of ASEAN's Outward FDI

This section analyses the changing trends and prospects of outward FDI from ASEAN countries. The prospect for increasing outward FDI from ASEAN countries is promising for a number of reasons. First, the capabilities to develop brand names and reputation at home as well as the strong growth in home market (which contributes to the building up of financial resources needed for investing abroad) exist in ASEAN countries. Second, the intense pressure from globalization forces a wider pool of firms to invest abroad in order to become more competitive. Third, many firms in ASEAN countries need and want to become global players and investing abroad is one channel to achieve their objectives. Fourth, many governments in ASEAN have liberalized their FDI policies during the last decade and this strategy is likely to be implemented further in the future. Fifth, the expansion of the regional production network also contributes to the higher outward FDI in the region. Sixth, the realization of AEC in 2015 is an increasingly influential factor supporting overseas investment.

There is a changing trend in the structure and composition of ASEAN FDI outflow. First, the share of services in outward FDI from ASEAN is increasing. Singaporean and Malaysian firms have dominated in overseas investment in the service sector, particularly in finance and real estate. Recently, the establishment of hotels and hospitals abroad by Thai firms has been led by prospective market growth (ASEAN Secretariat 2013). Second, even though ASEAN countries are a growing source of intra-regional investment and outward FDI to the developing economies, their investment in developed countries aimed at obtaining previously out-of-reach competitive advantages is rising. Recently, besides Singapore, countries such as Malaysia, Thailand, and Indonesia have started venturing in developed countries such as the United Kingdom, United States and Australia. Third, in general, ASEAN firms have been motivated to invest abroad mainly due to efficiency-seeking, market-seeking and resource-seeking reasons. Strategic asset-seeking FDI from ASEAN has become more noticeable. ASEAN firms invest abroad to acquire business networks, brand names and strategic production facilities.

From the data observation, many prominent investment activities were undertaken by SOEs or GLCs at the early stage. However, today, private firms are participating more in the outward FDI than in the past. For SMEs, unlike in the past, they do not need to grow to a certain size before they internationalize. There is a growing number of SMEs investing at the regional level.

4. EXPERIENCES FROM EAST ASIAN ECONOMIES AND LESSONS FOR ASEAN

This section examines the lessons learnt from the experience of the global players from East Asia, namely, China, Hong Kong, Taiwan and Korea.

4.1 Experience of Outward FDI from China, Hong Kong, Taiwan and Korea

Taiwan and Korea started liberalizing their outward FDI policies since the late 1980s. In Taiwan, the rising pressures from sharp increases in labour costs and land prices have forced Taiwanese firms to invest abroad to boost their competitiveness. The government introduced policies and measures to promote outward FDI such as the "Go South" policy which encouraged firms to invest in Southeast Asia. Taiwan has long been a net investor since the early stage of its development. The government has supported overseas acquisitions in order to access technology and to secure their position at the higher end of the value chain, especially after 1998 (Thurbon and Weiss 2006). However, the Taiwanese government has maintained significant control over the kind of investment that helps sustain its technological position. In the electronics industry, for example, the government has allowed Taiwanese firms to increase their manufacturing investments in China while at the same time keep high-technology firms at home to safeguard its competitive advantage.

For Korea, domestic constraints — increasing land and labour costs as well as the need to maintain the firms' competitiveness — have triggered OFDI since 1987. After 1997, Korean firms, such as Samsung and Hyundai, have actively participated in investing abroad because of the country's outward investment policy in the 1990s. For the labour-intensive manufacturing industry, firms shifted their production to lower-wage countries such as those in Southeast Asia while keeping higher value-added production at home. Firms from Korea with market-seeking and strategic asset-seeking purposes tend to invest in North America and Europe whereas the efficiency-seeking firms invested in Asia for low-cost labour. One interesting characteristic of Korean investment is that the developed economies were the destinations for acquiring new technology especially at the early stage. Gradually, Korean overseas investment diversified to cover both developed and developing countries (Kim and Rhe 2009). Korean inward and outward FDI have increased together since the end of 1980s; however, after 2005, the growth of outward flow exceeds the inward growth. Their outward FDI flow reached a peak of US$30,632.1 million in 2012.

China started and continues to be a net recipient of FDI even though their investment outflow has increased substantially over the past decade. Aside from being a global manufacturer, China is also recognized as a global investor. In 2014, China became the third largest global investor with the outflow of US$116 billion. Chinese government has played an important and active role in promoting these outflows including the "Go Global" strategy in 2000. It has implemented measures to relax and streamline the approval process and procedures for OFDI (Sauvant 2005). In terms of the destinations for Chinese FDI, the lion's share of outward FDI went to Hong Kong (58% in 2013). Latin America was the second most important destination for Chinese OFDI (13%), followed by Europe (6%). Other regions — Southeast Asia, North America, Australia and Africa — each accounted for 3–4 per cent of the overall Chinese OFDI in 2013.

Recently, the focus of Chinese outward investment has shifted from the natural resource industry to the high technology consumption-oriented sector. Chinese investment has been diversified mainly from the energy and mining industry in Asia, Latin America and Africa to mergers and acquisitions in technology, agriculture and real estate sectors in developed countries such as Europe and America. Moreover, private-owned enterprises (POEs) in China are more active in investing abroad. By the end of 2013, more than half of China's total accumulated outward FDI were from the non-SOEs. With this new force, the Chinese POEs, the country is likely to gain better results and benefits from outward FDI because they are more flexible, faster growing, more diversified outward FDI and more welcome in the host countries (Ernst & Young 2015).

The inward and outward FDI have moved together in the case of Hong Kong with an increasing trend since the 1990s. For OFDI, Hong Kong is registered as one of the largest investors; however, the data on OFDI include significant amounts of round-tripping and indirect FDI which is the investment from the foreign affiliates established in Hong Kong. China is the largest destination of Hong Kong's investment, accounted for 63.3 per cent in 2013. The advantages arising from Hong Kong's privileges under the Close Economic Partnership Arrangement for investing in China has attracted indirect FDI which contributed to the Hong Kong's role as a major investor (UNCTAD 2004).

4.2 Lessons for ASEAN

To sum up, the experiences of outward FDI from major investors in Asia — China, Hong Kong, Taiwan and Korea serves the following lessons for ASEAN.

First, the development of outward FDI does not follow the revised IDP. The constraints in domestic markets in these countries such as increasing land and labour costs and the active role of governments are the major drivers of outward FDI. In Hong Kong, Korea and Taiwan, the outward and inward FDI have moved together, like in cases of Singapore and Malaysia.

Second, the role of the government in fostering the FDI outflow is a significant factor for overseas investment. Examples include China's "Go Global" strategy in 2000 and Taiwan's "Go South" policy in 1994. The liberalization of FDI policy and measures which includes the relaxation

FIGURE 1.6

Outward FDI Flows from ASEAN, China, Hong Kong, Taiwan and Korea, 1980–2013

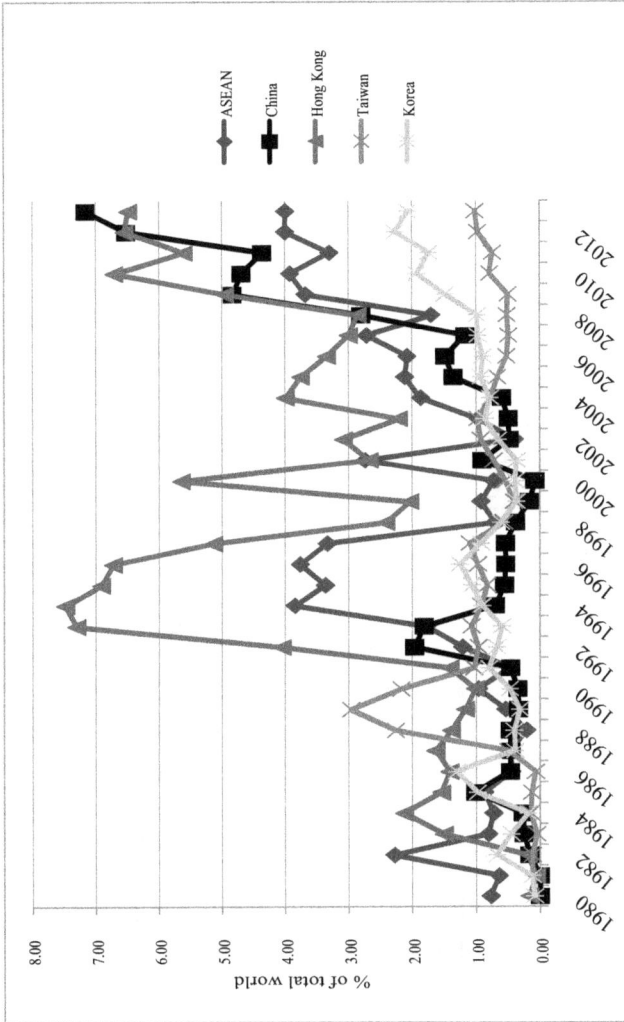

Source: UNCTAD.

FIGURE 1.7
China, Hong Kong, Korea and Taiwan Inward and Outward FDI Flows, 1980–2013 (US$ million)

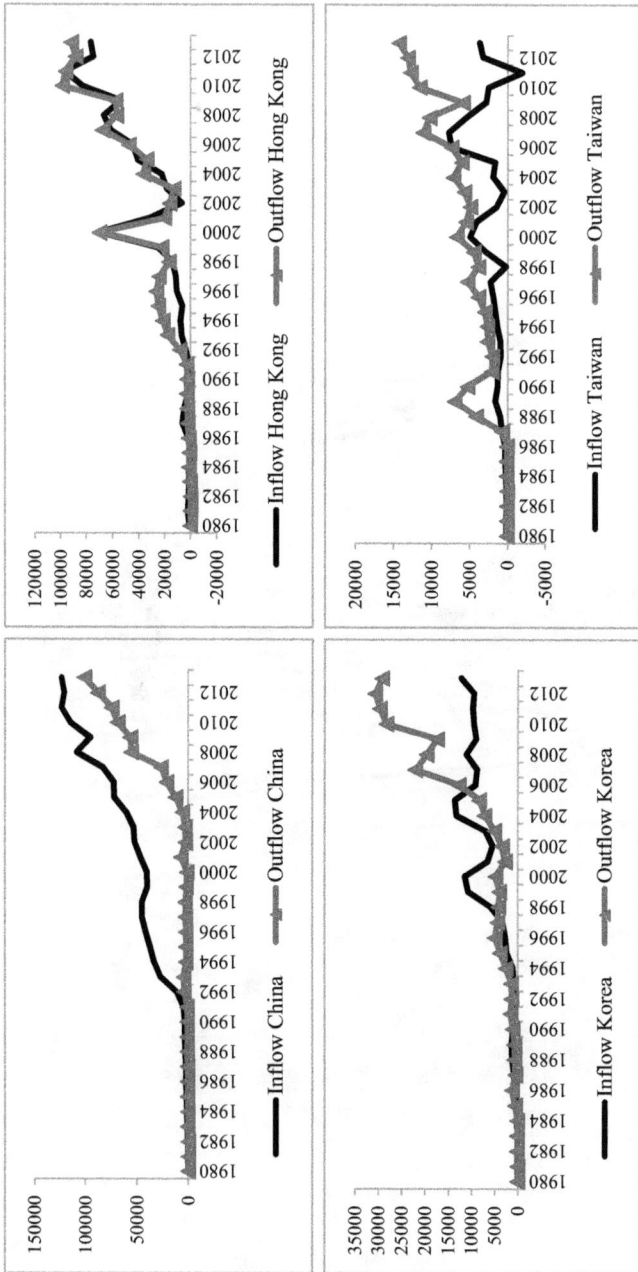

Source: UNCTAD.

and streamlining of the approval processes and procedures are examples of government support. Similar policies are observed in ASEAN countries such as Singapore and Malaysia. One lesson learnt for ASEAN countries is that governments have to maintain control over the kind of investment that needs to be kept at home and those that should relocate to overseas in order to sustain the competitive advantage of the home countries.

Third, once the internationalization process has started, firms would seek markets, natural resources and efficiency in the early stage. Later on, the focus of the outward FDI is on the high technology consumption-oriented sector. The same pattern can be found in case of South Korea where firms in the country first invest to have technology catch-up and then to become the technology leader. Strategic asset-seeking FDI gains more significance and tends to expand further (in terms of destination country) from the ASEAN region. Many firms from this region invest abroad to gain access to brand name, network and technology. In order to make access to strategic asset possible, government has to support and enhance the capabilities of local investors to venture abroad.

Fourth, investors tend to diversify the geography of investment after the internationalization process takes place at certain level. Driven by a shift in investment objective from acquiring production factor such as resource and market access to acquiring advanced technology and brands, the investment destinations are becoming increasing diversified. Beside developing countries such as Asia, Africa and Latin America, the developed countries — Europe and America — have become a new focus of outward FDI.

Fifth, despite SOEs and GLCs being leaders of outward FDI from many developing countries, the role of private firms in these outflows has continued to expand. The advantages of players from private sector include flexibility, fast-growth and more diversified investments. However, additional support to enhance capabilities of these firms is needed. The assistance from the government may take the form of measures such as reforms of the administration and approval processes, financial support, guidance and coordination between private firms and SOEs.

5. CONCLUSION

Globalization and more intense competition have forced firms from developing countries to actively undertake outward FDI. China, Hong

Kong, Korea, Taiwan and two countries from ASEAN, Singapore and Malaysia, are major investors from the developing Asia. Given the changing landscape in ASEAN which shifted the region from a major recipient of FDI to become an emerging source of outward FDI, it is necessary to understand the extent to which OFDI from ASEAN countries is explicable by referring to the theory of FDI from developing countries. This chapter examines the development of ASEAN's outward FDI, its characteristics, motives, trends and prospects as well as the lessons learned from other major Asian investors such as China, Hong Kong, Korea and Taiwan.

Observations from data indicate that outward FDI in ASEAN countries has been driven mainly by domestic constraints such as the cases of Singapore and Malaysia which started investing abroad since the 1980s. For other ASEAN countries with a relatively larger domestic market and abundance in resources such as Thailand, Indonesia and Vietnam, they started as major destinations for FDI. The intensification in competition from liberalization and rising costs of land and labour during the past decade have forced firms in these countries to actively invest abroad. Governments have played important roles in promoting the internationalization process in many ASEAN countries through the active roles of SOEs and GLCs as well as by initiating policies and measures aimed at liberalizing outward FDI and supporting the outflow process.

Most ASEAN countries, like other developing countries, invested in neighbouring countries in the early stage with the objective securing natural resources for their extractive industry, to access market and achieve efficiency in manufacturing industries. Intra-regional investment accounts for approximately one-fourth of the outward stock. Some outward FDI went to developed countries such as Europe and United States to acquire high technology. Manufacturing, finance and insurance, and real estate industries are the major sectors for intra-ASEAN investment.

Outward FDI from ASEAN has the potential to increase further because some ASEAN firms have gained higher capabilities, desire to become global players and are pressured to escape from their intense competition in domestic markets. The support from governments, the expansion of production networks and the coming of AEC have enhanced this process. In addition, larger share of investments in services sector will take place in the next stage. Strategic asset-seeking FDI and the FDI flow to developed countries will be the future trend for ASEAN. Both private firms and SMEs will become important players in outward investment in the future.

The experiences from China, Hong Kong, Korea and Taiwan can provide important lessons for ASEAN countries. Governments of ASEAN countries need to be aware of the increasing significance of outward FDI as a mean to gain and maintain their competitiveness. Government are important players in the internationalization process of the businesses. They need to initiate and design policies and measures to create an optimal environment to support outward investment. Playing an active role at the right time and fostering private sector to have higher capabilities to compete in the global market are what the government should consider doing. Investing abroad may drain domestic resources or disadvantage home countries. The way out for this situation is a careful sequencing of supports and FDI liberalization. At the industry level, investments in some activities need to be shifted overseas while keeping some within the country in order to gain and maintain their advantage. In some cases, investing abroad is a way to gain competitiveness and will expand the rest of the value chain. Optimal outward FDI strategy is a key to success.

References

ASEAN Secretariat. *ASEAN Investment Report 2012: The Changing FDI Landscape.* Jakarta: ASEAN Secretariat, 2013.
————. *ASEAN Investment Report 2013–2014: FDI Development and Regional Value Chains.* Jakarta: ASEAN Secretariat, 2014.
Aykut, D. and A. Goldstein. "Developing Country Multinationals: South-South Investment Comes of Age". Working Paper No. 257. OECD Development Centre, 2006.
Banga, R. "Drivers of Outward Foreign Direct Investment from Asian Developing Economies". In *Towards Coherent Policy Frameworks: Understanding Trade and Investment Linkages,* pp. 195–215. New York: United Nations ESCAP, 2007.
Blonigen, B.A. "A Review of the Empirical Literature on FDI Determinants". *Atlantic Economic Journal* 33 (2005): 383–403.
Cai, K.G. "Outward Foreign Direct Investment: A Novel Dimension of China's Integration into the Regional and Global Economy". *China Quarterly* 160 (1999): 856–80.
Dunning, J.H. *Multinational Enterprises and the Global Economy.* Harlow: Addison-Wesley, 1993.

———. "The Eclectic Paradigm as an Envelope for Economic and Business Theories of MNE Activity". *International Business Review* 9 (2000): 163–90.

——— and R. Narula. "The Investment Development Path Revisited: Some Emerging Issues". In *Foreign Direct Investment and Governments: Catalysts for Economic Restructuring*, edited by J.H. Dunning and R. Narula. London: Routledge, 1996.

———, Van Hoesel, R., and R. Narula. "Explaining the 'New' Wave of Outward FDI from Developing Countries: The Case of Taiwan and Korea". MERIT Working Paper Series No. 96–103, 1996.

Ellingsen, G., W. Likumahuwa, and P. Nunnenkamp. "Outward FDI by Singapore: A Different Animal?". *Transnational Corporations* 15, no. 2 (2006): 1–40.

Ernst & Young. *Riding the Silk Road: China Sees Outbound Investment Boom, Outlook for China's Outward Foreign Direct Investment*, 2015.

Goh, S.K. and K.N. Wong. "Malaysia's Outward FDI: The Effects of Market Size and Government Policy". *Journal of Policy Modeling* 33 (2011): 497–510.

Hill, H. and J. Jongwanich. "Emerging East Asian Economies as Foreign Investors: An Analytical Survey". *Singapore Economic Review* 59, no. 3 (2014): 1–26.

Kim, J.M. and D.K. Rhe. "Trends and Determinants of South Korean Outward Foreign Direct Investment". *Copenhagen Journal of Asian Studies* 27, no. 1 (2009): 126–54.

Nayak, D. and R.N. Choudhury. "A Selective Review of Foreign Direct Investment Theories". ARTNeT Working Paper Series No. 143, Bangkok, ESCAP, March 2014.

Sauvant, K.P. "New Sources of FDI: The BRICS, Outward FDI from Brazil, Russia, India and China". *Journal of World Investment & Trade* 6, no. 5 (2005): 639–709.

———, P. Economou, K. Gal, S. Lim, and W.P. Wilinski. "Trends in FDI, Home Country Measures and Competitive Neutrality". In *Yearbook on International Investment Law & Policy 2012–2013*, edited by A.K. Bjorklund. New York: Oxford University Press, 2014.

Thurbon, E. and L. Weiss. "Investing in Openness: The Evolution of FDI Strategy in South Korea and Taiwan". *New Political Economy* 11, no. 1 (2006): 1–22.

UNCTAD. *World Investment Report 2004: The Shift Towards Services*. Geneva: UNCTAD, 2004.

———. *World Investment Report 2006: FDI from Developing and Transition Economies: Implications for Development*. Geneva: UNCTAD, 2006.

———. *World Investment Report 2014: Investing in the SDGs: An Action Plan*. Geneva: UNCTAD, 2014.

———. *World Investment Report 2015: Reforming International Investment Governance*. Geneva: UNCTAD, 2015.

Vernon, R. "International Investment and International Trade in the Product Cycle". *Quarterly Journal of Economics* 80, no. 2 (1966): 190–207.

2

ASEAN'S OUTWARD FOREIGN DIRECT INVESTMENT

Aekapol Chongvilaivan and Jayant Menon[1]

1. INTRODUCTION

Foreign direct investment (FDI) has long been a key driver of economic growth and industrialization in the Association of Southeast Asian Nations (ASEAN) countries. ASEAN countries have traditionally been attractive destinations for foreign enterprises and multinational companies (MNCs), thanks to abundant natural resources, cheap and motivated labour force, and its strategic location in Asia. Inward FDI ushers in not only capital resources and jobs, but also knowledge, know-how, technology, and organizational expertise through spillovers as well as backward and forward linkage effects. Through these mechanisms, inward FDI has been part and parcel of economic and industrial development strategies and has seen the region play host to FDI since the 1980s.

However, the past two decades have witnessed rapidly evolving global and regional business environments. China and India have emerged as competing hubs for low-cost production since the 2000s, due in no small part to their large domestic markets and improving connectivity through regional production networks. Many ASEAN countries such as Indonesia,

Malaysia, and Thailand have also experienced rising labour costs, thereby making them less conducive for low-cost production. These recent developments caution that the conventional FDI strategies will soon reach the limit of offering the pace of economic growth and industrialization they once achieved.

Given the emerging challenges, ASEAN countries have exhibited a shift in FDI strategies towards outward FDI. Although inward FDI has been, and will continue to be, an important element of economic development, it has been vividly observed that more enterprises, especially government-linked and large businesses, have started to seek new business opportunities overseas and venture in foreign markets. This implies that regionalization and industrialization among firms will serve as another catalyst of economic growth and industrialization in the region.

Against this backdrop, this chapter aims to examine the emerging trends of outward FDI from ASEAN countries and characteristics of outward FDI strategies among three major players, namely Singapore, Thailand, and Malaysia. The lessons learnt from the experience of these ASEAN countries potentially provide interesting insights into the essential policies and reforms which will enable other ASEAN countries to successfully ride the waves of internationalization.

The remainder of the chapter is organized as follows: Section 2 looks into the overall trends of outward FDI from ASEAN countries; Section 3 attempts to identify the key players of outward FDI; Section 4 contemplates outward FDI strategies adopted by the three major players; and Section 5 concludes with policy implications.

2. TRENDS OF OUTWARD FDI FROM ASEAN COUNTRIES

ASEAN countries experienced an exponential increase in outward FDI in the run-up to the global financial crisis in 2008–09. Figure 2.1 compares the trend in outward FDI from ASEAN with that from Japan and China. Outward FDI from ASEAN rapidly surged from merely US$2.3 billion in 1990 to about US$62 billion in 2007; this rise was particularly pronounced during 2002–07, as companies in ASEAN recovered from the 1997 Asian Financial Crisis (AFC), strengthened their financial positions, and marched towards internationalization. As a proportion of gross fixed capital formation, outward FDI from ASEAN also increased from less than 3 per

FIGURE 2.1
Outward FDI Flows from ASEAN, 1990–2013

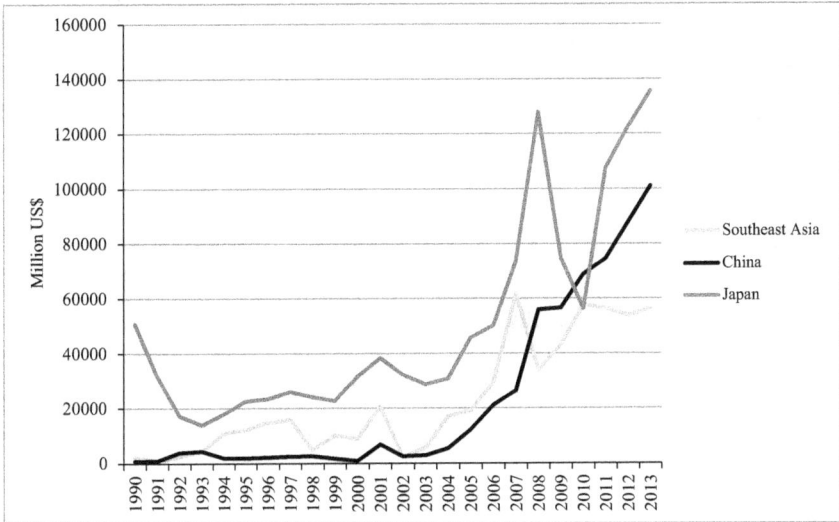

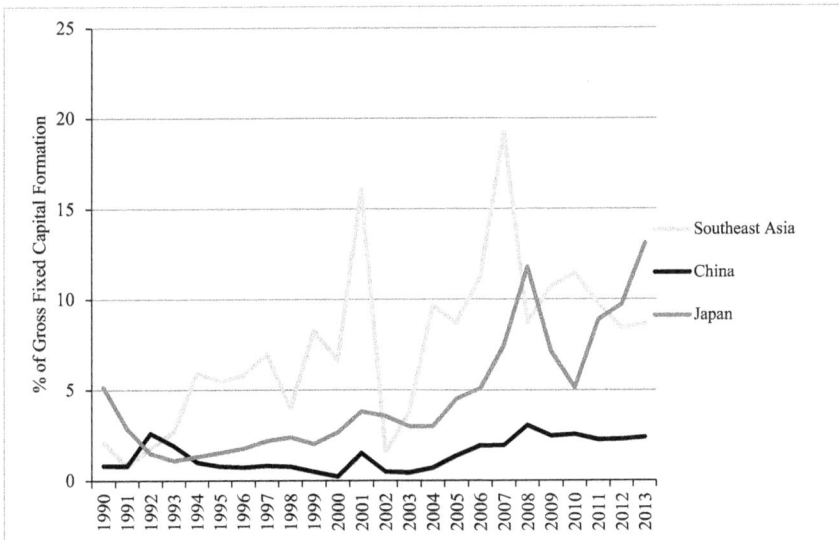

Source: *World Investment Report*, UNCTAD, various years.

cent in 1990 to almost 20 per cent in 2007. These trends imply that ASEAN — traditionally known as a low-wage production base and a host of FDI from advanced economies — has begun establishing its global footprint by venturing into new business opportunities overseas.

The rise in intra-ASEAN FDI flows is a major contributing factor to the spike in outward FDI from ASEAN (ASEAN Secretariat 2013). Since the mid-2000s, intra-ASEAN FDI has increased steadily, notwithstanding a drop during the 2008–09 global financial crisis. It reached a peak of US$26.3 billion — nearly 50 per cent of total outward FDI from ASEAN — in 2011.

Three factors account for burgeoning intra-ASEAN FDI. Firstly, the global financial crisis has significantly reduced the attractiveness of traditional investment destinations for ASEAN firms in the United States and the European Union (EU). As a consequence, ASEAN multinationals have moved their investment away from advanced economies towards emerging markets in the region, such as Cambodia, Lao PDR, Myanmar, and Vietnam, where natural resources are abundant and economic outlooks have been buoyant and relatively resilient to global economic shocks.

FIGURE 2.2
Intra-ASEAN FDI, 2005–14 (US$ million)

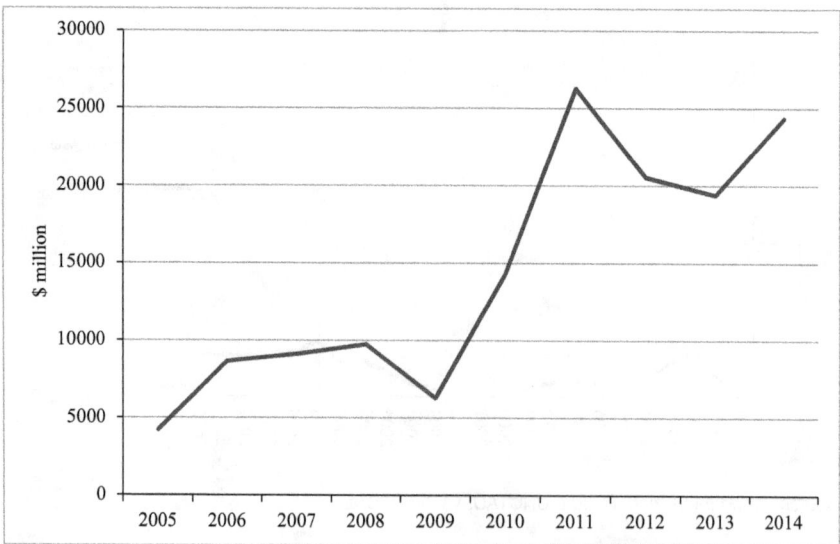

Source: ASEAN Secretariat.

Secondly, increasing regional economic integration under the platform of ASEAN has significantly reduced barriers to cross-border trade and investment and improved business sentiments in the region. Lastly, most ASEAN economies have embarked on export-oriented growth strategies and accrued a substantial amount of foreign exchange reserves, especially after the 1997 AFC. While advanced economies were the hardest hit by the global financial crisis, ASEAN economies increasingly redirected their excess savings within the region where emerging economies are fast-growing and demonstrating better economic prospects. Hill and Jongwanich (2014) posit that apart from resource-seeking motives, the rise of outward FDI from ASEAN has been driven principally by exceptionally high domestic saving rates.

3. THE KEY PLAYERS

Outward FDI from ASEAN has by and large been dominated by Singapore, Malaysia, and, to a lesser extent, Thailand. Figure 2.3 reveals the contribution of outward FDI stock by ASEAN country during 1990–2012. Prior to the global financial crisis in 2008–09, outward FDI from the region was dominated by Singapore and Malaysia; the former appeared to boost its outward FDI profile at a much faster pace than the latter. In the aftermath of the global financial crisis, Thailand, the Philippines, and Indonesia also implemented outward FDI strategies and started to venture overseas. As of 2013, Singapore accounted for approximately 70 per cent of outward FDI from ASEAN, followed by Malaysia with 19 per cent, and Thailand with 8 per cent. The rest of the region accounted for only 3 per cent of outward FDI.

Table 2.1 presents a ranking of ASEAN MNCs by foreign assets. Consistent with Figure 2.3, MNCs from Singapore and Malaysia dominate the rankings and are in the forefront of outward FDI. The proliferation of outward FDI from Singapore and Malaysia has been fuelled by their Governments' internationalization strategy, whereby government-linked companies spearhead investment in relatively advanced countries to acquire new knowledge and technology. Industrial parks and infrastructure projects in developing countries such as China, India, Indonesia and Vietnam were also established to induce investment by MNCs (Ellingsen, Likumahuwa and Nunnenkamp 2006). As of 2012, PETRONAS — the Malaysian government-linked petroleum company — topped the rankings

TABLE 2.1
Rankings of Top TNCs from ASEAN by Foreign Assets, 2012

Foreign assets	Corporation	Home economy	Industry	TNI[a]
4	PETRONAS - Petroliam Nasional Bhd	Malaysia	Petroleum expl./ref./distr.	39.2
13	Singapore Telecommunications Ltd	Singapore	Telecommunications	63.5
18	Wilmar International Limited	Singapore	Food, beverages and tobacco	75.5
25	CapitaLand Ltd	Singapore	Construction and real estate	71.1
28	Genting Bhd	Malaysia	Other consumer services	72.3
39	Golden Agri-Resources Ltd	Singapore	Food	100.0
41	YTL Corporation Bhd	Malaysia	Utilities (Electricity, gas and water)	75.8
54	San Miguel Corp	Philippines	Food, beverages and tobacco	21.7
56	Flextronics International Ltd	Singapore	Electrical & electronic equipment	91.9
72	Sime Darby Bhd	Malaysia	Diversified	46.4
75	Olam International Ltd	Singapore	Electrical & electronic equipment	57.5
80	Keppel Corp Ltd	Singapore	Diversified	33.3
86	Fraser & Neave Ltd	Singapore	Food, beverages and tobacco	53.1
91	City Developments Ltd	Singapore	Other consumer services	57.8

Note: a. TNI stands for the Transnationality Index.
Source: UNCTAD.

FIGURE 2.3
Outward FDI Stock by ASEAN Country, 1990–2013

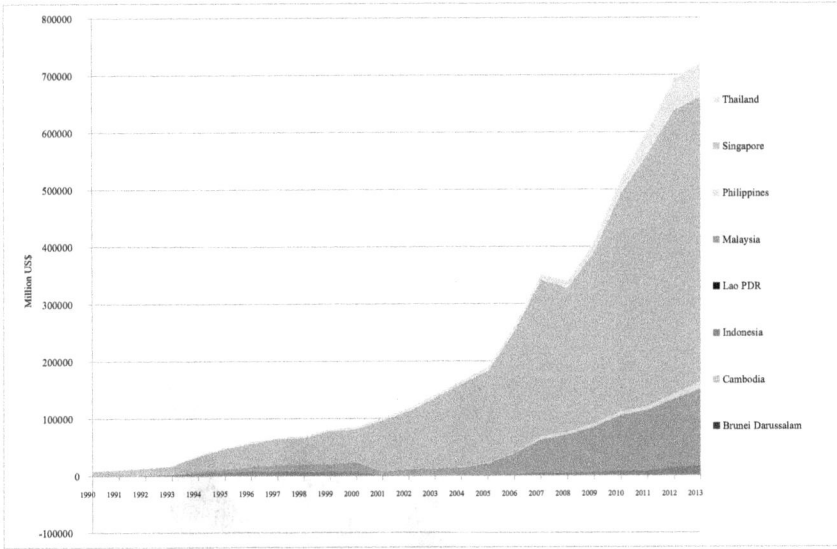

Note: Myanmar and Vietnam are excluded due to missing information.
Source: *World Investment Report*, UNCTAD, various years.

of MNCs from ASEAN and was ranked 4th worldwide with foreign assets
amounting to US$49 billion, followed by Singapore's government-linked
corporations including Singtel Limited (2nd), Wilmar International Limited
(3rd), and CapitaLand (4th). Other major MNCs are linked with Singapore's
Government, including Golden Agri-Resources Limited (6th), Flextronics
International Limited (9th), Fraser & Neave Limited (12th), and Keppel
Corporation Limited (13th).

The aftermath of the global financial crisis drove a shift in outward
FDI strategies among ASEAN MNCs, toward merger and acquisition
(M&A) and away from Greenfield FDI. Figure 2.4 shows the value of
M&A purchases from ASEAN by country during 1990–2013. While the
volume of M&A deals declined during the global financial crisis in
2008–09, it bounced back strongly from a mere US$5 billion in 2010 to an
all-time high level of US$27 billion in 2013. Escalating M&A purchases
from ASEAN are being led by Singapore and Malaysia, and, increasingly
Thailand. In contrast, Greenfield FDI appears to have lost its momentum
in recent years. As shown in Figure 2.5, the value of Greenfield projects
from ASEAN sources has steadily declined from a peak of US$47 billion

FIGURE 2.4
Value of Cross-border M&As by Purchasers from ASEAN Countries, 1990–2013

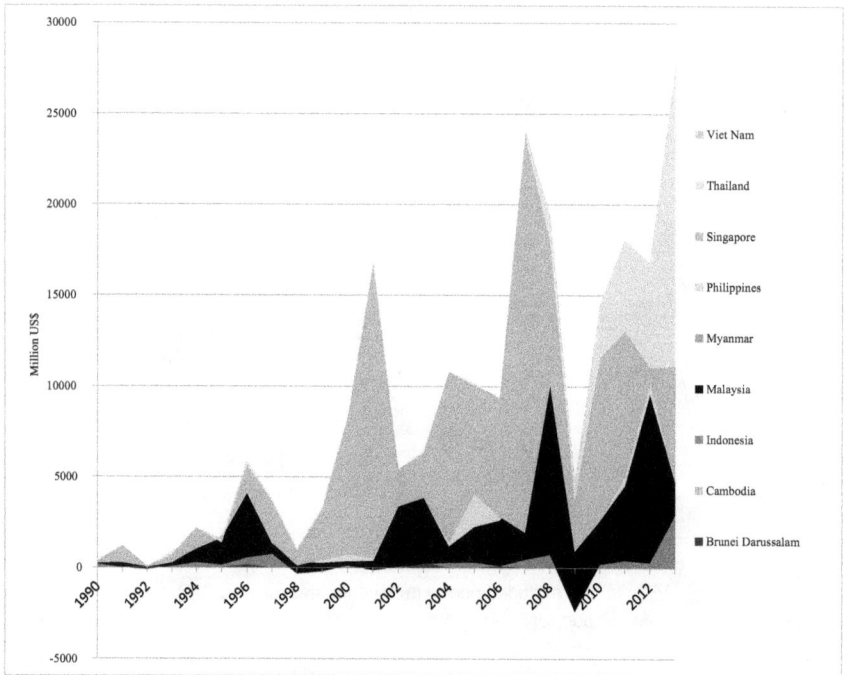

Note: Lao PDR is excluded due to missing information.
Source: *World Investment Report*, UNCTAD, various years.

in 2008 to merely US$23 billion in 2013. As is well known, Greenfield FDI is the most stable form of FDI. That MNCs from ASEAN are gearing towards M&A and away from Greenfield FDI implies that outward FDI from the region is becoming more footloose.

Apart from MNCs, Sovereign Wealth Funds (SWFs) are also a critical element of the success story of outward FDI from ASEAN. As shown in Table 2.2, three SWFs from ASEAN in 2007 topped the rankings of SWFs from developing Asia, namely the Government of Singapore Investment Corporation (GIC), Temasek Holdings, and Khazanah Nasional Berhad. The establishment of GIC and Temasek Holdings date back to 1981 and 1974, respectively. This reflects the Singapore Government's regionalization and internationalization strategies, whereby SWFs serve as a key vehicle of expanding "external wings" through outward FDI (Okposin 1999; Chongvilaivan and Rajan 2012).

FIGURE 2.5
Value of Greenfield FDI Projects by Sources from ASEAN Countries, 2003–13

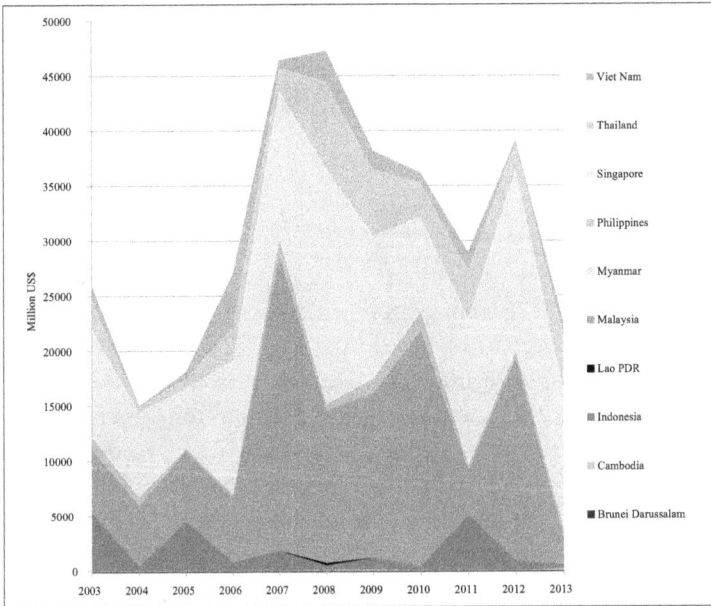

Source: World Investment Report, UNCTAD, various years.

TABLE 2.2
Top Sovereign Wealth Funds (SWFs) of Developing Asia,
Ranked by the Value of Assets, 2007

Name of SWF	Economy	Asset (US$ bn.)	Year of Inception	Type
Government of Singapore Investment Corp.	Singapore	330.0	1981	Non-commodity
China Investment Corp.	China	200.0	2007	Non-commodity
Temasek Holdings	Singapore	100.0	1974	Non-commodity
Hong Kong Monetary Authority Investment Portfolio	Hong Kong	100.0	1998	Non-commodity
Brunei Investment Agency	Brunei	30.0	1983	Oil Commodity
Korea Investment Corp.	Korea	20.0	2005	Non-commodity
Khazanah Nasional Berhad	Malaysia	15.0	1993	Non-commodity
National Oil Fund	Kazakhstan	15.0	2000	Oil, gas, metals
National Stabilization Fund	Taiwan	15.0	2000	Non-commodity
State Oil Fund	Azerbaijan	1.6	1999	Oil commodity

Source: Park and Estrada (2009).

4. ASEAN EXPERIENCE OF OUTWARD FDI STRATEGIES

Having discussed the recent trends and major players of outward FDI from ASEAN, this section turns the attention to examining the outward FDI strategies adopted by the three key players in the region: Singapore, Malaysia, and Thailand.

4.1 Singapore

In the 1960s–80s, the central thrust of Singapore's development strategy was on (inward) FDI-driven, export-led industrialization. Various fiscal and tax incentives were introduced to attract MNEs to set up operations in Singapore for export markets. However, with limited resources, tightening labour markets, and rising competition from emerging markets, this strategy's usefulness eventually reached its limit. To overcome these limitations, Singapore had to establish itself as a "business hub" that would tap into economic complementarities with Asia-Pacific region.

Since its first economic recession in the mid-1980s, Singapore has emphasized outward FDI as a key engine of economic growth and international competitiveness. Singapore correctly saw that the strategies of global sourcing offered a way to overcome its city-state limitations. Several policy initiatives were implemented to increase Singapore's outward FDI. For instance, the International Direct Investment Programme was launched in 1988 to offer tax incentives to direct investors, provide financial support, and evaluate outward FDI projects. In the early 1990s Singapore also pioneered the concept of a growth triangle that provided an economic nexus with Johor of Malaysia and the Riau Islands of Indonesia. This concept allowed Singaporean firms to invest in these neighbouring areas, thereby generating economic synergies and complementarities that strengthened attractiveness of the sub-region as a whole. Additionally, the Committee to Promote Enterprise Overseas was set up in 1993 to recommend measures to assist Singapore companies venturing overseas. In 1999, the US$1 billion Technopreneurship Investment Fund was inaugurated to spur the development of Singapore's venture capital industry.

To date, Singapore's outward FDI performance remains exceptional. Singapore has successfully leveraged its leading role in outward FDI as a means to maintain, if not enhance, international competitiveness through structural adjustment and industrial development. In the run-up to the global financial crisis, Singapore consistently ranked second in Asia in terms of outward FDI, after Hong Kong.[2] However, Singapore lost this position to China after the global financial crisis, as the deleveraging attempts of Singaporean investors reversed the mounting trend of outward FDI. China has continued to outpace Singapore in terms of both stock and flows of outward FDI, due mainly to its persistent current account surpluses in addition to efficiency-seeking motives.

Singapore's outward FDI has profoundly affected the financial services industry. Foreign investment in the financial services sector accounted for approximately 50 per cent of total outward FDI flows, with investment volume rising substantially from US$38.5 billion in 2000 to US$149.2 billion in 2008 (see Table 2.3). Market-seeking incentives have been a crucial driver of this trend, with Singapore's financial companies seeking to tap economies of scale and scope in larger markets abroad. Singapore also appears to be an active investor in non-financial service sectors. The stock of outward FDI in service sectors like construction, wholesale and retail trade, real estate services, and professional and technical services approximately doubled over the period 2000–08; in particular, foreign investment in the transportation and communication services increased exponentially from US$2.8 billion in 2000 to US$17.8 billion in 2008.

Another key component of Singapore's outward FDI is the manu-facturing sector. The outward FDI stock in the manufacturing sector exhibited a sharp spike from US$14.0 billion in 2000 to US$51.3 billion in 2008 (see Table 2.3). At least two forces account for this trend. The first is efficiency-seeking: in the last decade, Singapore's manufacturing sector was losing comparative advantage to its neighbour developing countries, especially China and India, where manufacturers have cheap labour costs and abundant raw materials. To maintain its competitiveness in the global market, Singapore's manufacturing firms had to relocate their manufacturing plants to bolster their overall production efficiency. The other catalyst was the Government's policy to keep technology-intensive, high value-added manufacturing at home and relocate labour-intensive, low value-added production to plants abroad (Yeung 2001).

4.2 Malaysia

Malaysia is ASEAN's second largest player when it comes to outward FDI. However, compared with Singapore, Malaysia is a latecomer. Although the

TABLE 2.3
Distribution of Outward FDI Stock by Economic Sector and Industry,ª 2000, 2008
(US$ billion)

Sector/industry	2000	2008
All sectors/industries	53.4	210.7
Primaryᵇ	n.a.	n.a.
Agriculture, hunting, forestry, and fishing	n.a.	n.a.
Mining, quarrying and petroleum	n.a.	n.a.
Secondary	14.0	51.3
Manufacturing	14.0	51.3
Services	38.5	149.2
Construction	0.5	1.0
Wholesale and retail trade	4.4	11.3
Transport and communication	2.8	17.8
Financial and insurance services	25.7	105.7
Real estate, rental and leasing	4.0	9.6
Professional and technical, administrative and support services	1.2	3.7
Unspecified other sectors/industries	0.8	8.2

Notes:
a. Singapore direct investment abroad (consolidated), by country and activity abroad.
b. Primary industries are not in the list of activities in Singapore investment abroad.
Source: *Singapore's investment abroad*, 2000, 2008, Department of Statistics, Ministry of Trade and Industry, Republic of Singapore, April 2010, available at <http://www.singstat.gov.sg/pubn/business/sia2008.pdf>.

Malaysian government has been encouraging outflows of FDI for some time now (Menon 2000), it has had limited success. Income repatriated from overseas investments — in all sectors except banking, insurance, and sea and air transport — was made tax-exempt as far back in 1995 as an inducement.

Malaysia's investments overseas remained low between 1980 and 1992, hovering around US$200 million annually and never exceeding US$300 million in a single year. They increased sharply to just over US$1 billion in 1993 and peaked at US$3.7 billion in 1996. It then fell sharply during the AFC, returning to negligible levels. On the whole, outward FDI from Malaysia prior to the 2000s was rather modest and concentrated around the finance and banking sectors in advanced economies such as the United States and Australia (see Figure 2.3). As noted by Goh and Wong (2011), the turning point arrived in the aftermath of AFC after the lifting of capital controls, when the Financial Sector Master Plan and Capital Market Master

Plan were implemented to further liberalize the capital account. These plans were aimed to facilitating cross-border investment by Malaysian companies. The second-round effect of this policy is that it tried to induce firms to invest abroad, thereby limiting the upward pressures on the ringgit exchange rates due to an influx of capital in the post-AFC period.

Outflows of capital from Malaysia started increasing sharply after the AFC to the point where Malaysia has become a net exporter of capital since 2005. During 2006–09, total outflows reached US$40.4 billion, almost double the inflows of US$23.2 billion over the same period. With the gap between inflows and outflows increasing over time, total outflows peaked at almost US$15 billion in 2008. UNCTAD (2012) suggest that outflows have started rising sharply again after the global financial crisis (GFC), amounting to US$13.3 billion and US$14.8 billion in 2010 and 2011, respectively. Malaysia is also the only net exporter of capital among the ASEAN countries.

As in Singapore, the Malaysian government has tried to promote outward FDI by domestic and government-linked enterprises. For instance, the Third Industrial Master Plan and the Ninth Malaysia Plan stipulated that the government encourages both privately owned and government-linked companies to venture abroad to foster the creation of successful Malaysian MNEs. Chan (2005) documented the former Prime Minister Dr. Mahathir's statement that encouraged Malaysian manufacturers to "relocate overseas, go large scale, and shift into high technology".

A significant portion of the outflows appears to be taking place in the services sector, which is dominated by oil and gas, as well as in mining and banking. There are also substantial outflows directed at the agriculture sector, especially plantations. As of 2012, the largest MNE from ASEAN is PETRONAS, a government-linked petroleum company from Malaysia, with US$49 billion in assets (see Table 2.1). PETRONAS has been investing heavily in offshore oil and gas operations in a wide range of countries in several continents, including Australia, Algeria, Chad, Cameroon, Mauritius, and Iraq, as well as closer to home in Indonesia, Myanmar, and Vietnam.

Several other Malaysian MNEs have also topped the rankings, such as YTL Corporation and Sime Darby. Sime Darby is the largest agriculture multinational corporation in the world. Two other Malaysian government-linked corporations (GLCs) are among the world's ten largest in this sector: Kuala Lumpur Kepong (KLK) and Kulim (UNCTAD 2009). There have been increasing levels of outward FDI in the oil palm sector, mostly going to Indonesia due to lower land and labour costs. In a move to diversify horizontally, Sime Darby also purchased rubber plantations in Liberia at a total value of US$800 million in 2009 (UNCTAD 2009). Meanwhile, the MSC Group has investments in mining in Australia, Canada, Indonesia, and the Philippines (UNCTAD, 2011). Singapore appears to be a large recipient covering a wide range of sectors.[3] A lot of these outward investments in almost all sectors are associated, predictably, with M&A activity.

Khazanah Nasional Berhad was also among the largest SWFs from ASEAN, with US$15 billion in assets, following GIC and Temasek Holdings from Singapore and Brunei Investment Agency from Brunei Darussalam (see Table 2.2).

4.3 Thailand

Thailand has been heavily reliant on inward, rather than outward, FDI. Thanks to passive strategies towards overseas investment, outward FDI from Thailand prior to the global financial crisis in 2008–09 was quite modest (see Figure 2.3). Following the global financial crisis, however, there was a remarkable surge in outward FDI from Thailand. The ranking of Thailand in terms of the Outward FDI Performance index are reported in Table 2.4. Although Thailand is consistently ranked among the least competitive economies in the region in terms of outward FDI performance, its performance has been consistently improving. As of 2005–07, Thailand's

TABLE 2.4
Country Rankings by Outward FDI Performance Index, 2000–07

Economy	Outward FDI Performance		
	2000–02	2003–05	2005–07
Singapore	5	12	10
Malaysia	29	29	22
Philippines	122	60	49
India	63	65	50
Indonesia	80	42	52
China	59	61	59
Thailand	84	70	66
Vietnam	n.a.	89	84

Note: The ranking covers 125 economies.
Source: UNCTAD, World Investment Report 2011, available at <www.unctad.org/wir>.

outward FDI performance was ranked the 66th, up from the 70th in 2003–05 and the 84th in 2000–2002. Nonetheless, Thailand still lags far behind countries like Singapore (10th), Malaysia (22nd), the Philippines (49th), India (50th), Indonesia (52nd), and China (59th). It has not been able to catch up with the well-established outward FDI players like Singapore and Malaysia. More recently, Thai MNCs concluded a number of mega cross-border M&A purchases, both intra- and inter-regional, exceeding US$500 million (ASEAN Secretariat, 2013). For instance, Thai Beverage acquired a 22 per cent stake in Fraser & Neave Ltd (Singapore) for US$2.2 billion. PTT-EP acquired Cove Energy (United Kingdom) with a deal worth US$1.9 billion. Banpu acquired an 80 per cent stake in Centennial Coal (Australia) for US$1.6 billion. Thai Union Frozen Products spent US$884 million to acquire MW Brans (France). More recently, CP Group closed an M&A deal with Ping An (China), worth US$9.4 billion.

The push factor for outward FDI from Thailand is by and large structural and market-driven, rather than policy-driven as in Singapore and Malaysia. In most cases, MNCs that engage in foreign investment are privately owned as opposed to government-linked corporations and SWFs. With an ever-increasing degree of globalization, Thai companies are hard pressed to become regional and international to maintain their competitiveness in the global market. That said, as Wee (2007) posited, the traditional motives of outward FDI from Thailand tend to be market-seeking, especially among large corporations, while resource-seeking FDI remains relatively limited. Efficiency-seeking FDI, albeit still modest, is on a rising trend.

5. CONCLUSION

ASEAN has traditionally been a major recipient of FDI. With the rapidly changing global economic environment, more and more enterprises are striving to venture abroad and tap new business opportunities through internationalization. For some ASEAN countries such as Singapore and Malaysia, outward FDI has exceeded inward flows of foreign capital in recent years. These developments suggest that ASEAN has evolved into an important source of foreign investment, both within and outside the region.

Nevertheless, the degree to which enterprises are able to invest abroad and leverage on internationalization differs remarkably within the region.

While Singapore, Malaysia, Thailand, and, to a lesser extent, Indonesia and the Philippines have firmly established their regional and global footprint, outward FDI from the rest of ASEAN countries remains modest. In light of closer economic ties and rising global competition, outward FDI from ASEAN will become a much more crucial source of growth and competitiveness than ever before. As some less developed ASEAN countries may fall out from the regionalization and internationalization waves, appropriate policies must be put in place to enable firms, particularly small and medium enterprises (SMEs), to competitively venture overseas. Otherwise, the full benefits and potentials of regional economic integration will not be realized.

Notes

1. The usual disclaimer applies. This paper represents the views of the author and not those of the Asian Development Bank, those of its Executive Directors or of the member countries that they represent.
2. "Singapore is biggest FDI draw in Asia after China, HK", *Business Times*, 30 September 2005.
3. Asia Sentinel. *Malaysia's Disastrous Capital Flight*. 11 January 2010.

References

ASEAN Secretariat. *ASEAN Investment Report 2012: The Changing FDI Landscape*. Jakarta: ASEAN Secretariat.

Chan, H.C. "Boosting Competitiveness through Reversed Investments". Paper presented at MIER, National Economic Outlook Conference 2006–07, Hilton Hotel Kuala Lumpur, Malaysia, 6–7 December 2005.

Chongvilaivan, A. and R. Rajan. "How Has Singapore Expanded Its Global Footprint through FDI?". In *Exchange Rates and Foreign Direct Investment in Emerging Asia: Selected Issues and Policy Options*, edited by Ramkishen S. Rajan. London: Routledge, 2012, pp. 145–64.

Ellingsen, G., W. Likumahuwa, and P. Nunnenkamp. "Outward FDI by Singapore: a different animal?". *Transnational Corporations* 15, no. 2 (2006): 1–40.

Goh, S.K. and Wong, K.N. "Malaysia's outward FDI: The effects of market size and government policy". *Journal of Policy Modeling* 33 (2011): 497–510.

Hill, H. and J. Jongwanich. "Emerging East Asian Economies As Foreign Investors: An Analytical Survey". *Singapore Economic Review* 59, no. 3 (2014): 1–26.

Menon, J. "How Open is Malaysia? An Analysis of Trade, Capital, and Labour Flows". *World Economy* 23, no. 2 (2000): 235–55.

Okposin, S.B. *The Extent of Singapore's Investment Abroad*. Brookfield: Ashgate, 1999.

Park, D. and G. Estrada. "Developing Asia's sovereign wealth funds and outward foreign direct investment". *Asian Development Review* 26, no. 2 (2009): 57–85.

UNCTAD. *World Investment Report 2009: Transnational Corporations, Agricultural Production, and Development*. Geneva: UNCTAD.

————. *World Investment Report 2011: Non-Equity Modes of International Production and Development*. Geneva: UNCTAD.

————. *Global Investment Trends Monitor*, 12 April 2012. Geneva: UNCTAD.

Wee, K.H. "Outward Foreign Direct Investment from Enterprises in Thailand". *Transnational Corporations* 16, no. 1 (2007): 89–116.

Yeung, H.W. "Organising regional production networks in Southeast Asia: implications for production fragmentation, trade, and rules of origin". *Journal of Economic Geography* 1, no. 3 (2001): 299–321.

3

THE IMPACT OF THE ASEAN ECONOMIC COMMUNITY ON OUTWARD FDI IN ASEAN COUNTRIES[1]

Pitchaya Sirivunnabood

1. INTRODUCTION

The Association of South East Asian Nations (ASEAN) has continued to pursue a free and open investment regime to promote more investment flows and investment integration in the region. On one hand, an increase in investment flows will sustain economic growth and improve social conditions in terms of employment and technology transfer. On the other, integration will create better investment environment with lower cost and time efficiency.

Despite the global economic turbulence in 2008–09, the trend of foreign direct investment (FDI) inflows to ASEAN has continuously improved due to strong macroeconomic foundations, increasingly favourable investment climate, and improving policy environment in ASEAN. The attractiveness of ASEAN has considerably increased since the Blueprint of ASEAN

Economic Community (AEC) was signed in November 2007. The Blueprint incorporates several high-impact agreements such as the ASEAN Trade in Goods Agreement (ATIGA), ASEAN Framework Agreement on Services (AFAS), and ASEAN Comprehensive Investment Agreement (ACIA). These agreements help create a more favourable economic environment for investors and traders in the region by increasing the region's attractiveness for investment, production and trade. Additionally, the ASEAN Agreement on the Movement of Natural Person (MNP) that was signed in November 2012 also aims to facilitate movement of businessmen and professionals in the region. Institutional capacity was also strengthened with the establishment of the ASEAN Investment Forum (AIF) in 2011, with the participation of lead investment agencies from each ASEAN country. Altogether, many regional measures have been undertaken to promote investment climate and strengthen the region's investment environment, resulting in a more free flow of investment across ASEAN.

In addition to the regional initiatives, each ASEAN Member State (AMS) has also introduced measures to further improve their investment climate and facilitate investment flows, i.e., liberalizing their investment regimes, opening up more industries for investment, providing more attractive investment incentives, and simplifying investment procedures and taxation.

This chapter aims to describe the transitional process of ASEAN's regional investment integration as well as its impacts on FDI flows in the region, both inflows and outflows. Empirical evidence are presented together with a discussion on the implications of ASEAN's efforts towards regional integration under the AEC initiatives and key deliverables. The availability of ASEAN investment data, particular the outflow foreign direct investment (OFDI), is limited. Most of the data presented in this chapter is used to explain the impact of the AEC on the investment outflows of each ASEAN member states. Since the AEC is a major initiative of ASEAN aimed at achieving regional economic integration, a major result presented in this chapter is how this initiative create intraregional investment flows.

Section 2 will provide an overview of FDI flows in ASEAN, for both inward and outward FDIs. Section 3 will discuss the background, process, and progress of ASEAN investment integration through its regional initiatives. Section 4 will examine the impact of AEC on FDI flows in the region. Challenges and outlook will be included in Section 5. Finally, Section 6 concludes.

2. REGIONAL ECONOMIC INTEGRATION AND OUTWARD FOREIGN DIRECT INVESTMENT

Regional economic integration affects the flows of foreign direct investment, both inward and outward flows. Basically, regional economic integration can lead to an increase in FDI by opening up sectors for investment. It aligns policies for treatment of foreign investors through direct and indirect effects of trade and investment liberalization as well as market integration (UNCTAD 2013). This includes the process of harmonization of general policy and regulatory frameworks across the member states through direct cooperation at the regional level. For example, a common FDI regime or a single integrated market for trade and investment can been designed to encourage increasing FDI from outside and inside within a region. Table 3.1 summarizes the relationship of regional integration and FDI flows. With the complementation of indirect effects of trade liberalization and market integration, an increase in FDI flows is accommodated by harmonization of policy and regulations and direct cooperation on investment projects at the regional level.

Regional integration can stimulate FDI flows through the rationalization of production facilities by transnational corporations (TNCs) due to the benefit from lower costs due to reduced trade barriers and economies of scale by focusing their production locally as serving broader regional markets. Taking a closer look at outward FDI, in relation with regional economic integration, it is evident that intra-regional FDI flows will increase due to implementation of initiatives under the regional economic integration framework. An increase in FDI from one member country to another will be evident, which implies more outward FDI flows moving among the participating countries. It could happen through enlarged markets and regional supply chain. More developed countries in ASEAN, such as Malaysia, Singapore, and Thailand, have moved their investment to less developed member countries, such as Cambodia, Lao PDR, and Myanmar, for lower production costs, particular in labour-intensive industries such textile and garment. This pattern of investment movement is enhanced by the ASEAN's initiatives for investment liberalization as a part of regional economic integration framework. The details of such initiatives will be discussed further in the later section.

Brenton Di Mauro and Lucke (1999) suggested that regional economic integration provides an important stimulus not only to trade, but also FDI.

TABLE 3.1
Mechanisms of the Impacts of Regional Economic Integration on FDI

Mechanisms	Effects on Intraregional FDI Flows	Effects on FDI Inflows from outside the region
Investment liberalization and/or provisions in regional agreements	Enables/encourages increased flows from regional investors per se, including existing third-country investors from outside the region	Enables/encourages increased flows from third-country investors not currently established inside the region
Trade and market integration provisions in regional agreements	Enables the reorganization of production at the regional level, including investment and divestments	Attract new third-country investment through enlarged markets, including within global value chains
Policy harmonization implicit in the implementation of regional agreements	Encourages investment through reduction in transaction costs and perceived risk	Enables/encourages increased inflows if harmonization encompasses investment regulations applicable to third-country investors
Broader pan-regional investment projects (e.g., infrastructure or research and development) made possible by, or integral to, regional agreements	Provides increased investment opportunities	Provides increased investment opportunities

Note: the mechanisms and effects are not mutually exclusive.
Source: UNCTAD, 2013.

Generally, regional economic integration is often considered as a means to improve member countries' attractiveness to FDI. Nonetheless, Kubny, Molders and Nunnenkamp (2008) indicated that FDI-related benefits gained from the regional economic integration depend on incentives of integration, e.g., market-seeking or efficiency-seeking. Basically, the market-seeking type relates to the local market of a host country or region, involving a horizontal replication of similar production line in different locations. The efficiency-seeking type is vertical phenomenon driven by international cost differentials and involving slicing up the value chain through re-locating specific stages of the production process to where they are most cost effective to undertake. As a result, under the horizontal scheme, removal of trade barriers reduces FDI flows in the region by weakening the incentive of companies based within the regional integration scheme to use FDI as a tariff jumping device. On the other hand, intra-regional FDI of the vertical scheme may be stimulated by the removal of internal trade barriers when the member countries have different level of economic development. Cost differentials among the member countries may strengthen the incentive of companies to relocate their production and investment to seek for more efficiency. Regarding this framework and the nature of development in the region, ASEAN's regional economic integration under the ASEAN Economic Community (AEC) is then considered as the efficiency-seeking integration. According to the World Investment Report (UNCTAD 2015), most of the investment in developing economies, including most ASEAN countries, tends to arise within each economy's immediate geographic region. Familiarity eases a company's early internationalization drive and regional markets. Together, regional value chains are a key driver for successful investment. Table 3.2 shows the relative bilateral FDI intensity of Malaysia and Singapore (as home economies) as an example to demonstrate the familiarity of these countries with the host economies.

ASEAN FDI Trends and Development

Fundamentally, investment flows in ASEAN countries tend to follow the global economic situation and investment trends. In other words, if the global FDI inflows increase, the FDI inflows to ASEAN would potentially increase too. Figure 3.1 shows the ASEAN's inward FDI trend in the past two decades under different global circumstances.

TABLE 3.2
Relative Bilateral FDI Intensity of Selected ASEAN Countries
as Home Economies, 2012

Malaysia		Singapore	
Indonesia	13.4	Malaysia	10.1
Cambodia	10.9	Indonesia	7.1
Vietnam	7.3	Philippines	7.0
Singapore	5.3	Taiwan	4.6
Thailand	4.7	China	4.2
Philippines	3.4	Thailand	4.0
Australia	2.3	Lao PDR	3.1
Taiwan	2.1	Australia	2.4
		India	1.8
		Vietnam	1.8

Source: World Investment 2015, UNCTAD.

Although it is apparent that ASEAN's FDI flows are affected by adverse external factors, such as the global/regional crisis, such flows in ASEAN usually rebound with steady growth. This suggests that the solid FDI performance in the region could be due to improved investment environment and its ability to gain back investors' confidence. The three consecutive years of increases (2010–13), and a high absolute level of inflows, indicate a growing confidence of foreign investors in ASEAN countries as an investment destination of choice. By the end of 2013, total inward FDI to ASEAN reached US$122.4 billion or approximately 6.6 per cent growth from the previous year. Intra-ASEAN FDI accounted for 17.4 per cent or US$21 billion. New investment and expansion of existing operations by transnational corporations (TNCs) continued to surge into the region while a record increase in intra-ASEAN investment was evident as well as a rise in FDI from emerging sources, particularly from China.

There are several factors underlying this period of sustainable and increasing FDI inflows. First, a strong growth momentum was maintained after the global financial crisis. Second, despite the economic slowdown and fiscal crises in many advanced economies, a considerable increase in FDI inflows took place against these backdrops. Third, reinvestment remained high, which reflects existing investors' favourable experience of ASEAN investment climate, increasingly recognized as a competitive place to do business and invest. Lastly, the rise in numbers of mergers and

FIGURE 3.1
ASEAN's Inward FDI Trend, 1995–2013 (US$ million)

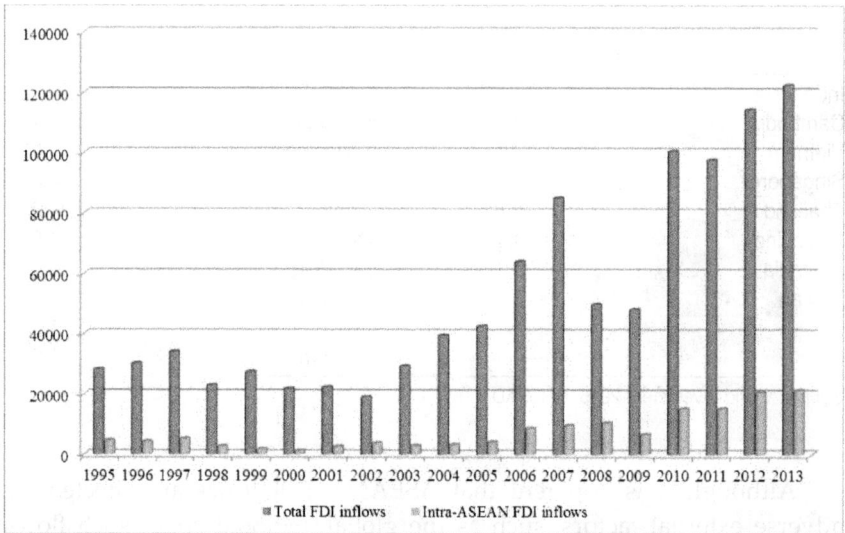

Source: ASEAN Investment Report 2012 and ASEAN Statistics, ASEAN Secretariat.

acquisitions (M&As) in the region implies growing maturity of ASEAN's M&As environment.[2]

ASEAN's dialogue partners (DPs)[3] are normally the largest sources of FDI inflows to the region, reaching US$70.76 billion in 2013 while the average share of the DPs' FDI inflows to the region accounted for almost 55 per cent. Figure 3.2 shows the region's top ten investors in 2013. While developed economies e.g., EU28, Japan, and the United States, remained the biggest contributors, new sources of FDI from developing countries have been witnessed in the past couple years. The significant rise in FDI from China and India as well as an increase in intra-ASEAN FDI flows have made these countries and the region the new emerging FDI contributors to ASEAN countries. The combined FDI from China and ASEAN countries grew by 75.3 per cent, from US$17.1 billion in 2010 to US$29.97 billion in 2013.

The various economic arrangements and developments involving ASEAN such as the ASEAN-China Free Trade Agreement (ACFTA) and the ASEAN Economic Community (AEC) have accentuated investment and

FIGURE 3.2
Top 10 Investors in ASEAN, 2012–13 (US$ million)

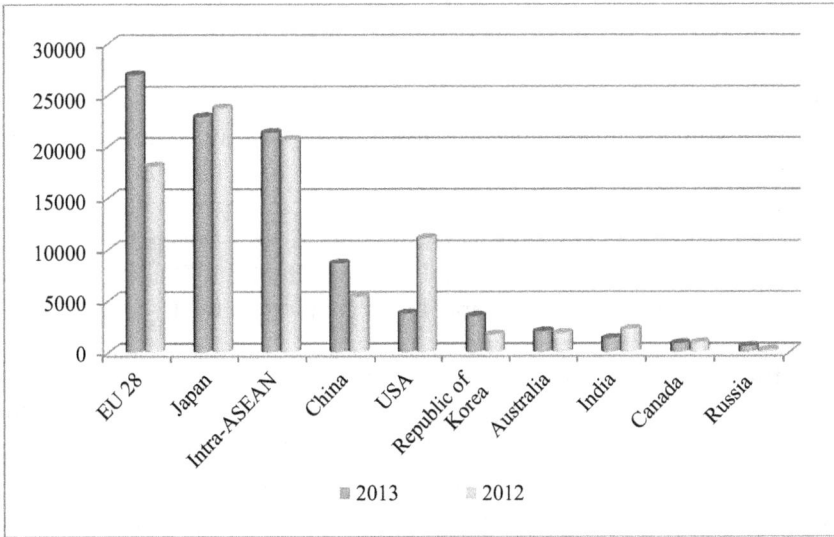

Source: ASEAN Secretariat, July 2014.

trade ties among ASEAN member countries and between ASEAN and other countries. These FTA arrangements enhance the regional investors' interest and confidence in investing in ASEAN. A series of investment promotion events, and a greater cooperation among the private sector, has facilitated investment and raised awareness of investment opportunities and benefits in the region. One of the most important factors that stimulate the FDI flows among ASEAN and the dialogue partners is the establishment of free trade agreement (FTA) between ASEAN and the DPs. More details shall be discussed in the later section in this chapter.

In addition, *ASEAN is not only a major recipient of FDI, but also an evolving source of investment to many economies outside and inside the region.* There has been a rapid increase in enterprise internationalization from ASEAN to elsewhere and among its members. Outward ASEAN FDI has continuously risen since the regional economic initiatives under the AEC is in place. Though the volume of ASEAN's outward FDI has remained lower than its inflows, there has been some improvement in the past decade (Figure 3.3). Some ASEAN countries have experienced a continual increase in FDI outflows, e.g., Singapore, Malaysia, and Thailand. The gap in FDI outflows between the largest regional investor such as Singapore and other potential ASEAN countries (i.e., Malaysia, Thailand, and Indonesia) are actually narrowing. In other words, ASEAN investors have become increasingly regionalized as initiatives have been gradually implemented for regional investment integration.

The volume of outward FDI in ASEAN countries jumped from US$33.96 billion in 2008 to US$56.37 billion at the end of 2013. Outward FDI from ASEAN countries rose by 5 per cent. Singapore experienced a double increase in FDI outflows from US$13 billion in 2012 to US$27 billion in 2013 while the OFDI from Malaysia (US$13.6 billion) and Thailand (US$6.6 billion) dropped by 21 per cent and 49 per cent, respectively, possibly due to slowdown in the global economy.

Most of the multinational enterprises (MNEs) from developing countries have expanded their foreign operations through greenfield investments and cross-border M&As. Though there was a drop in the OFDI in some economies, the outlook is still positive for ASEAN; partly because of the accelerated regional economic integration process under the AEC initiatives (see the section of ASEAN investment integration reforms). Rising intra-regional FDI flows is expected through the proactive regional

FIGURE 3.3
ASEAN's Outward FDI, 2003–13 (US$ million)

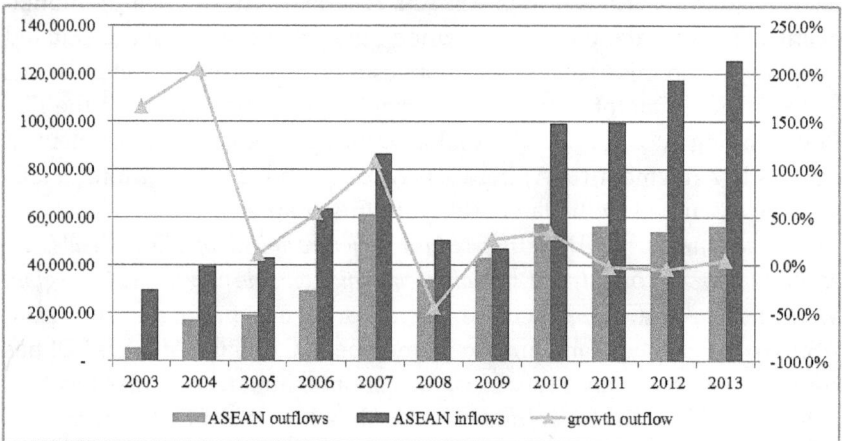

Source: FDI data, World Investment Report, UNCTAD.

investment cooperation effort. Evidently, China, India, Japan, the Republic of Korea, Singapore, Malaysia, and Thailand have made considerable advances as sources of FDI to ASEAN, at the possible costs of the United States and European Union (UNCTAD 2014).

3. ASEAN INVESTMENT INTEGRATION REFORMS

ASEAN Investment Agreements

ASEAN's efforts towards regional investment integration have been gradually constructed. Many steps were taken to deepen investment liberalization in the region. Initially, ASEAN cooperation in promoting investment flows was implemented through separate agreements. In 1987, ASEAN initiated agreements on its investment integration with the ASEAN Agreement for the Promotion and Protection of Investment, or commonly known as the ASEAN Investment Guarantee Agreement (IGA). The main objective of IGA back then was just only to promote investment through guaranteeing investment protection. Basically, the term "investment promotion" was set in a general context of encouraging and creating favourable conditions for foreign investment. A legal framework to protect investments in member states was created on the premise of Most Favoured Nation (MFN) treatment, but not national treatment.

After the Asian financial crisis in 1997–98, ASEAN members realized a need to review and deepen ASEAN's investment framework for higher cooperation. Thus, the framework agreement on ASEAN Investment Area (AIA) was signed in 1998. The AIA focused on three main pillars of liberalization, facilitation, and promotion. A specific provision was made for the term "promotion" which covers the process of facilitation, promotion, and liberalization as well as taking appropriate measures to ensure the attractiveness of the investment environment. A more comprehensive approach was added under the AIA Framework by including market access and national treatment which covered six main sectors namely, manufacture, agriculture, mining, fisheries and forestry, and services incidental. Together with this approach, exceptions were listed in the Exclusion and Sensitive lists. In accordance with the AIA, ASEAN investors should benefit from national treatment by 2010 and all other ASEAN investors by 2020. The goal of the AIA is to attract FDI not only within the region, but also from outside through more competitive and transparent investment climate in ASEAN through deregulation and jointly promoting the region as an optimal investment destination.

Further reforms and implementation of new regional initiatives were officially introduced later in the AEC Blueprint. The AEC's priority goal is the creation of a single market and production base that will generate a dynamic and competitive ASEAN. As a result, to ensure achievement of this priority goal, free flow of investment was added as an integral element of the ASEAN single market and production base. An open and non-discriminatory investment regime has become a key driver of ASEAN's global competitiveness, economic diversification, and ultimately shared growth. A major impact from promoting the free flow of investment shall be further development of intra-ASEAN investment and more dynamic investment flows across the region, especially among multinational corporates (MNCs) based in ASEAN.

In February 2009, the ASEAN Comprehensive Investment Agreement (ACIA) was signed as a comprehensive agreement for regional investment integration for ASEAN. It covers investment liberalization, protection, facilitation, and promotion. Although ACIA has a similar structure to the AIA (4 pillars and 6 sectors), its framework is actually more comprehensive than AIA and IGA combined. The ACIA is composed of new provisions and improved versions of provisions that currently exist in the AIA and IGA. These include efforts to accelerate the ASEAN investment integration process. Upon ACIA's entry into force in March 2012, the ASEAN's IGA and AIA Agreement were terminated while a three-year transition period was applied to investors who wished to keep existing investment within the realm of the IGA and the AIA Agreements.

Fundamentally, the ACIA was developed to provide a single framework for relevant investment provisions in investment liberalization and protection. Clear and transparent procedures and definitions in line with international investment agreements are provided under the Agreement. Several liberalization provisions are included, which improve the ACIA over the IGA. For example, the Agreement sets up a target to achieve an ASEAN open investment regime to all investors in 2015, instead of 2020 as previously stated in AIA. This will provide opportunities for both ASEAN and foreign investors to enjoy the same benefits at the same time. The ACIA maintains automatic MFN provision of AIA as preferential treatment granted by any AMS under any existing or future agreement (which must be extended to all other AMS).

Moreover, the coverage of the Agreement was extended to portfolio investment, which followed the practice of many bilateral investment treaties, e.g., the one modelled in the North America Free Trade Agreement (NAFTA). The Agreement also includes new articles on the prohibition of performance requirements under Trade-Related Investment Measures (TRIMs) as defined by the World Trade Organization (WTO) as well as nationality requirements in the appointment of managers. This is to make the agreement more comprehensive by incorporating TRIMs-Plus elements. Importantly, the ACIA provides detailed procedures for dispute settlement, including consultation among the AMS. This gives more confidence and understanding to foreign investors who are interested in investing in the region. Technically, ACIA has taken into account several international best practices, e.g., US Model Investment Text, NAFTA, OECD Guidelines for multinational enterprises, and the draft ASEAN FTAs (investment element) with China, Republic of Korea, and Australian and New Zealand.

One of the major crucial improvement is the change in the liberalization scheduling approach to a single negative list regime. In principal, exceptions to liberalization are listed in a single negative list replacing the prior lists in AIA, i.e., Tentative Exclusion List (TEL) and Sensitive List (SL). Therefore, the ACIA's consolidated Reservation List consists of the remaining exceptions in the TEL and SL, plus additional amendments and inclusions. The Reservation List of each ASEAN member state is then intended to state those sectors that are not subjected to future elimination or improvement as well as those whose reservations are expected to be improved or eliminated over time i.e., permanent and temporary exclusions, respectively.

ACIA also includes special and differential (S&D) treatment for newer ASEAN member states as a narrowing development gap initiative. This S&D can be implemented through technical assistance, capacity-building programmes, and other related facilitations. Flexibility is also given to the newer AMSs to assist them in terms of catching up and adjusting to this regional integration dynamics.

The complete implementation of the ACIA will offer primary benefits of an open investment regime, enhanced investment protection, further development of intra-ASEAN investment, and enhanced economic integration. First, a free and open investment regime will reduce and/or eliminate investment barriers (Reservation List). Second, the ACIA's comprehensive provisions will upgrade the investment protection and improve confidence of investors in investing in ASEAN. In case of dispute settlement with a host government, investors have a choice of bringing a claim to a domestic court, where applicable, or international arbitration. Furthermore, the ACIA encourages higher flow of intra-region investments, especially among the ASEAN-based MNCs, through expansion, industrial complementation, and specialization. The ASEAN-based investors can enjoy the benefits of non-discrimination treatment when they invest in other ASEAN countries. At the same time, the ACIA also grants similar treatment given to domestic investors to non-ASEAN investors and also similar treatment vis-à-vis other ASEAN-based investors. As a result, fair and equitable treatment is expected to be granted to investors and their investment as well as full protection and security.

In addition, the ACIA has developed several guidelines to further facilitate business sector in ASEAN. These include initiatives to ensure free transfer of funds, capital, profit, and dividends. Clear provisions on compensation based on fair market value are also included, together with non-discriminatory treatment for compensation for losses arising from civil strife, riots, etc. Last, but not least, the cooperation from ASEAN governments in terms of promotion and facilitation of investment are highlighted to accelerate regional investment and economic integration. Table 3.3 summarizes ASEAN's key investment efforts along with their objectives.

ASEAN Investment-Complementary Agreements

In addition to the ACIA, the main regional investment agreement, ASEAN has implemented other complementary agreements and initiatives to promote the regional investment integration and to facilitate free flow of investment in the region. Since ACIA does not cover the whole services sector, the ASEAN Framework Agreement on Services (AFAS) is a complementary agreement to help facilitate investment. It covers some sectors that are not included in ACIA. Basically, AFAS covers the liberalization of services sector and facilitates trade in services in the region. The overlapping issues include the foreign ownership ratio and restrictions on foreign equity. Moreover, in cognizance of the importance of the professional movement, ASEAN has signed and implemented the Agreement on Movement of Natural Persons (MNP) in 2012. This will

TABLE 3.3
ASEAN's Key Investment Efforts

Year	Initiative	Objectives
1983	ASEAN Industrial Joint Venture (AIJV)	• To provide an investment framework for industrial joint venture, • To promote greater utilization of industries and expand trade, • To improve economic infrastructure.
1987	Investment Guarantee Agreement (IGA)	• To create favourable conditions to increase private investment flows by nationals and companies of any AMS within their territories, • To provide equitable treatment to investors of the most favoured nations. • The amendment of GIA to simplify the investment procedures and approval processes, as well as enhance transparency, was done in 1996.
1995	ASEAN Plan of Action on Cooperation and Promotion of FDI and intra-ASEAN Investment	• To facilitate and promote investment and trade through promotional seminars and activities, • To upgrade transparency and simplification of procedures and regulations, • To establish cooperation among ASEAN investment agencies for information sharing and best practices.
1996	ASEAN Industrial Cooperation Scheme (AICO)	• To promote greater industrialization and expand trade and investment in the ASEAN economies, • To strengthen the process of industrialization and industrial cooperation among ASEAN and non-ASEAN economies. • The amendment of AICO to update the preferential tariff rates and basic agreement was done in 2004.
1998	ASEAN Investment Area (AIA)	• To stimulate investment flows from ASEAN and non-ASEAN sources, • To strengthen and increase competitiveness of ASEAN's economic sectors and eliminate investment restrictions, • To achieve the free flow of investment for AMS by 2010 and for all investors by 2020.
2009	ASEAN Comprehensive Investment Agreement (ACIA)	• To consolidate IGA and AIA as well as related Protocols in response to more competitive global environment, • To expand the scope of investment industries for eligible sectors, • To encourage further development of intra-ASEAN investment, particular among MNCs based in the region via expansion, industrial cooperation, and specialization.

Source: ASEAN Secretariat.

improve the investment environment in ASEAN countries, specifically in terms of employment aspects.

A number of major economic agreements between ASEAN and its dialogue partners have established free trade areas. These have crucial implication on FDI decisions in terms of market size (as an integrated region), economic liberalization, as well as trade and investment facilitation. The ASEAN's free trade agreements (FTAs) that have been negotiated between ASEAN and its dialogue partners (such as Australia, New Zealand, China, Japan, India, and the Republic of Korea) provide investment opportunities and increase the two-way investment flows among the parties involved. This so-called "ASEAN +1" FTAs have helped facilitate both trade and investment flows among these sixteen economies. Over time, ASEAN has broadened its scope of regional economic integration, alongside with its trading/investment partners through the ASEAN+3 and ASEAN+ Cooperation. According to the 2014 World Investment Report (UNCTAD, June 2014), it was suggested that the proactive regional investment cooperation efforts in East Asia and Southeast Asia have contributed to a significant rise in total and intra-regional FDI. Despite the stagnation in outward FDI from advanced economies, the outflows from developing countries remained resilient in 2013, particularly from developing Asia which rose by 8 per cent to US$325 billion. Table 3.4 assesses the strength of existing ASEAN+1 FTAs that may lead to an increase in OFDI of ASEAN and its member countries. In terms of trade in goods, all of the DPs have a progressive implementation on tariff elimination schedules. Therefore, the template of some ASEAN+1 FTAs is characterized by vertically integrated trade and complementary FDI which has driven production in manufacturing supply chains (Sally 2013).

Subsequently, ACIA and these complementary agreements have been working together in promote FDI and investment flows in the region. However, ASEAN needs to put more efforts in terms of establishment of negotiation frameworks and implementation in order to witness significant results from its regional economic integration measures/initiatives.

4. ASEAN INTEGRATION IMPACTS

Increase in Outward FDI

Since the signing of the AEC in 2007 and the entry into force of ACIA in 2012, there has been a gradual rise in the share of intra-ASEAN FDI

TABLE 3.4
Assessment of ASEAN+1 FTAs

FTA	Measure	Results
ASEAN-China (ACFTA)	• Trade in Services Agreement was signed in 2007, • Investment Agreement was implemented in 2010.	• Investment provisions follow the template of AIA, but with absence of MRAs, government procurement, IPRs, and movement of business persons, • Economic cooperation on infrastructural projects.
ASEAN-Japan Comprehensive Economic Partnership Agreement (AJCEP)	• Agreement of Trade in Goods came into effect in 2008, • Agreements on services and investment are based on bilateral Economic Partnership Agreements (EPAs).	• Japan has EPAs with seven countries in ASEAN, • Most EPAs cover economic cooperation.
ASEAN-Korea (AKFTA)	• Agreement on services and investment cane into effect in 2009.	• Similar to ACFTA, the framework does not cover government procurement, government services, movement of business persons, and IPRs, • Economic cooperation is included.
ASEAN-India (AIFTA)	• Services and investment are in coverage, but negotiations are still ongoing.	• Similar to others, the framework may not cover government procurement, government services, movement of business persons, and IPRs, • Poor customs performance in India would limit trade and investment activity between the two economies.
ASEAN-Australia-New Zealand (AANZFTA)	• Trade in goods, services, and investment were negotiated and concluded concurrently in 2010.	• Though the negotiations were concluded, not all AMS implemented AANZFTA, • GATS-Plus commitments by some AMS and the service agreement operates on a positive list, • The most advanced ASEAN+1 FTA that includes investor-state dispute settlement, investment protection agreement, movement of business persons, IPRs, and future negotiations on sectoral MRAs and cooperation on SPS.

Source: The AEC Work in Progress, ADB, 2013.

in the region. Intra-ASEAN FDI accounted for 17.4 per cent of total FDI by the end of 2013. This implies not only a higher degree of regionalism in ASEAN, but also increasing investment from one ASEAN member to another. Table 3.5 shows the FDI outward flows from each ASEAN country to the other AMS (intra-ASEAN) since 2005. The trends indicate a significant increase from Singapore and gradual increase from Brunei Darussalam, Cambodia, and Myanmar. A drop in FDI flow to ASEAN was evident in Indonesia, Malaysia, the Philippines, Thailand, and Vietnam.

Indonesia has made significant progress and has become a predominant source of intra-ASEAN FDI outflows to ASEAN, followed by Singapore and Malaysia. Singapore and Indonesia were also the predominant FDI destinations, and to lesser extent Thailand and Malaysia (Table 3.6). In addition, Table 3.7 shows the progress of ASEAN's outward FDI in annual average value. An obvious trend of increasing FDI outflows has been presented in ASEAN 6 in the past decade. A big increase was observed between the period of 2000–05 and during 2006–11. One factor that has driven the investment outflows is the propensity for AMS to increase OFDI as development occurs.[4] Despite the increase in the OFDI of ASEAN, most of these flows were initiated by Singapore which accounted for almost 40 per cent of total ASEAN's OFDI.

The rising share of intra-ASEAN FDI inflows is consistent with global trend in rising South-South investment. Particularly, the outward FDI flows originating in developing countries have been increasing with the biggest share from East and Southeast Asia, which accounted approximately for 65 per cent of total FDI outflows from developing economies (WIR 2013, UNCTAD). On the other hand, the FDI outflows from advanced countries have demonstrated a fluctuating trend, mainly due to the global economic situation. Fundamentally, such outflows are driven with an intention to search for new markets, natural resources, and technological and management know-hows.

From Figure 3.4, it can been that the volume of ASEAN's OFDI has increased since 2000. A parallel trend of increasing intra-ASEAN FDI outflows is also highlighted in this figure. This development could imply a considerably cumulative effect of regional agreements on the investment behaviour of ASEAN member states. This change in investment pattern in ASEAN is also explained by the factors discussed below.

TABLE 3.5
FDI Flows of each AMS to ASEAN (US$ million)

	2005	2006	2007	2008	2009	2010	2011	2012	2013
Brunei Darussalam	25.67	–37.57	–3.00	81.64	128.55	–37.63	150.83	295.46	545.69
Cambodia	0.03	0.03	1.35	8.50	–11.54	17.17	33.07	2.43	1.72
Indonesia	128.17	603.72	792.90	853.46	1,375.94	1,455.57	2,133.87	3,721.16	2,648.01
Lao PDR	–0.60	41.58	9.67	–72.10	0.35	34.48	0.80	–0.09	–44.61
Malaysia	830.40	979.59	961.52	3,720.17	2,640.62	3,422.77	1,802.91	2,854.43	1,296.94
Myanmar	10.52	32.69	62.91	64.54	71.08	68.90	120.63	105.31	98.45
Philippines	135.27	153.69	359.35	155.71	–441.10	262.55	–506.15	826.35	330.36
Singapore	2,907.65	6,614.35	6,381.44	4,611.24	2,218.21	7,989.20	11,769.20	10,254.44	14,385.71
Thailand	54.18	298.62	889.61	882.52	589.14	1,565.14	–605.76	2,044.69	1,725.58
Vietnam	6.39	6.82	179.69	138.17	94.34	395.14	303.29	413.49	346.08

Source: ASEAN Secretariat, 2014.

TABLE 3.6
Flows of Intra-ASEAN FDI in 2013 (US$ million)

FDI Outward by / FDI Inward to	BRD	CAM	IND	LAO	MAL	MYA	PHI	SIN	THA	VIE	TOTAL
Brunei Darussalam	—	—	—	—	-57.76	—	—	-14.84	—	—	-72.60
Cambodia	1.17	—	-0.00	—	97.88	—	—	83.68	61.81	54.31	298.85
Indonesia	-2.98	0.02	—	0.00	-656.32	—	7.22	9,257.89	109.87	5.41	8,721.11
Lao PDR	—	—	—	—	—	—	—	—	—	—	—
Malaysia	1.79	2.22	56.04	0.04	—	-0.51	-40.10	1,788.08	240.19	144.19	2,187.50
Myanmar	0.70	—	16.40	—	4.00	—	—	654.80	494.50	16.40	1,186.80
Philippines	0.02	0.02	0.10	—	99.78	—	—	-138.04	-3.55	—	-41.71
Singapore	510.20	—	2,483.90	—	1,501.40	98.00	344.40	—	655.80	124.90	5,718.60
Thailand	0.64	3.52	75.14	-44.66	248.57	0.96	18.70	953.05	—	0.88	1,256.79
Vietnam	34.15	0.41	16.43	—	59.39	—	0.15	1,801.09	166.96	—	2,078.59
Total ASEAN Outward	545.69	1.72	2,648.01	-44.61	1,296.94	98.45	330.36	14,385.71	1,725.58	346.08	21,333.93

Source: ASEAN Secretariat, 2014 (no data available for Lao PDR).

TABLE 3.7
Outward FDI Flows from ASEAN, annual average (US$ million)

	1990–95	2000–05	2006–11	2011–13
ASEAN	5,538	12,189	42,350	55,534
Brunei Darussalam	35	26	9	–182
Cambodia	–	8	15	36
Indonesia	967	1,190	4,321	5,604
Lao PDR	1	2	–3	–9
Malaysia	1,050	1,784	11,445	15,321
Myanmar	n/a	n/a	n/a	n/a
Philippines	154	187	814	3,388
Singapore	2,981	8,682	21,082	21,307
Thailand	350	229	4,147	8,703
Vietnam	–	11	520	1,369

Source: World Investment Report 2014, UNCTAD.

FIGURE 3.4
ASEAN's Outward Foreign Direct Investment Trends, 2000–13

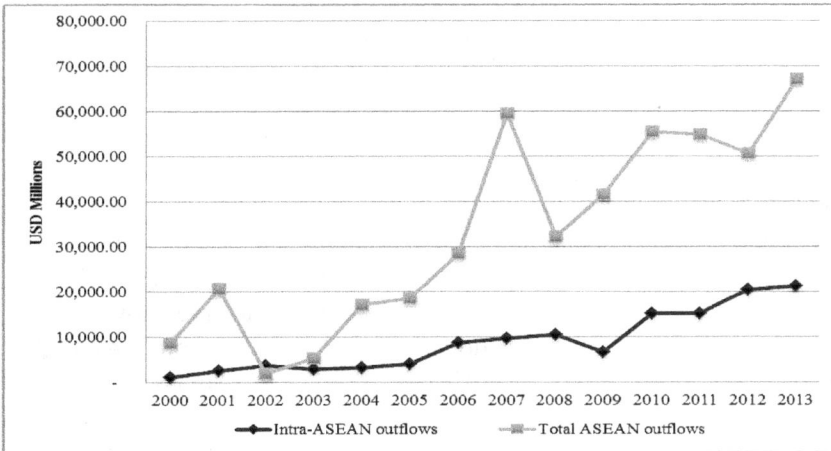

Source: ASEAN Statistics and World Investment Report, UNCTAD.

Rise of Regionalization

In the past decade, a changing pattern of FDI in ASEAN has been witnessed. ASEAN is no longer just an FDI recipient, but it has evolved to be an important source of investment for many developing markets, including the investment flows within the region. Some ASEAN members have experienced annual outward FDI flows that are consistently higher than inward FDI flows in recent years. At the same time, the gap between the biggest ASEAN FDI source such as Singapore and other countries in the region (e.g. Indonesia, Thailand, and Malaysia) has been narrowing. This implies that investors in some countries in ASEAN are now becoming more regionalized than ever. In other words, *regionalization has emerged considerably in the ASEAN.*

In the current era of regionalization driven by the AEC, a rapid rise in enterprise internationalization from ASEAN and a continual improvement of ASEAN's FDI outflows have been increasingly demonstrated in recent years. More companies from ASEAN are going regional or strengthening their regional footprint in light of closer economic integration (ASEAN Investment Report 2012). The volume of intra-ASEAN FDI reached US$21.3 billion in 2013. According to the ASEAN Investment Report 2012, many ASEAN companies have expressed their interest in regionalization after the signing of the AEC by expanding their investment and operations across ASEAN. These include companies such as CIMB, Maybank, Axiata, Air Asia, Siam Cement, PTT, Thai Beverage, S&P, Central Group, Ayala, San Miguel, Ciputra, DBS, Far East Hospital Group, Keppel Group, and Petro Vietnam. This recent expansion reflect a growing financial competence and capacity to regionalize/internationalize amongst ASEAN multinational enterprises (MNEs). Complementarily, AMSs have encouraged their national companies to invest regionally by taking up the advantages and benefits of the AEC. With the full implementation of initiatives and agreements under the AEC Blueprint, ASEAN offers a favourable investment climate to investors. The free movement of resources — goods, services, and investment — will encourage a higher degree of regionalization in ASEAN which will increase financial resources and economic complementary between countries across the region. This will drive forward the current wave of enterprise regionalization. It is noteworthy that, despite the increase in the volume of intra-ASEAN FDI, the traditional sources of FDI such as EU28, Japan, and the United States remain important.

An increasing number of ASEAN MNEs moving across the region has confirmed the positive impacts of regional integration and the ingenuity of AEC. Many ASEAN and non-ASEAN MNEs have expanded their investment in the region in recent years. It is evident that specific regional policy measures have actually stimulated the growth of regional production networks in ASEAN, along with regional value chains. The main initiatives are not only the AIA and ACIA, but also the ASEAN Free Trade Agreement (AFTA), ATIGA, AFAS, and MNP. To upgrade the regional financial competence in supporting real sectors and investment, serious efforts are now undertaken under the ASEAN Financial Integration Framework (AFIF).

For AFTA, the emphasis is on elimination/reduction of tariff lines which has lowered the cost of production as well as offer an attractive regional market with more than 600 million consumers with continuously increasing purchasing power. ATIGA, AFAS, and MNP are being implemented to facilitate doing business in the region. This involves the harmonization of regulations, standard and conformance, quality of products and services, and customs procedures, as well as movement of professionals. All in all, with the implementation of the AEC, FDI in ASEAN countries is being shaped into a new landscape where regionalization has become a big part. FDI flows in the ASEAN countries will become even more regional oriented with a greater flow of professionals and stronger regional production networks. The ASEAN Investment Report 2012 provides examples of cases on regional MNEs' production networks and value chain arrangements in ASEAN including interesting cases such as Procter & Gamble (P&G) and Toyota. Consequently, investment-specific efforts have been witnessed in the regional integration process of ASEAN. Besides encouraging intra-ASEAN FDI by granting ASEAN investors national treatment and greater access to industries, this process of regionalization has expanded the regional market and enhanced awareness of the attractiveness of ASEAN as a regional location for international investment.

In parallel with the process of regionalization, ASEAN has also internationalized through its FTAs with dialogue partners. A growing number of FTAs and similar agreements[5] of ASEAN with other dialogue partners have strengthened ASEAN's competitiveness and attractiveness to investors and producers. Although the FTAs have not yet included comprehensive agreements in the investment areas as mentioned earlier, they open an opportunity for ASEAN investors to go internationally with a larger combined market and higher advantages underlined by the ASEAN+1 agreements. For example, the establishment of the ASEAN-China FTA (ACFTA) has strengthened regional economic cooperation and contributed to the promotion of two-way FDI flows. Figure 3.5 demonstrates ASEAN's FDI outflows to its FTA dialogues in the past decade. A big jump in ASEAN's OFDI can be observed in 2007 the same year as the AEC Blueprint was signed. However, this may not be entirely due to the AEC because the impact of the AEC is likely to require more time. In any case, the volume of OFDI continued to increase after 2007. Tracking the record of ASEAN+1 FTAs, some implications can be drawn. First, the economies that are ASEAN's FTA dialogue partners — China, Australia and New Zealand — received the most OFDI from the region. Second, as mentioned in the section on ASEAN+1 Assessment, the AANZFTA is the most comprehensive trade agreement that ASEAN have signed with its trading partners. As a result, after the conclusion of the FTA in 2010, an increasing trend of OFDI was observed.

Moreover, the recent initiative of Regional Comprehensive Economic Partnership (RCEP)[6] under Pillar 4 — integration to global economy — is also offering benefits of a larger combined market and some advantages. The RCEP has become a priority to ASEAN since its initiation. It combines sixteen negotiating members with FDI inflows that amounted to US$343 billion or 24 per cent of global FDI inflows. At the same time, it promotes

FIGURE 3.5
ASEAN's Outward FDI, by Destination, 2001–12 (US$ million)

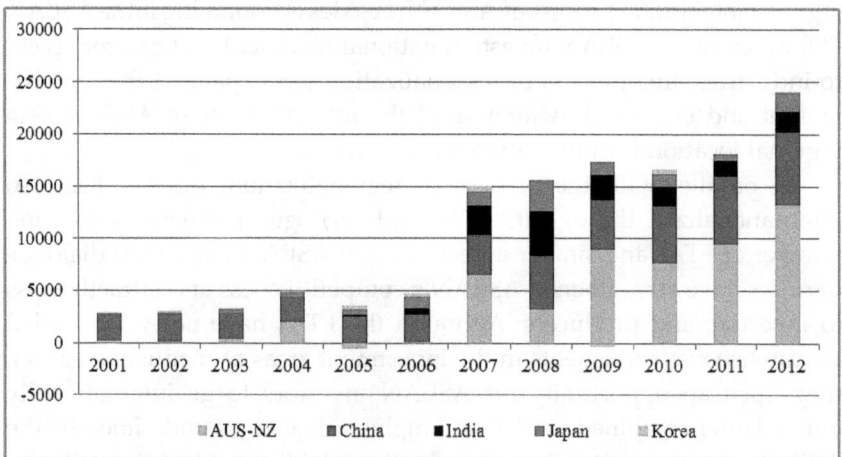

Source: FDI data, World Investment Report, UNCTAD.

intra-regional FDI flows across ASEAN. The FDI outflows from one AMS to others would be encouraged. Rising intra-ASEAN FDI flows have focused increasingly on infrastructure and manufacturing, which is bringing development opportunities to ASEAN, particularly for newer members such as Cambodia, Lao PDR and Myanmar. Recently, these countries have emerged as attractive investment destinations, not only for foreign investors outside the region, but also for ASEAN investors. For example, Siam Cement Group from Thailand has expanded its operations to the CLMV economies. Under the theoretical framework of the regional industrial upgrading, increased intraregional FDI has accelerated the development of international production networks within ASEAN. In parallel, the proactive investment cooperation and regional investment integration framework also promote cross-border investment by regional TNCs. These effective institutional mechanisms of investment facilitation and promotion coordinate national efforts within the bloc and compete effectively with other countries in attracting FDI (WIR 2014, UNCTAD). In sum, ASEAN regional integration and AEC have increased intra-regional FDI inflows and outflows.

Investment Facilitation — Ease of Doing Business

One important impact of the ASEAN regional integration process on the region's FDI outflow, especially via the AEC initiatives, is the investment facilitation that makes doing business in ASEAN easier. The favourable investment environment has been recognized by views of companies investing in the region, as reported in the findings of the 2010 ASEAN BAC Survey. The positive findings were indicated in the Survey for investment in ASEAN. At the same time, it is evident from the World Bank's Doing Business reports that ASEAN members have further improved their overall business regulatory practices. ASEAN has shown a good record in terms of business startup, business regulatory practices relating intellectual property registration, construction permits, tax payment, and trade procedure.

Figure 3.6 shows divergence in starting up businesses in ASEAN countries. Member countries such as Singapore, Malaysia, and Thailand offer more favourable conditions than the average of East Asia and Pacific. One interesting point is that the variance in terms of days it takes to start a foreign business among ASEAN countries is significantly higher than the

FIGURE 3.6
Starting Up a Foreign Business in ASEAN, 2014

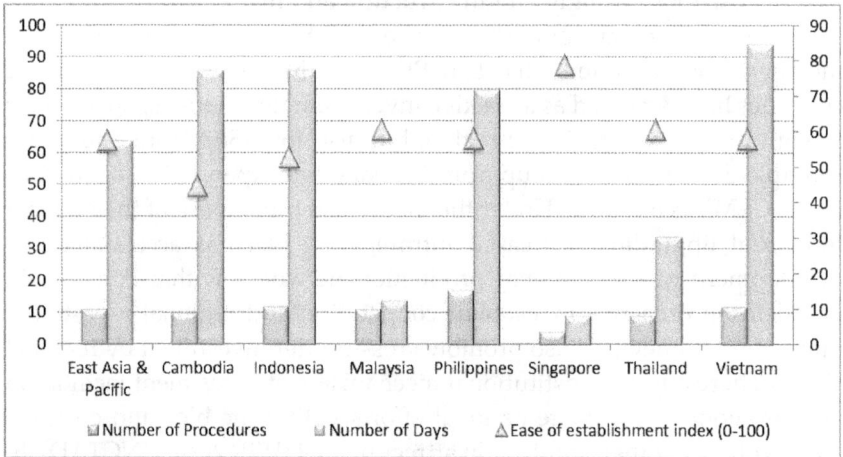

Source: Investing Across Borders.

variance for the number of procedures. This indicates the fact that each additional administrative step has compounding effects and lengthens the whole process.

This kind of survey, and the indicators included, influence investors' decision-making in the region. Under the AEC agreements and initiatives, ASEAN is expecting to implement more investment liberalization, promotion, and protection which will stimulate investment flows, both inflows and outflows. To measure the effectiveness and capability to increase investment flows within the region, these indicators can be used as tools that can help us to understand the progress of policy/initiative implementation of ASEAN.

In addition to the investment facilitation, improvements in infrastructure connectivity is another key major factor that can stimulate FDI flows in the region. Connectivity between countries and economies in ASEAN (as well as with East Asia) is intensifying across the infrastructure sector, business connections, and institutions (UNCTAD 2014). Improved regional infrastructure connectivity through regional cooperation and investment initiatives will help to upgrade investment climate and enhance attractiveness for efficiency-seeking manufacturing FDI. This will stimulate the intra-ASEAN FDI flows in particular. The regional infrastructure connectivity initiatives should include electricity, road, railway, ICT and financial development. According to the World Investment Report 2015 (UNCTAD 2015), the OFDI in infrastructure industries from East and Southeast Asia has increased dramatically and is targeted to connect the region, particular East Asia and countries in Southeast Asia, and to develop basic infrastructure to support regional production networks.

5. CHALLENGES AND OUTLOOK

The recent increase in intra-ASEAN FDI flows reflects the potential of AEC. However, challenges still remain. A major concern is on how to improve the region's investment climate through further enhancement of investment facilitation procedures in order to smooth investment flows across the region. Three components are always referred to when discussing the investment environment — political and macroeconomic stability, sound regulatory framework and efficient supporting in-stitutions, and sufficient physical and social infrastructure (World Bank 2005). For ASEAN, these components are still work in progress. ASEAN has put efforts to smooth investment flows by taking guidelines of good business practices and identifying the best practices for critical area that would get them to achieve the AEC realization goal. Particularly, the focus is most likely to lay on strengthening legal institutions that protect property and investor rights while continuing to promote efficient regulatory processes.

Findings from a survey conducted by Accenture in 2011 with 407 observations[7] from ASEAN-5 (Indonesia, Malaysia, Singapore, Thailand, and Vietnam) indicated that foreign businesses are still facing significant barriers in pursuing investment expansion across national borders in the region despite the many attractive factors such as strong economic growth prospects, increasing consumer confidence and spending power. Figure 3.7 shows the survey's result on barriers to business expansion. Generally, non-conducive regulatory environment is the most important barrier, followed by challenging business environment.

The survey also found that the most crucial business expansion enabler was improvement in the business environment, followed by promotion of regional trade and facilitating regional investment (Figure 3.8). Identified key business expansion enablers include regulatory transparency and policy consistency, especially for cross-border investment. It is essential

FIGURE 3.7
Barriers to Business Expansion in Southeast Asia
(% of business survey respondents)

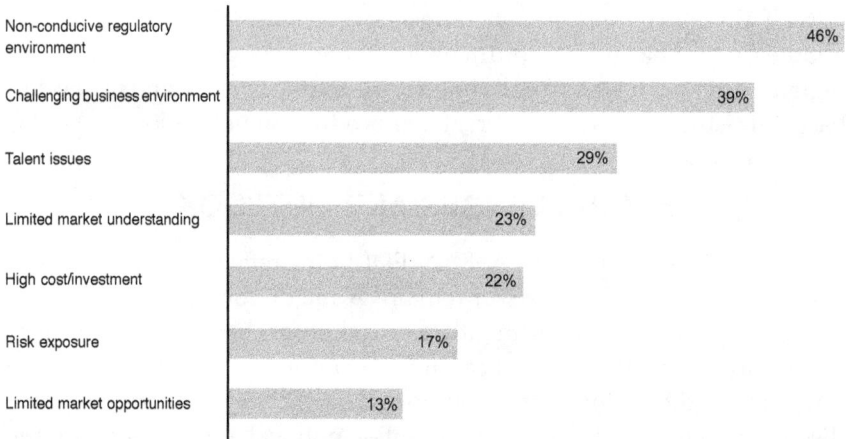

Barrier	%
Non-conducive regulatory environment	46%
Challenging business environment	39%
Talent issues	29%
Limited market understanding	23%
High cost/investment	22%
Risk exposure	17%
Limited market opportunities	13%

Source: Accenture SEA Business Expansion Survey, 2011, Figure 15.

FIGURE 3.8
Critical Business Expansion Enablers in ASEAN (% of businesses)

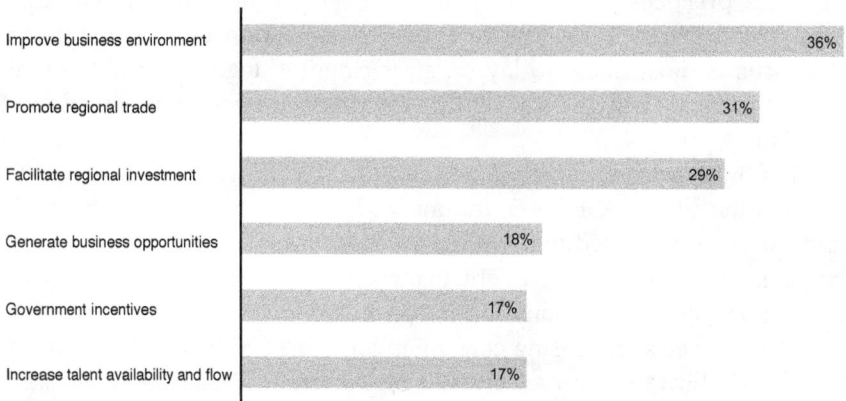

Enabler	%
Improve business environment	36%
Promote regional trade	31%
Facilitate regional investment	29%
Generate business opportunities	18%
Government incentives	17%
Increase talent availability and flow	17%

Source: Accenture SEA Business Expansion Survey, 2011, Figure 17.

for ASEAN to work more towards this direction in achieving free flow of investment and enhancing both FDI inflows and outflows in the region.

In conclusion, as ASEAN emerges as a distinct, potentially high growth region for businesses, greater certainty in investment environment is crucial to accelerate businesses' expansion plans that would lead to an increase in the intra-ASEAN investment. As a result, cross-border integration of the ASEAN's ten economies is highly essential to create greater scale of investment/production such that markets and companies in the region become truly competitive and efficient.

An important idea to further promote intra-ASEAN FDI is the focus on *regional production networks* in the context of the regional integration agenda in the ASEAN 2020 Vision. A proposal was made towards a promotion of regional clusters and production network through the ASEAN industrial cooperation initiatives. Fundamentally, production networks, together with complementary FDI and trade flows as well as technological transfer, are considered as foundations of ASEAN industrialization. It is known that integrated production networks leads to greater cross-border investment amongst members of the networks. This would make the region more resilient or less vulnerable to global economic uncertainties by enhancing its productivity and growth potentials. Nonetheless, for ASEAN, the challenge is how to broaden and deepen the reach of production networks.

In the recent discussions on global value chains (GVCs) in the context of investment and trade for development, the global economy has been characterized by the presence of GVCs in which intermediate goods and services are traded in fragmented and internationally dispersed production process (UNCTAD, 2013). It is noted that GVCs have contributed considerably to the global economy by upgrading value-added trade, especially in developing economies. GVCs directly impact value added, jobs, and income while participation in GVCs and GDP growth rates have been found to be positively correlated. In this context, *the development of regional value chains has come into view and highlighted the importance of regional cooperation.* Regional industrial development could stimulate integrated regional trade and investment along with improving liberalization, facilitation, trade and investment mechanism and institution. The creation of cross-border industrial clusters through joint financing for GVC-enabling infrastructure and joint-productive capacity building could create region-wide impacts.

To accommodate this scheme, several recommendations are put forward. First, regional cooperation must be further strengthened through regional agreements. Stronger commitment in achieving regional integration is highly needed. Policy makers need to evaluate countries' capabilities in order to set up their national supply chains to access pragmatic GVC development path for strategic positioning. It is also important to establish a favourable environment for trade and investment to promote the path of GVC growth as well as to develop software and hardware infrastructures within a nation and across the region. Moreover, partnership between governments in the region, between governments and international organizations, and between public and private sectors are required to create positive impacts under this regional value chain development.

Second, the regional investment agreement, ACIA, must be fully implemented to strengthen the links of regional value chain in the region. It is also crucial to review and enhance ACIA to promote regional investment flows and growth. Further socialization of ACIA is also essential to increase businesses' understanding and awareness of the investment opportunities that come with ACIA implementation. According to the Survey on ASEAN Community Building 2012 released by ASEAN Secretariat in 2013, the results indicated investors as having positive perceptions of the AEC and ASEAN's effort on regional integration. Their expectations were directed towards the overall improvement of ASEAN economy in such a way that will help them compete in the global economic arena. In particular, the ACIA as a regional investment agreement needs to be aligned with other milestones and commitments in the AEC Blueprint in order to ensure progressive implementation that would bring about optimal investment outcomes to ASEAN.

Thus, investment facilitation must be upgraded to encourage the linkages in production networks among MNEs in ASEAN countries. The development of ASEAN SMEs is another complementary industrial factor that should not be overlooked. To deepen the networks, SME development is required. This involves extending the reach of regional production networks in the region through SME integration. This can be achieved by creating an enabling environment that would facilitate SME's operation and participation in the regional market and production networks. Generally, initiatives that focus on improving business and investment facilitation for SMEs at the national and regional level are essential. The challenge is how ASEAN could extensively and strategically develop a regional SME agenda that would accommodate a new framework for regional value chain that promotes investment flows in the region.

Furthermore, to broaden the reach of production networks, it is essential to include the newer members of ASEAN in the loop in terms of economic development. This is to support the ASEAN's goal of equitable economic development (Pillar 3). Despite all the technical assistance and capacity building programmes provided to the CLMV countries, it is still quite a challenge for ASEAN to fully implement the ASEAN Framework of Equitable Economic Development (AFEED) towards the end of 2015. All actions and initiatives under the IAI Work Plan 2 also need to be accelerated to enhance the CLMV economies' regional integration capability.

Consequently, ASEAN connectivity — particularly physical infrastructure development — is one of the key strategies to achieve cross-border integration; thus, promote investment flows across the region. Gradual establishment of efficient transport links would facilitate not only the flow of investment, but also flow of labour, raw materials and goods — all factors that optimize intra-ASEAN investment, trade, and production networks. ASEAN Master Plan on Connectivity could also be exploited more broadly to improve the competitiveness of ASEAN and to connect with South Asia and East Asia for a more integrated pan-Asia. This will then become a foundation for ASEAN to become a hub of investment and the link of regional value supply chains in East, South, and Southeast Asia.

6. CONCLUSION

ASEAN has strived to achieve greater regional economic integration. Despite the progress achieved, some shortfalls remain. Stronger commitment and political will are needed for deeper regional economic integration. In terms of investment, ACIA was extended to cover investment facilitation, promotion, and protection. At the current stage, most of initiatives focus on inward foreign direct investment (FDI). The main goal is to facilitate and stimulate more investment flows into the region. Though the empirical evidence is still limited and it is too soon to measure the whole impact of AEC on ASEAN's OFDI, it is plausible that the AEC could facilitate intra-ASEAN FDI rather than facilitate the ASEAN FDI outflows to outside-the-region economies.

New frameworks are needed to stimulate investment flows while many existing initiatives still need to be further realized. The regional value supply chain is an idea that involves the creation of both investment inflows and outflows in the region involving the movement of ASEAN MNEs. ASEAN must continue to develop strategic agendas and directions to support this process. This is the next chapter of ASEAN regional economic integration, the so-called AEC beyond — 2015 Vision.

Notes

1. This chapter was written in November 2014 when the author did not work as a staff of the ASEAN Secretariat. As a result, the writing represents solely the author's individual view. There is no context in this chapter that represents the Secretariat's view.
2. ASEAN Secretariat. *ASEAN Investment Report 2012: the Changing FDI Landscape*. Jakarta: ASEAN Secretariat, 2013, p. 3.
3. ASEAN Dialogue Partners (DPs) include Australia, Canada, China, European Union (EU-28), India, Japan, Korea, New Zealand, Pakistan, Russian Federation and US. Of the DPs, six have existing free trade agreements (FTAs) with ASEAN. These ASEAN Free Trade Partners (AFPs) are Australia, China, India, Japan, Korea and New Zealand.
4. Countries with higher GDP per capita tend to have the greater outward FDI stocks.
5. ASEAN's major dialogue partners with FTAs are Australia, New Zealand, China, Japan, Republic of Korea, and India.
6. The ten ASEAN member states have launched negotiation with its six FTA partners — Australia, China, India, Japan, the Republic of Korea, and New Zealand in late 2013.
7. The survey comprised global MNCs, Southeast Asian businesses who operated across the region and only operated domestically.

References

Accenture. *The Time for Regional Expansion is Now: Why Businesses are Gravitating Towards South East Asia as a New Growth Destination*. Singapore: Accenture, 2011.

Association of Southeast Asian Nations (ASEAN) Secretariat. *ASEAN Comprehensive Investment Agreement (ACIA) Booklet*. Jakarta: ASEAN Secretariat, 2012.

———. *ASEAN Community Progress Monitoring System 2012*. Jakarta: ASEAN Secretariat, 2013.

———. *ASEAN Integration Monitoring Report (AIR)*. Jakarta: Joint Report between ASEAN Secretariat and World Bank, 2013.

———. *ASEAN Investment Report 2012*. Jakarta: ASEAN Secretariat, 2013.

———. *ASEAN Community in Figure (ACIF) 2013*. Jakarta: ASEAN Secretariat, 2014c.

Bhaskaran, Manu. "The ASEAN Economic Community: The Investment Climate".

In *The ASEAN Economic Community: a Work in Progress*. Singapore: ADB and ISEAS Publishing, 2013.

Brenton, Paul, Francesca Di Mauro, and Matthias Lucke. "Economic Integration and FDI: An Empirical Analysis of Foreign Investment in EU and in Central and Eastern Europe". *Empirica* 26, pp. 95–121. Netherlands: Kluwer Academic Publishers, 1999.

Kubny, Julia, Florian Molders, and Peter Nunnenkamp. "Regional Integration and FDI in Emerging Markets". Kiel Working Paper no. 1418. German: Kiel Institute for World Economy, 2008.

Sally, Razeen. "ASEAN FTAs: State of Play and Outlook for ASEAN's Regional and Global Integration". In *The ASEAN Economic Community Working in Progress*, edited by Basu S., J. Menon, R. Severino, and O. Shresta. Singapore: ADB and ISEAS, 2013.

UNCTAD. *World Investment Report 2015: Reforming International Investment Governance*. Geneva: United Nations, 2015.

———. *World Investment Report 2014: Investing in SDGs: an Action Plan*. Geneva: United Nations, 2014.

———. *World Investment Report 2013*. Geneva: United Nations, 2013.

———. *Note on Regional Integration and Foreign Direct Investment in Developing and Transition Economies*. Geneva: United Nations, 2013.

World Bank. *Doing Business 2005: Removing Obstacles to Growth: an Overview*. Washington, D.C.: World Bank, 2005.

———. *Doing Business 2013: Smart Regulations for Small and Medium-Size Enterprises*. Washington, D.C: World Bank, 2013.

———. *Investment Across Borders: Indicators of Foreign Direct Investment Regulation*. World Bank Group, 2015.

4

DETERMINANTS OF SINGAPORE'S OUTWARD FDI

Cassey Lee, Chew Ging Lee and Michael Yeo

1. INTRODUCTION

For a long time, inward foreign direct investment (IFDI) has more often been studied than outward foreign direct investment (OFDI) in Southeast Asia as most countries in the region are developing countries. IFDI can generate technology transfer and positive spillovers to domestic firms (Blomstrom and Kokko 1997; Alfaro et al. 2003) and promotes economic growth in developing countries (Balasubramanyam, Salisu and Sapsford 1996). Most Southeast Asian countries are still experiencing net inward FDI, with the exception of Singapore. From a comparative advantage perspective, Singapore is a small and open economy with factor endowments skewed towards human and physical capital. Thus, it is not surprising that the country has received and still receives the largest amounts of OFDI in the region. However, given the uniqueness of the Singaporean economy — a city state entrepôt and regional financial centre — a question that arises is whether the country's experience is similar to that of other countries.[1] This question can be answered partially by an econometric analysis of the determinants of Singapore's OFDI.

A number of studies have been conducted on this issue, both qualitatively and quantitatively. None of these studies have, however, covered sectoral OFDI beyond the Global Financial Crisis (GFC). This paper seeks to examine the state and determinants of Singapore's OFDI using a dynamic panel data estimation for the period 1994–2012. This study compares the determinants of OFDI stock and flow. It also provides an analysis of total and sectoral OFDI to uncover sector-specific determinants.

The outline of the rest of the paper is as follows. Section 2 presents a discussion on the Singaporean government policy towards OFDI. Trends and patterns are discussed in Section 3. The general and country-specific literature on the determinants of OFDI is discussed in Section 4. This is followed by a presentation of the modelling strategy employed in Section 5. The empirical results are discussed in Section 6. Section 7 concludes.

2. GOVERNMENT POLICY TOWARDS OFDI

Singapore's policy of promoting OFDI is rooted in its post-independence economic history. The city-state's approach towards OFDI was nurtured under the auspices of a government that recovered from its first serious recession in 1985, determined to guard against the vicissitudes of the global economy.

Since its independence, Singapore's core economic strategy has been to remain adaptable to changing circumstances in order to keep abreast of global and regional competition. Its economic development is characterized by a constant struggle against a lack of natural resources and the limitations associated with its small land size and population. In the 1960s and the early 1970s, the city-state focused on the manufacture of labour-intensive products such as food, paper, simple electronics, textiles, and wood. By the 1970s, international competition, protectionism, unpredictable energy costs, and labour scarcity threatened Singapore's labour-intensive industries and prompted an adjustment of its economic strategy. The economy began to concentrate on higher value-added industries from the mid-1970s — such as chemicals, precision engineering equipment, and shipbuilding — but these still utilized large numbers of unskilled workers.

It was only from 1979 — under a plan known as Singapore's "Second Industrial Revolution" — that Singapore moved from labour-intensive manufacturing towards more capital-intensive manufacturing, in order to increase the productivity of its limited labour resources (Chia 2005). It planned to achieve this by raising wages, improving the education sector, investing in physical infrastructure, and providing fiscal incentives for companies to shift towards high value-added production. Despite experiencing considerable economic gains in the early 1980s, Singapore faced an extreme recession in 1985 — its first experience of negative economic growth since independence — caused by a global economic slowdown, intensifying international competition, and high local operating costs without corresponding productivity increases. Additionally, the recession was exacerbated by the high-wage policy of the "Second Industrial Revolution".

This setback forced Singapore to rethink its economic strategy; a committee was formed in April 1985 to assess the state of Singapore's economy and identify new growth areas. In February 1986, the committee published a report — the proposals of which were later officially adopted — that recommended the economy move beyond manufacturing to become an exporter of services, especially business and financial services (Ministry of Trade and Industry Singapore 1986, pp. 12–13). More importantly, the report endorsed the export of capital in order to exploit opportunities beyond Singapore's shores (Ministry of Trade and Industry Singapore 1986, p. 17). This involved the reduction of taxes on the remittance of foreign income to encourage profit remittance back to Singapore, and thus stimulate offshore investment (Ministry of Trade and Industry Singapore 1986, p. 94). Therefore, the idea of engaging in OFDI was introduced in and gradually gained state support from as early as the mid-1980s.

It was in the early 1990s, after decades of struggling against its land and labour constraints, that the importance of reaping the benefits of OFDI — by investing in land-, labour-, and technology-abundant countries — became urgent. On 8 January 1993, then Senior Minister Lee Kuan Yew gave the first major policy speech on the need for Singapore to develop its external wing by investing in foreign high-growth markets as had its competitors — Hong Kong, Korea, and Taiwan (Lee 1994, pp. 1–2). Soon after, in the same year, Singapore accelerated the drive to promote OFDI with the formation of a special Committee to Promote Enterprise Overseas. It provided suggestions on how to stimulate overseas enterprise by examining the role of the state in facilitating such activities — through tax incentives and partnerships (Tan 1995, p. 22). Heeding the Committee's proposals, the Minister for Finance introduced a variety of tax credit, deduction, and exemption schemes in the 1993 Budget (Tan 1995, p. 24). In a rather far-sighted measure, the Committee's final 1993 report also focused on how the state could provide personal and family support for Singaporeans venturing overseas and develop an entrepreneurial spirit amongst Singaporeans (Ministry of Finance Singapore 1993).

The state-led promotion of OFDI also included roles for government agencies such as the Economic Development Board (EDB) and the Trade Development Board (TDB). The Committee's final 1993 report recommended that EDB focus on both inward and outward investments, which remains one of its core functions to date. On the other hand, TDB was to focus on facilitating trade and exports (Ministry of Finance Singapore 1993). However, with the shift away from manufacturing exports, TDB was restructured in 2002 into International Enterprise Singapore (IE Singapore), which focuses on the internationalization of Singapore companies (IE Singapore 2015). Both organizations remain key agencies that spearhead the state's OFDI initiatives.

Despite the shock of the Asian Financial Crisis (AFC) — which severely affected Singapore companies with regional operations — the government remained committed to strengthening its external wing. A 1998 report by the Committee on Singapore's Competitiveness concluded that: "Developing an external wing is a key strategy to hone Singapore's competitiveness and strengthen our economic resilience" (Ministry of Trade and Industry Singapore 1998, p. 64). However, the crisis demonstrated the importance of diversifying Singapore's OFDI portfolio geographically to spread risks and avoid similar region-centric mishaps. The 1998 report recommended companies to tap on opportunities in the Asia-Pacific and beyond — to emerging economies such as China, India, Latin America, and Eastern Europe — in order to "achieve efficiency in resource allocation and diversify risks from economic shocks in any one region" (Ministry of Trade and Industry Singapore 1998, pp. 63–64).

Presently, Singapore has continued to develop its external economy, as it restructures its economy towards service-led and higher value-added activities. Recently, under the Singapore Budget for 2015, the Government announced three tax-incentive schemes — worth an estimated S$240 million — to help Singapore companies internationalize. These are schemes to raise grant levels for SMEs, co-share risks and initial costs, and a new tax incentive to support the internationalization of larger Singapore companies (Ministry of Finance Singapore 2015, pp. 43–44).

Overall, the government's policies on OFDI have brought about significant increase in the country's OFDI. This is discussed in the next section.

3. SINGAPORE'S OFDI TRENDS AND PATTERNS

Trends

The stock of Singapore's investment abroad has increased consistently over the years (Figure 4.1).[2] Of the various types of investment abroad, OFDI, measured as direct investment stock, remains the most important type of investment (Figure 4.2). Whilst direct investment stock shows an overall and consistent increase over time, the annual direct invest flow —

FIGURE 4.1
Singapore's Investment Abroad (S$ billion)

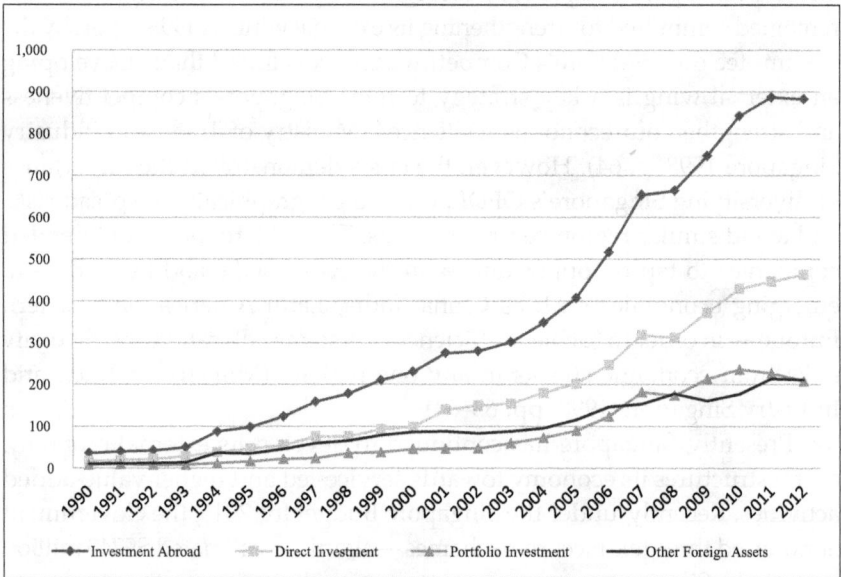

Source: Singapore Department of Statistics.

FIGURE 4.2
Composition of Singapore's Investment Abroad

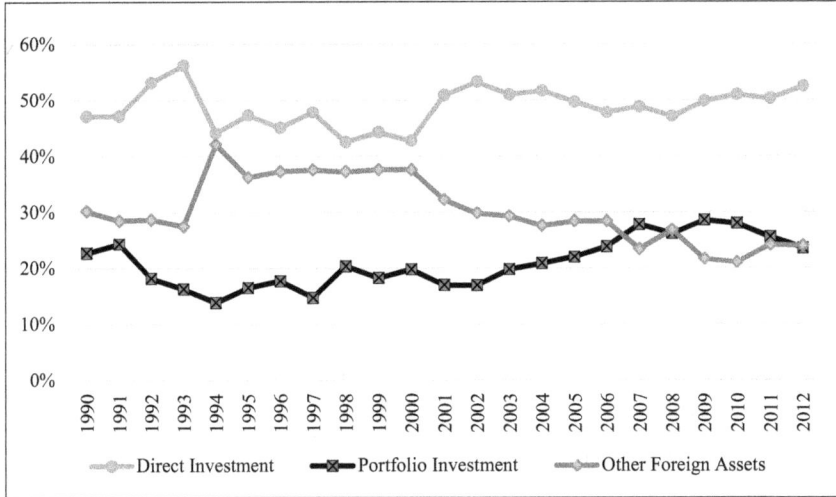

Source: Singapore Department of Statistics.

in absolute terms (Figure 4.3) as well as a percentage of GDP (Figure 4.4) — has been rather erratic.

In terms of destination country, China has emerged as the single most important country (Figure 4.5). China (including Hong Kong) accounts for about 28.0 per cent of Singapore's outward investments in 2012. Singaporean OFDI in China grew rapidly after diplomatic relations between China and Singapore were established in 1990 (Chia 2011). Other important destinations are United Kingdom (9.3 per cent) and Australia (8.3 per cent).

ASEAN countries account for 22 per cent of Singapore's OFDI in 2012. The top three investment destinations are Indonesia (8.1 per cent in 2012), Malaysia (7.0 per cent) and Thailand (4.0 per cent). They account for 87.4 per cent of Singapore's investments into ASEAN countries. Thus, it can be argued that ASEAN economic integration has not had much effect on Singapore's OFDI, as the stock has remained relatively low in countries other than the three aforementioned (Table 4.1). The percentage share has even declined for countries such as Malaysia and Thailand, especially

FIGURE 4.3
Singapore's OFDI Flow (S$ billion)

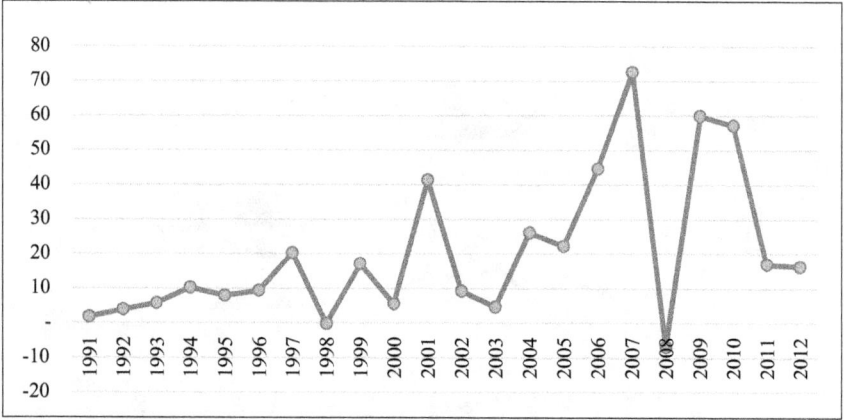

Source: Singapore Department of Statistics.

FIGURE 4.4
OFDI Flow as a Percentage of GDP

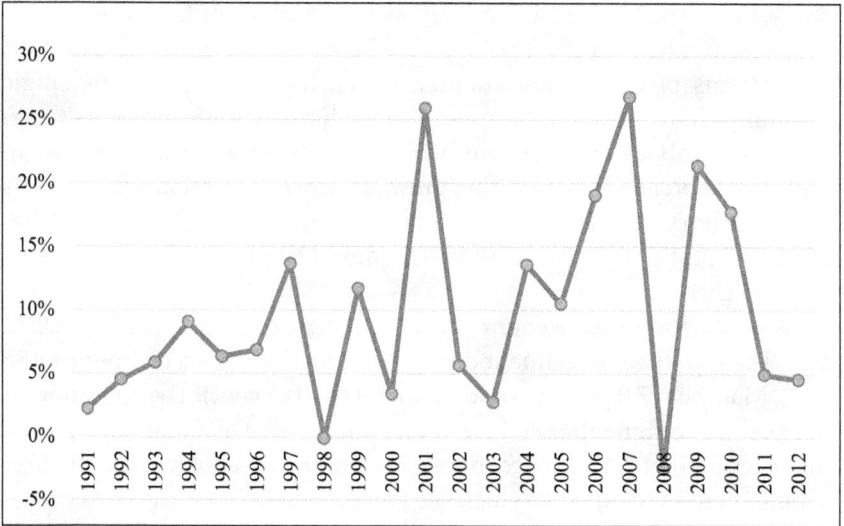

Source: Singapore Department of Statistics.

FIGURE 4.5
Main OFDI Stock Country Destinations (percentage share)

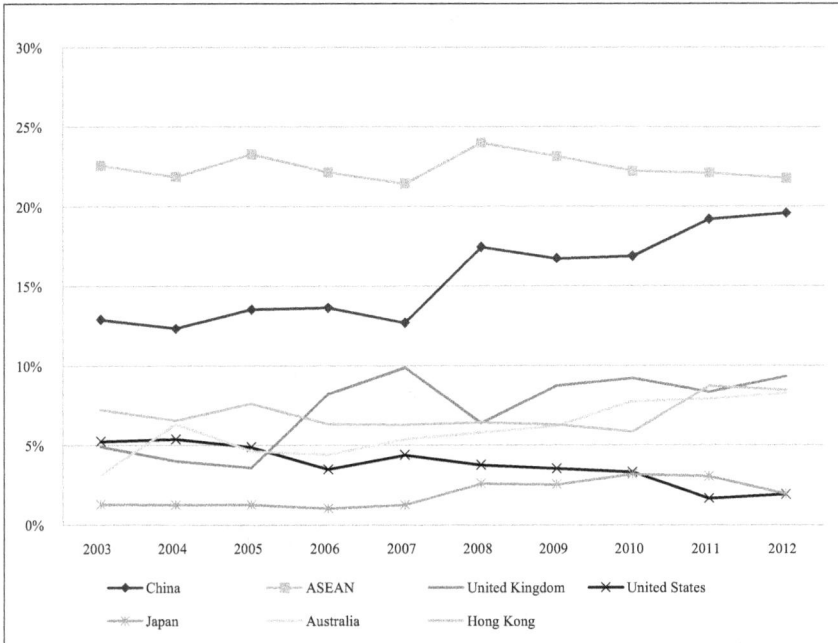

Source: Singapore Department of Statistics.

after the GFC. The only exception is Indonesia, which saw a resurgence in Singaporean OFDI since 2007. Incidentally, Indonesia was also the least affected by the GFC among countries in ASEAN.

Aside from an overall trends analysis, it might also be interesting to examine the sectors Singapore invests in. As discussed in Appendix 1, there are two ways in which Singapore's OFDI has been classified. In terms of investors' activity, much of the OFDI comes from investors in the financial and insurance services (Table 4.2). This sector continues to be important when OFDI is classified in terms of the activity abroad (in host country). The financial and insurance services sector accounted for 44.9 per cent of total OFDI in 2012. The second most important sector is manufacturing, which accounted for 21.4 per cent.

It is also useful to examine whether the sectoral composition of Singapore's OFDI varies from country to country. An analysis of the key

TABLE 4.1
ASEAN Country Share of Singaporean OFDI Stock, 1997–2012
(percentage share)

Year	1997	1998	1999	2000	2001	2002	2003	2004	2005	2006	2007	2008	2009	2010	2011	2012
Brunei Darussalam	0.1	0.08	0.09	0.10	0.04	0.10	0.04	0.04	0.03	0.05	0.06	0.05	0.05	0.04	0.03	0.03
Cambodia		0.16	0.16	0.11	0.16	0.17	0.15	0.07	0.06	0.06	0.05	0.09	0.07	0.06	0.05	0.05
Indonesia	8.60	5.93	5.94	5.56	5.44	5.17	6.70	6.65	7.26	6.79	6.33	7.15	7.57	7.30	7.81	8.05
Laos		0.02	0.00	0.01	0.00	0.03	0.04	0.05	0.05	0.05	0.05	0.07	0.06	0.05	0.05	0.04
Malaysia	11.75	11.39	9.19	9.92	8.09	8.95	8.83	8.18	8.31	7.44	7.14	7.81	7.12	6.91	6.89	6.99
Myanmar		0.84	0.87	1.05	0.75	0.71	0.74	0.39	0.73	0.40	0.50	0.40	0.59	1.32	0.97	0.81
Philippines	1.42	1.72	2.47	2.60	1.96	1.92	2.05	1.63	1.61	1.36	1.29	1.37	1.34	1.22	1.20	1.07
Thailand	1.66	2.63	3.56	3.56	3.23	2.76	3.06	4.01	4.38	5.32	5.33	6.15	5.49	4.65	4.40	3.99
Vietnam	1.10	1.39	1.24	1.09	0.76	0.93	0.95	0.85	0.85	0.68	0.67	0.91	0.84	0.64	0.68	0.73

Note: (s) — negligible.
Source: Singapore Department of Statistics.

TABLE 4.2
Singapore's OFDI by Sector, 2012
(percentage share)

	Activity of Investor	Activity Abroad
Manufacturing	3.8	21.4
Construction	0.4	0.3
Wholesale & Retail Trade	7.9	8.0
Accommodation & Food	0.4	1.0
Transport & Storage	1.6	2.7
Information & Communications	(s)	4.4
Financial & Insurance Services	77.5	44.9
Real Estate Activities	2.0	8.5
Professional, Scientific & Technical, Administrative & Support Services	2.60	1.8
Others	(s)	7.1
	96.1	100.0

Note: (s) — negligible.
Source: Singapore Department of Statistics.

destination countries reveals that there are generally two groups of country destination (Table 4.3). The first are destination countries where primary investments are in financial and insurance services. Such destination countries include United Kingdom and Hong Kong. The second group are countries in which OFDI are more diversified with significant contributions to the manufacturing sector. This includes country destinations such as China, Indonesia, Malaysia and Thailand.

4. FACTORS AFFECTING SINGAPOREAN OFDI

4.1 The Theoretical and Empirical Literature on IFDI and OFDI

The theories on outward foreign direct investment are, in a sense, the same as the theories of IFDI. Instead of examining the determinants of IFDI from a host country perspective, the theories of OFDI take the perspective of the home country. The theories of IFDI are very diverse in levels of analysis (macro, industry or firm) and sources (economics and international business studies).[3] The neoclassical trade theory focuses on

TABLE 4.3
Sectoral Composition of Singapore's OFDI for Main Destination Countries, 2012
(percentage share of total OFDI stock to each country)

	China	UK	Hong Kong	Australia	Indonesia	Malaysia	Thailand	Total
Manufacturing	48.5	−0.3	1.9	2.5	28.7	32.4	30.7	21.4
Construction	0.3	0.0	0.1	0.0	0.0	0.3	0.4	0.3
Wholesale & Retail Trade	12.3	0.6	20.5	10.1	4.0	8.6	11.4	8.0
Accommodation & Food	0.4	0.0	0.0	0.0	0.7	1.6	2.9	1.0
Transport & Storage	2.0	0.4	2.3	2.1	1.9	1.0	2.0	2.7
Information & Communications	0.3	0.4	2.1	21.9	0.0	0.5	3.7	4.4
Financial & Insurance Services	8.7	67.6	67.0	40.3	29.9	49.2	45.8	44.9
Real Estate Activities	22.3	0.1	0.0	5.0	6.1	2.5	1.3	8.5
Professional, Scientific & Technical, Administrative & Support Services	2.2	0.3	0.6	0.5	0.9	1.4	0.3	1.8
Others	2.9	0.0	0.0	16.2	18.8	2.5	1.6	7.1

Source: Singapore Department of Statistics.

the differences in relative factor endowment and how this drives FDI as capital move from economies with low returns on capital to those with high returns to capital (Faeth 2009). A number of macro factors could affect IFDI flow such as taxes, exchange rate and interest rate. Other aggregate level variables that could be important are GDP, GDP per capita, GDP growth, trade barriers, transport cost and physical proximity. These variables are regarded as being related to market sizes. The theoretical justification for the inclusion of such variables in IFDI models could be through the gravity model (Kleinert and Toubal 2010).

Theories of IFDI from international business studies tend to be more micro-oriented. These include the influential works of John Dunning (1973) who proposed an eclectic theory of IFDI based on three groups of factors, namely, ownership advantages, location advantages and internalization advantages. Ownership advantages take the form of multinational enterprises' (MNEs) propriety assets (that confer competitive advantages in host countries) whilst location advantages are factors that makes it more profitable to produce a good in host country than export it from the home country. Internalization advantages are factors that make firms prefer internalizing production rather than outsourcing it.

The theoretical literature also often makes the distinction between horizontal and vertical FDI. The former refers to FDI that substitutes exports from the home country with FDI to produce for the host country market. Vertical FDI refers to fragmentation of the production chain to take advantage of the differences in cost of production across the supply chain in different countries. Thus, the market size of host country is important for horizontal but not vertical FDI.

In general, the empirical evidence that has emerged provides evidence for the role of the following macro factors as determinants of IFDI — country size, transport cost, tax rates, openness to trade, and exchange rate appreciation. At the micro-level, scale economies, firm size, R&D intensity, capital intensity, labour skills and experience have been found to be important factors determining IFDI (Faeth 2009). Finally, there is also evidence that government policies affect many of the factors that affect both IFDI and OFDI. Of those macro variables that are measurable, tax rates and investment incentives have been identified as having a significant effect on FDI. There is another set of government policies that is less studied — home-country policies to encourage OFDI. This is examined further in the next subsection.

4.2 Literature on Singapore's OFDI

A few studies on Singapore's OFDI have been published since the late 1990s. One of the earliest studies on Singapore's OFDI is the study by Low, Ramstetter and Yeung (1998); they examined such investments by country of the capital source during the period 1981–91. This is particularly important for an entrepôt economy such as Singapore in which a large proportion of the country's OFDI may come from MNEs rather than locally-owned firms. The study also found that MNEs share of OFDI was 26 per cent in 1985 but grew rapidly in the late 1980s to 51 per cent in 1991. It was further noted that government-linked corporations (GLCs) dominate OFDI by locally controlled firms in Singapore. However, no statistics were available on the extent of GLC involvement in OFDI.

Another early study is that of Yeung (1999) who examined Singapore's OFDI from a "regulationist perspective".[4] In the study, Singapore's OFDI or "regionalization strategy" is seen as a solution to economic crises caused by foreign-capital-driven and export-oriented industrialization. With regards to OFDI, the government's "Regionalization 2000" strategy or "Second Wing" was launched in 1993 to enhance the business and scale economies of firms based in Singapore. This strategy was a formalization and intensification of an ongoing process in which GLCs partnered with private sector firms to invest abroad (Yeung 1999; Pereira 2005). These GLCs include Temasek Holdings, Singapore Airlines and Singapore Technologies Pte Ltd. Leung also identified three forms of regionalization, namely, (i) private-sector-led regionalization, (ii) partnership between private firms and GLCs to undertake regional investment projects; and (iii) state or private firms' investment in development of industrial sites. These strategies also reduce the cost and risks of Singaporean firm venturing abroad.

By early 2000s, with larger datasets becoming available, scholars began undertaking econometric analyses of Singapore OFDI. The earliest example of this is the paper by Blomqvist (2002), a study which covered the years 1990, 1995 and 1999 (pooled data). The empirical part of the paper attempts to estimate the determinants of OFDI stock. The explanatory variables used in the study include GDP of host country, ten-year growth rate of host country, ratio between manufactured exports to total exports, ratio between manufactured imports and total imports (proxy for import substitution), labour cost per worker in host country, economic freedom index and a dummy variable for ASEAN host countries. The only explanatory variables that are statistically significant are manufactured imports and total imports ratio (+) and labour cost (–).

An OFDI gravity model is used by Ellingsen, Likumahuwa and Nunnenkamp (2006) to investigate the determinants of OFDI as well as the relationship between OFDI stock and trade. The authors used data covering the period 1990–2003. In their estimation of the determinants of FDI stock, the statistically significant variables include population (+), distance (–), lagged FDI (+), proportion of population of Chinese origin (+) and ASEAN dummy variable (–). When regressing trade (imports and exports) against lagged OFDI stock, the authors found a positive relationship between trade and OFDI — suggesting that a complementary relationship exists between OFDI and trade.

With the availability of longer datasets, more recent studies have utilized the time series properties of Singaporean OFDI. Kueh, Chin and Liew (2010) undertake an econometric analysis of the macro determinants of Singapore's aggregate OFDI using data from UNCTAD's World Investment Report covering the period 1975–2007. Explanatory variables that are statistically significant in the long run include: national income (+); trade openness (+); interest rate (+); and exchange rate (–/appreciation).

The study by Lee (2010) uses the bounds testing approach (based on ARDL framework) to examine the reverse causality between OFDI and economic growth. The OFDI data takes the form of annual net outflows of FDI as a percentage of GDP for the period 1972–2006. The OFDI data is obtained from World Development Indicators Online. Using the Granger causality test, the author finds that increased OFDI leads to higher GDP per capita for Singapore. However, higher GDP per capita could result in a decline in OFDI.

5. MODELLING THE DETERMINANTS OF OFDI

The existing literature on OFDI, both general and specific to Singapore, suggests that data availability constrains empirical work. OFDI data for Singapore is only available at the aggregated level. Bilateral OFDI stock and flow data is used for this study.

The basic model for the determinants of bilateral OFDI between country i (Singapore) and country j can be estimated using the following specification:

$$OFDI_{ij,\,t} = \beta_0 + \beta_1 OFDI_{ij,\,t-1} + \beta_2 FTA_{ij,\,t} + \beta_3 X_{ij,\,t} + \varepsilon_{ij,\,t}$$

where *FTA* represents the existence of a free trade agreement (between Singapore and destination country), X is the vector of factors that can affect OFDI and ε is the random error term. The OFDI data is from the Department of Statistics, Singapore. The variables in X include the GDP of Singapore and the GDP of OFDI destination countries, GDP per capita of Singapore and destination countries, bilateral exchange rate (host currency per Singapore dollar) and destination country corporate tax rate. All data for these variables are obtained from the World Bank with the exception of tax rate and FTA. The tax rate is average corporate tax rate in destination countries and is obtained from KPMG's Corporate and Indirect Tax Rate Surveys. The bilateral exchange rate variable is obtained from the World Bank database and is constructed by taking the ratio of annual average (based on monthly averages) of the Singapore dollar relative to the U.S. dollar.[5] The FTA variable is a dummy variable constructed from the existence of FTA between Singapore and the OFDI destination countries. This is summarized in Appendix 2.

This study uses the Arellano-Bond dynamic panel-data method to estimate the above relationship. In terms of expected signs, current OFDI is likely to be positively correlated with lagged OFDI. If FTA has an effect on OFDI, the coefficient is likely to be positive. The gravity-type models suggest that GDP and GDP per capita are likely to be positively related to OFDI. The results from the existing literature on the complementarity between trade and OFDI also suggest a positive relationship between the trade ratio and OFDI. The coefficient for the real exchange rate is likely to be negative indicating that higher levels of OFDI are associated with an appreciation in the Singapore dollar. Some of the factors determining OFDI are likely to be different for different sectors such as finance and manufacturing. Thus, aside from estimating the determinants for total OFDI, separate estimations are undertaken for key sectors such as finance and manufacturing.

Finally, unlike previous studies, both stock and flow data are used in this study. As the stock data is likely to have more persistence due to its cumulative nature, the results from flow and stock OFDI may be different.

6. EMPIRICAL RESULTS

The empirical results are presented below by two categories: OFDI stock; and OFDI flows.

6.1 OFDI Stock

The results OFDI stock is summarized in Table 4.4. As expected, lagged OFDI is statistically significant for all four estimations. The GDP variable is only significant with a positive sign for total OFDI and retail OFDI. The latter is consistent with the idea that retail OFDI is attracted to host country market size. Interestingly, the GDP per capita variable is negative

TABLE 4.4
Determinants of OFDI Stock — Arellano-Bond Dynamic Panel-Data Estimation

VARIABLES	(1) OFDI Total	(2) OFDI Manuf	(3) OFDI Finance	(4) OFDI Retail
OFDI Total L1	0.583*** (0.0609)			
OFDI Manuf L1		0.588*** (0.0684)		
OFDI Finance L1			0.545*** (0.0631)	
OFDI Retail L1				0.413*** (0.0665)
GDP	2.503** (1.173)	1.698 (1.314)	1.003 (1.626)	6.675*** (1.318)
GDP PC	−2.289* (1.322)	−1.520 (1.582)	−0.0865 (1.931)	−6.274*** (1.528)
Exch Rate	6.45e-06 (4.50e-05)	2.39e-05 (5.16e-05)	1.19e-05 (6.98e-05)	−3.22e-06 (5.35e-05)
Tax	−0.00943 (0.00737)	−0.0232** (0.0103)	0.00382 (0.0115)	−0.0197** (0.00858)
FTA	0.212** (0.0985)	0.0496 (0.130)	−0.0236 (0.148)	0.295** (0.129)
Constant	−43.39** (20.06)	−28.88 (21.97)	−22.97 (27.42)	−120.6*** (22.37)
Observations	132	106	114	119
Number of id	16	14	15	15

Note: *, ** and *** indicate significance at 10 per cent, 5 per cent and 1 per cent level, respectively. Standard errors are in parentheses.

and significant — indicating that OFDI could be attracted to host country with low average income — perhaps indicating lower cost of production in these countries. The corporate tax rate is only significant for manufacturing and retail OFDI. The negative sign for this variable suggests that higher corporate tax rate in host country discourages Singapore's OFDI to these countries. FTA is also found to have positive effect on OFDI especially for the retail sector.

6.2 OFDI Flows

Estimation of the determinants of OFDI flow reveal that the results are slightly different from those of OFDI stock (Table 4.5). The lagged OFDI variable has a negative sign indicating that a deceleration of OFDI flows with higher levels of OFDI flows. Interestingly, finance OFDI flows have a negative relationship with GDP and a positive relationship with GDP per capita. This suggests that higher OFDI flows towards countries with lower GDP (smaller economies) but with higher income — a form of market-seeking activity. FTA has a negative sign for manufacturing but positive for retail. This is puzzling and needs further research.

7. CONCLUSION

Singapore's outward FDI policies since the mid-1980s have been fairly reactive in nature. The initiatives undertaken to support OFDI were primarily responses to external stimuli rather than pre-emptive measures. Singapore's foray into outward foreign investment — concentrated in neighbouring Asian countries — was precipitated by the 1985 recession and exacerbated by the country's factor endowments. Similarly, the shift towards OFDI opportunities beyond the Asia-Pacific region only transpired after the AFC in 1998 compelled Singapore to reconsider its concentration on Asia-based assets and diversify its investments. The Singaporean government has provided direct and indirect support for the country's OFDI. Singaporean GLCs have played a major role in the OFDI strategy of the country.

Singapore's OFDI has increased substantially over time in tandem with the rise in the country's GDP per capita. In recent years, China has become increasingly important as an investment destination for Singapore. Among ASEAN countries, the three most important country destinations are Indonesia, Malaysia and Thailand. Singapore's investments also have

TABLE 4.5
Determinants of OFDI Flow — Arellano-Bond Dynamic Panel-Data Estimation

VARIABLES	(1) OFDI Total	(2) OFDI Manuf	(3) OFDI Finance	(4) OFDI Retail
OFDI Total L1	−0.295***			
	(0.112)			
OFDI Manuf L1		−0.0741		
		(0.163)		
OFDI Finance L1			−0.289*	
			(0.149)	
OFDI Retail L1				−0.150
				(0.149)
GDP	−7.116	3.162	−30.14***	6.323
	(5.324)	(10.15)	(9.847)	(7.353)
GDP PC	5.998	−0.223	30.83***	−13.04
	(6.393)	(11.60)	(11.84)	(9.772)
Exch Rate	0.000175	−0.000810	−0.000113	0.00124*
	(0.000408)	(0.000555)	(0.000296)	(0.000642)
Tax	−0.00374	0.0538	0.0737	−0.0428
	(0.0538)	(0.0974)	(0.0823)	(0.0865)
FTA	0.518	−1.638**	0	2.927***
	(0.554)	(0.825)	(0)	(1.122)
Constant	142.3	−79.19	549.4***	−53.11
	(88.82)	(181.0)	(167.8)	(117.4)
Observations	65	41	42	47
Number of id	13	10	12	13

Note: *, ** and *** indicate significance at 10 per cent, 5 per cent and 1 per cent level, respectively. Standard errors are in parentheses.

important sectoral dimensions that differ across countries. On the one hand, OFDI in financial and insurance services are mostly concentrated in more developed economies such as United Kingdom and Hong Kong. On the other hand, OFDI in manufacturing is directed mostly towards less developed economies such as China, Indonesia, Malaysia and Thailand. This is also reflected in the econometric analysis of the determinants of OFDI in terms of the significance of explanatory variables in the different sectors. Furthermore, it appears to be important to distinguish between OFDI stock and flow. Further research is needed to understand the erratic behaviour of OFDI flows in the region.

APPENDIX 1
SINGAPORE'S OFDI DATA — SOURCES AND DEFINITIONS

Data Source
Singapore Department of Statistics (SDOS) has been publishing data on Singapore's investment abroad since 1976. The data is based on an annual survey of both local and foreign-owned enterprises that are incorporated in Singapore.

Definitions
The SDOS adopts a financial approach to measuring FDI. In this approach, FDI is measured in terms of equity and ownership-related financial transactions rather than capital expenditure on fixed assets. This also means that only actual investments are measured rather than committed investments.

Singapore's OFDI is measured in terms of direct investment abroad which has been defined as "an investment in which a Singapore direct investor owns 10 per cent of more of the ordinary shares or voting power in an overseas direct investment enterprise".[6]

Direct investment abroad comprises two components, namely:

— Direct equity investment abroad
— Net lending between the Singapore direct investor and overseas enterprise

Data on OFDI is available by sectors. Two sectoral classifications are provided, namely, in terms of the activity of investor (in Singapore) and activity abroad (in host country).

Published Data
Aggregate data on Singapore investment abroad is available for three major categories, namely, (i) direct investment, (ii) portfolio investment, and (iii) other foreign assets.

The OFDI data for country destinations are available for direct investment abroad and direct equity investment. Data on OFDI by country destination and sectoral/industrial classification are also available for direct investment abroad. However, the sectoral/industrial classification applies to the type of activities investors in Singapore are involved in (host country industry definition). This classification is available for ten industries are offered.

APPENDIX 2
LIST OF SINGAPORE'S FTAs

ASEAN Free Trade Area (AFTA)
ASEAN-Australia-New Zealand FTA (AANZFTA)
ASEAN-China (ACFTA)
ASEAN-India (AIFTA)
ASEAN-Japan (AJCEP)
ASEAN-Korea (AKFTA)
Australia (SAFTA)
China (CSFTA)
Costa Rica (SCRFTA)
GCC (GSFTA)
Hashemite Kingdom of Jordan (SJFTA)
India (CECA)
Japan (JSEPA)
Korea (KSFTA)
New Zealand (ANZSCEP)
Panama (PSFTA)
Peru (PeSFTA)
Switzerland, Liechtenstein, Norway and Iceland (ESFTA)
Trans-Pacific SEP (Brunei, New Zealand, Chile, Singapore)
United States (USSFTA)

Notes

1. For example, is the country's experience similar to that of Japan, South Korea and Taiwan? A survey of the literature on these countries and other NIEs is provided by Hill and Jongwanich (2014).
2. The data sources and definitions for Singapore's OFDI are explained in Appendix 1.
3. See Faeth (2009), Kleinert and Toubal (2010), and Hill and Jongwanich (2014) for discussions of the theoretical literature.
4. The regulationist perspective, which is influenced by Marxist economics, seeks to examine capitalism from a variety of angles such as capital-labour nexus, inter-capitalist competition, monetary-credit relationships, globalization of capital and state intervention.
5. An increase in the value of the bilateral exchange variable (between Singapore and a given trading partner) indicates a depreciation of the Singapore dollar against the currency of the trading partner (i.e. more Singapore dollar is needed to purchase a unit of the trading partner's currency).
6. This definition is broadly consistent with how economists define FDI as "investments in which a firm acquires a majority or at very least a controlling interest in a foreign firm" (Markusen 2008).

References

Alfaro, Laura, Areendam Chanda, Sebnem Kalemi-Ozcan and Selin Sayek. "FDI and Economic Growth: The Role of Local Financial Markets". *Journal of International Economics* 64, no. 1 (2004): 89–112.

Balasubramanyam, V.N., M. Salisu, and David Sapsford. "Foreign Direct Investment and Growth in EP and IS Countries". *Economic Journal* 106 (1996): 92–105.

Blomqvist, Hans C. "Extending the Second Wing: The Outward Direct Investment of Singapore". Department of Economics Working Paper no. 3. Vaasa: University of Vaasa, 2002.

Blomstrom, Magnus and Ari Kokko. "How foreign investment affects host countries". World Bank Policy Research Working Paper no. 1745. Washington, D.C.: World Bank, 1997.

Chia, Siow Yue. "The Singapore Model of Industrial Policy: Past Evolution and Current Thinking". Paper presented at the Second LAEBA Annual Conference, Buenos Aires, 28–29 November 2005.

————. "Inward and Outward FDI and the Restructuring of the Singapore Economy". In *Foreign Direct Investments in Asia*, edited by Chalongphob Sussangkarn, Yung Chul Park and Sung Jin Kang. Oxford and New York: Routledge, 2011.

Dunning, John H. "The Determinants of International Production". *Oxford Economic Papers* 25, no. 3 (1973): 289–336.

Ellingsen, Gaute, Winfried Likumahuwa and Peter Nunnenkamp. "Outward FDI by Singapore: A Different Animal?". *Transnational Corporations* 15, no. 2 (2006): 1–40.

Faeth, Isabel. "Determinants of Foreign Direct Investment: A Tale of Nine Theoretical Models". *Journal of Economic Surveys* 23, no. 1 (2009): 165–96.

Hill, Hal and Junthathip Jongwanich. "Emerging East Asian Economies as Foreign Investors: An Analytical Survey". *Singapore Economic Review* 59, no. 3 (2014): 1450019.

IE Singapore. "International Enterprise (IE) Singapore 30th Anniversary in 2013". <http://www.iesingapore.gov.sg/About-Us/IE-Singapore-30th-Anniversary> (accessed 8 August 2015).

Kueh, Jerome, Hong-Puah Chin, and Venus Liew. "Macroeconomic Determinants of Direct Investment Abroad of Singapore". MPRA paper no. 47243. Munich: Munich Personal RePEc Archive, 2010.

Lee, Chew-Ging. "The Nexus of Outward Foreign Direct Investment and Income: Evidence from Singapore". *Applied Econometrics and International Development* 10, no. 1 (2010): 187–94.

Lee, Tsao Yuan. *Overseas Investment: Experience of Singapore Manufacturing Companies*, pp. 1–2. Singapore: Institute of Policy Studies, 1994.

Low, Linda, Eric D. Ramstetter and Henry Wai-Chung Yeung. "Accounting for Outward Direct Investment from Hong Kong and Singapore: Who Controls What?". In *Geography and Ownership as Bases for Economic Accounting*, edited by Robert E. Baldwin, Robert E. Lipsey, and J. David Richardson, pp. 139–68. Chicago: The University of Chicago Press, 1998.

Markusen, James. "Foreign Direct Investment". In *The Princeton Encyclopedia of the World Economy*, edited by Kenneth A. Reinert and Ramkishen S. Rajan. New Jersey: Princeton University Press, 2008.

Ministry of Finance, Singapore. *Final Report of the Committee to Promote Enterprise Overseas*. Singapore: Ministry of Finance, 1993.

———. "Budget Statement 2015", pp. 43–44. <http://www.singaporebudget.gov.sg/data/budget_2015/download/FY2015_Budget_Statement.pdf> (accessed 8 August 2015).

Ministry of Trade and Industry, Singapore. *The Singapore Economy: New Directions*, pp. 12–13, 17, 94. Singapore: Ministry of Trade and Industry, 1986.

———. *Committee on Singapore's Competitiveness*, pp. 63, 64. Singapore: Ministry of Trade and Industry, 1998.

Pereira, Alexius. "Singapore's Regionalization Strategy". *Journal of the Asia Pacific Economy* 10, no. 3 (2005): 380–96.

Singapore Department of Statistics. *Singapore's Investment Abroad* [online]. Singapore: Department of Statistics, various years.

Singapore Economic Development Board. *Regionalization 2000*. Singapore: Economic Development Board, 1995.

Tan, Chwee Huat. *Venturing Overseas: Singapore's External Wing*, pp. 22, 24. Singapore: McGraw-Hill Book Co., 1995.

UNCTAD. *Case study on outward foreign direct investment by Singaporean firms: Enterprise competitiveness and development*. No. TB/D/COM.3/EM.26/2/Add.3. Geneva: United Nations Conference on Trade and Development, November 2005.

Yeung, Henry Wai-Chung. "Regulating Investment Abroad: The Political Economy of the Regionalization of Singaporean Firms". *Antipode* 31, no. 3 (1999): 245–73.

5

OUTWARD FOREIGN DIRECT INVESTMENT FROM MALAYSIA

Tham Siew Yean, Teo Yen Nee and
Andrew Kam Jia Yi

1. INTRODUCTION

Outward foreign direct investment (OFDI) from developing countries has progressively attracted research attention due to its increasing share in world outward flows. According to UNCTAD (2006a), only six developing and transition economies reported outward stocks of more than US$5 billion in 1990. By 2005, 25 developing and transition economies have exceeded that threshold, while contributing to 17 per cent of world outward flows. Malaysia is one of the contributors to this phenomenon. In 1980, Malaysia was ranked 11 in the top 15 developing and transition economies in terms of stocks of OFDI, but it moved up to the tenth position by 2013 (UNCTADSTAT 2014). OFDI in terms of flows surpassed inward flows after 2007, and Malaysia became a net capital exporter.

These changes inevitably lead to comparisons between OFDI from developed and developing economies. Based on the investment development path (IDP) theory, there are five stages of development whereby a country transits from being a net recipient of investment flows to becoming a net source of foreign direct investment (FDI). The first stage is characterized by little inflows and outflows as the country may not have acquired the necessary location-specific advantages to attract inflows, except for given endowments such as natural resources. The firms in the country are also at a nascent stage of development and therefore do not have as yet the firm-specific advantages and resources for investing abroad. In the second stage, inflows start to emerge with the development of location-specific advantages such as increases in per capita income. By the third stage, however, inward flows may start to decline due to erosion of some location-specific advantages such as low labour costs and the increasing competitiveness of local firms as they move up their learning path and acquire firm-specific advantages. Outward stock of FDI may equal or exceed inward stock by the fourth stage, while in the fifth stage, the net investment position hovers around zero with inward and outward stocks tending to be of the same magnitude. The increasing importance of OFDI from developing and transition economies, however, seems to deviate from the IDP theory in that transnationals in developing countries appear to be investing overseas at an earlier stage than the pattern outlined in the IDP theory. This in turn is attributed to the development of certain unique advantages of firms from developing countries such as expertise and technology, access to resources and activities and production and service capabilities (UNCTAD 2006a).

Given the importance of Malaysia as a supplier of OFDI, this paper seeks to examine the pattern of OFDI from the country, key motivations and some of its impact. The pattern of OFDI and some of its known impact is discussed in Section 2 while the main drivers are identified in Section 3. The conclusion in Section 4 provides the key findings of this paper and discusses some policy implications.

2. PATTERN OF OFDI FROM MALAYSIA

The overall pattern of OFDI from Malaysia indicates increasing participation in global outflows of FDI, especially to Southeast Asia. Malaysia's share as a percentage of total OFDI in Southeast Asia increased from 8 per cent in 1990 to 19 per cent in 2013 (UNCTADSTAT 2014). In fact, Malaysia is the second most active investor in Southeast Asia, after Singapore.

Figure 5.1 indicates that in terms of flows, OFDI increased perceptibly from 2004 to 2008. The sudden jump in 2004 is attributed to the increasing

FIGURE 5.1
Malaysia's Inward FDI and Outward FDI by Flows and Stocks,
1980–2013 (RM billion)

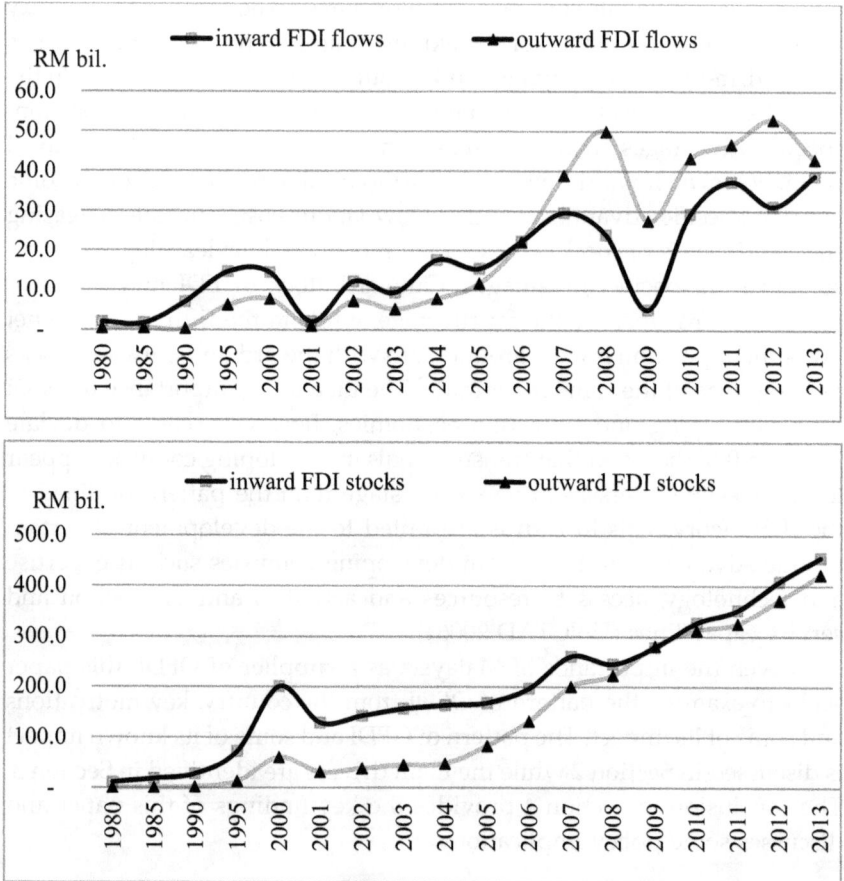

Source: UNCTADSTAT 2014.

importance of Labuan as a destination country. Since Labuan is an offshore financial centre, there is no data to indicate whether Labuan is the "ultimate" destination of these capital flows (Tham 2007). As offshore financial centres are also major sources of FDI, there may be "round-trip" capital involved, or capital that flows into Labuan and back again to Malaysia as FDI inflows. Later in 2005, government regulations regarding overseas investment were further relaxed and made more liberal compared to those prevailing prior to 1 September 1998 (Bank Negara Malaysia 2006). For example, resident companies with domestic borrowings are allowed to invest abroad using foreign currency funds maintained in Malaysia or offshore.

OFDI subsequently dipped in 2009 due to the global financial crisis (GFC), which affected the Malaysian economy negatively through its trade links with the United States and Europe. After recovering in 2010, it increased steadily until 2012, before dropping significantly in 2013. Outflows exceeded inflows since 2007 although the gap is narrowing over time, especially for 2013 when inflows increased while outflows declined. As for the stock OFDI, Figure 5.1 shows inward stock exceeds outward stock, with the gap narrowing significantly before the GFC and widening after the GFC. Given the pronounced upsurge in OFDI, it is not surprising that the stock of OFDI as a percentage of GDP increased significantly from less than 5 per cent in 1990 to 43 per cent in 2013 (UNCTADSTAT 2014).

By destination countries, according to Bank Negara Malaysia (2006), Malaysia's OFDI is dispersed over more than 100 destinations. Nevertheless, Figure 5.2 indicates more than 50 per cent of the total OFDI is channelled to 10 main countries for the period 2003 to 2013. Singapore, Indonesia, Australia, Sudan and the Virgin Islands (British) garnered more than 40 per cent of total OFDI. As in the case of Labuan, the presence of other international offshore financial centres (IOFCs) such as the Virgin Islands suggests the use of these tax havens for financial and other corporate reasons such as intra-company transfer of funds (Zainal 2006).

Figure 5.3 shows that investments in the Virgin Islands (British), Indonesia and Singapore are dominated by the services sector, specifically in financial services, whereas investments in Sudan and Australia are mainly in the mining sector, which includes petroleum and gas. Outward investments in this sector are led by Petroliam Nasional Berhad (PETRONAS), the national oil and gas company that was incorporated in 1974 and has remained a government-linked company (GLC) since its incorporation. PETRONAS started investing overseas since the early 1990s and has over hundred affiliates and associated companies with interests in more than thirty countries (Zainal 2006). Although the value of PETRONAS' overseas investments is not published, it is Malaysia's largest investor abroad in 2010 with a reported US$7.34 billion worth of assets overseas (EU Delegation to Malaysia 2013). It engages with a large range of petroleum activities, including both upstream and downstream. These

FIGURE 5.2
Stocks of Outward FDI by Top 10 Countries, 2003–13 (in %)

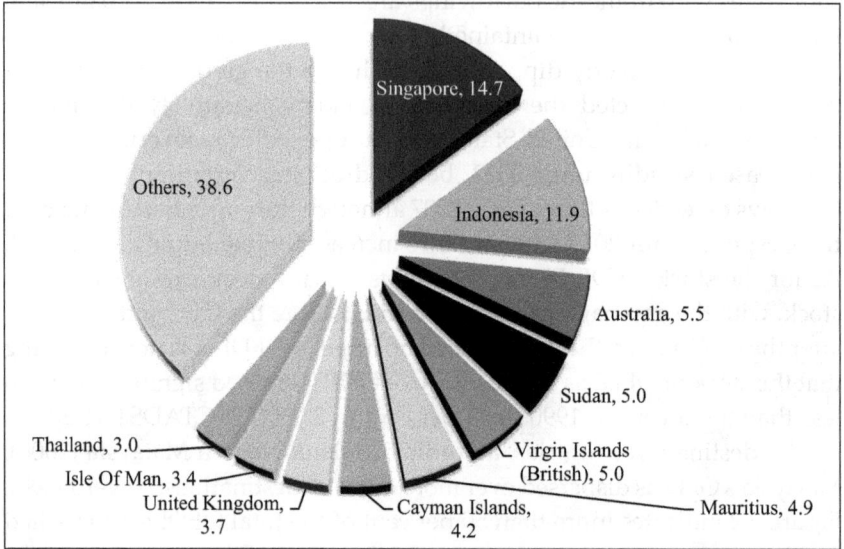

Source: Department of Statistics Malaysia (DOSM), unpublished.

FIGURE 5.3
Malaysia's Stock of Outward FDI by Top 5 Countries Sectors, 2003–13 (in %)

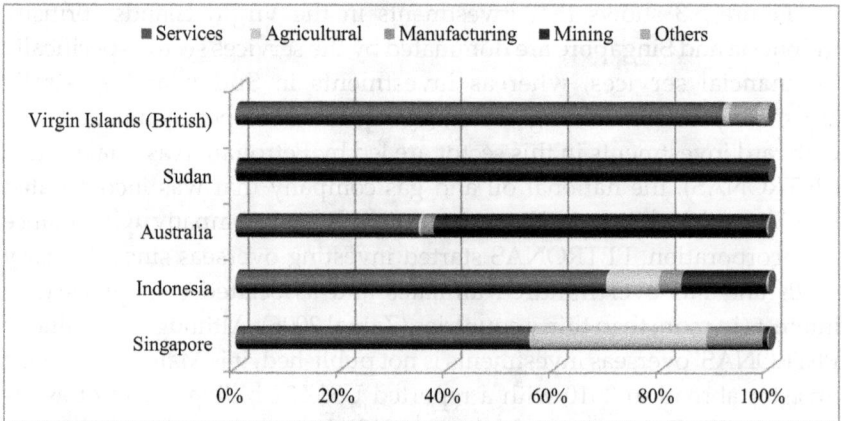

Source: Department of Statistics Malaysia, unpublished.

international activities are motivated by the need to enhance and sustain Malaysia's oil and gas reserves. In turn, oil revenue contributed 31.2 per cent of total government revenue in 2013 while there are plans to reduce this contribution to below 30 per cent by diversifying the government's revenue base.

Comparing OFDI by sectors in 2003 with 2013, Figure 5.4 shows a four-fold increase in investments in the mining sector within this ten-year period. This is attributed to the large investment flows to mining sectors of Australia, Canada and Bermuda in the last two years (Department of Statistics Malaysia, unpublished). Although services remain the largest sector invested by OFDI from Malaysia, its share in total OFDI stock declined from 61.9 per cent in 2003 to 56.2 per cent in 2013. This sector is mainly led by investments from GLCs in financial, telecommunications, and construction services. Bank Negara Malaysia's cumulative data for OFDI from 2000–09 indicate that 70 per cent of these cumulative flows are in services, and it is highly concentrated in the financial sector, with GLCs leading in the investment in this sector. GLCs have a mandate to establish a regional presence, especially in the banking sector (Tham and Loke 2014). For example, two leading GLCs in the banking sector, namely Maybank and CIMB reportedly have 342 and 212 branches abroad in 2009.

The impact of OFDI on the home economy is not well investigated. The literature so far examines its impact on trade. In both theoretical and empirical literature, the impact of investment on international trade is most commonly examined. Earlier theories assert that FDI may substitute or complement trade, depending on the nature of the investment. Horizontal FDIs that are market-seeking as well as investments to avoid trade costs or protection measures in host economies tend to lead to a substitutionary relationship while vertical FDI that engages with the fragmentation of the production process tend to lead to complementary trade relationship with FDI. The overall literature on the empirical evidence shows mixed findings with no consensus on the trade effects of OFDI. In the case of Malaysia, Goh, Wong and Tham (2013) find a complementary relationship between inward FDI with trade. However, in the case of OFDI, there were no significant trade linkages since OFDI is dominated by the services sector where trade is generally non-tradeable. In this case, OFDI in services serve primarily the market of its host economy due to the proximity burden of services, with local resources from the host economy.

FIGURE 5.4
Stocks of Outward FDI by Sector, 2003 Compared with 2013 (in %)

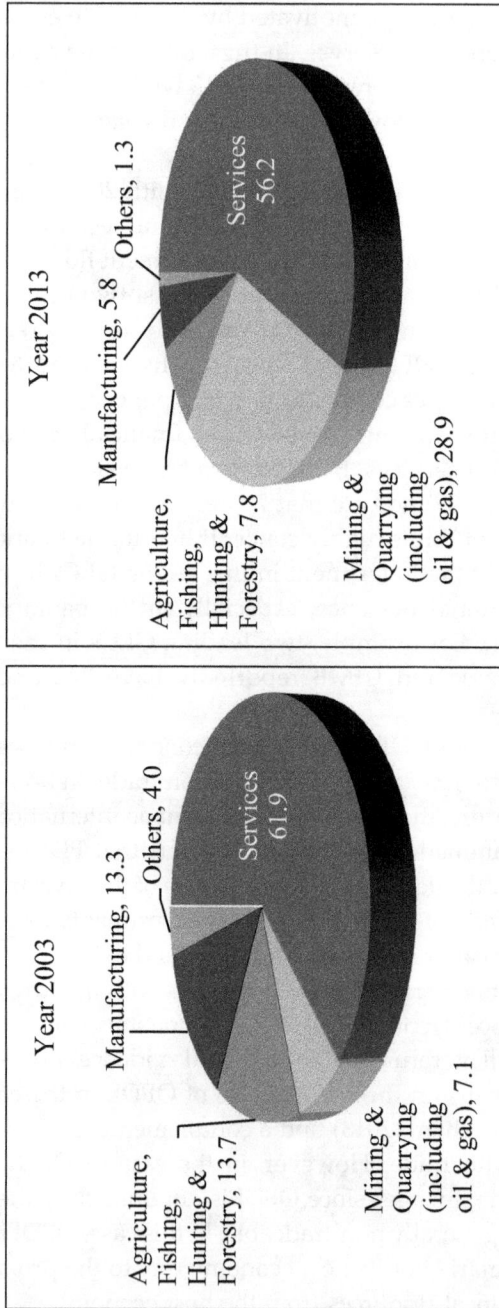

Source: Department of Statistics Malaysia, unpublished.

One of the benefits from overseas investment is the repatriation of profits earned from abroad as these are returns on risks taken by investing in a lesser known environment as compared to home grounds. Total profits, dividends and interests accrued to Malaysian companies that have invested abroad grew from RM0.4 billion in 1999 to RM4.1 billion in 2005 (Bank Negara Malaysia 2006). The data in Figure 5.5 indicates the trend increasing over time to a peak of RM29 billion in 2011 before dropping to RM16 billion in 2012 and increasing again to RM22 billion in 2013. The return to overseas investment that is repatriated back to Malaysia is important in view of the narrowing merchandise surplus in recent years if Malaysia is to avoid a deficit in its overall balance of payments while there is still an ongoing fiscal deficit.

3. DRIVERS OF OFDI IN MALAYSIA

Globalization intensifies competition while liberalization opens markets to foreign competition. Firms consequently resort to internationalization to stay

FIGURE 5.5
Investment Income Repatriation (Credit) from Direct Investment, 2005–13
(RM billion)

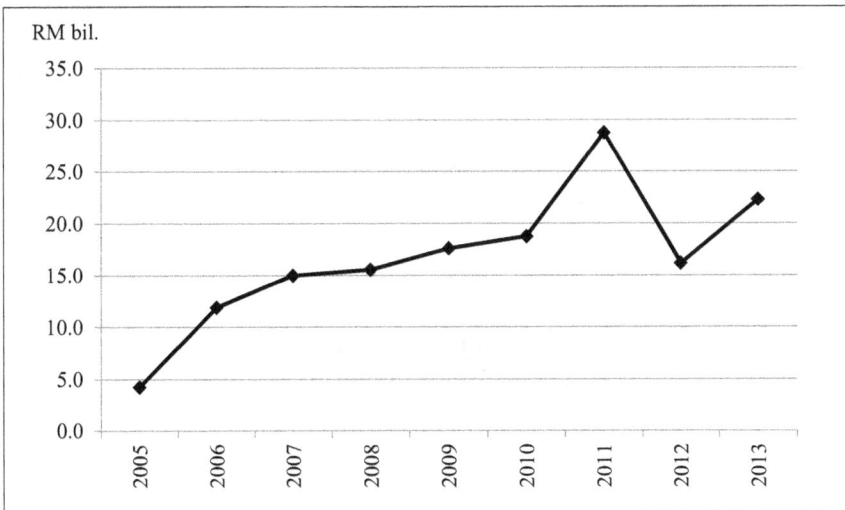

Source: Bank Negara Malaysia 2014.

competitive and to enlarge their markets beyond domestic shores (UNCTAD 2006b). Push and pull factors contribute to the internationalization of firms. Push factors include declining competitiveness at home due to rising factor costs such as labour, limited market size or increasing corruption in home country relative to other countries. Pull factors include the increasing attractiveness of host country conditions such as availability of scarce resources, growth prospects, liberalization and deregulation in host economies as well as the provision of incentives. Firms, however, venture forth for a variety of motives such as market-seeking, efficiency-seeking, strategic assets-seeking, and resource-seeking.

3.1 Determinants of OFDI in Malaysia[1]

As explained earlier, OFDI from Malaysia was led by PETRONAS' investment in the oil and gas sector in other countries. This together with investments from other GLCs formed 49 per cent of the total of Malaysia's overseas investment from 1999 to 2004 (Zainal 2006). Another sector of major interest to the GLCs is in the agricultural sector, mainly in plantation activities and in Indonesia. These investments are primarily for resources and new markets abroad to complement the saturated domestic market in some sectors such as telecommunications (Tham 2007).

For the period 1999–2005, according to Bank Negara Malaysia (2006), resident-controlled companies (RCC[2]) and GLCs accounted for 61 per cent of total gross outflows of funds for direct investment abroad. Assuming that the share of GLCs is constant, RCC's contribution to OFDI is about 12 per cent. The rest were contributed by non-resident controlled companies (NRCCs) (or 39 per cent), which are mainly in the form of inter-company loans to related corporations abroad (90 per cent). Investments from RCCs and NRCCs may be for a greater variety of reasons, including possibly push factors from the country (Menon 2014). Unfortunately, more recent data does not include the breakdown of OFDI by GLCs, RCCs and NRCCs and it is difficult to ascertain the motivations for investment abroad, without this and more detailed breakdown in the published data. We therefore use a simple push and pull model to analyse the determinants of OFDI based on more recent data made available from the Department of Statistics Malaysia (DOSM).

Using 2003 to 2013 OFDI data of the top-15 foreign countries[3] that have received the most investments from Malaysia, an econometric model is used to identify the main drivers of OFDI. Based on our literature review, the standard gravity model is used to estimate the determinants of foreign direct investment. It is considered as the "workhorse for empirical studies of (regional) to the virtual exclusion of other approaches" (Cheng and Wall 2005). We then "augment" the standard gravity model by incorporating pull and push factors. Using indicators (or variables) expressed in ratios, we are able to compare the relative locational advantage of foreign country (pull factors) with the locational disadvantages of home country (push factors). These variables explain the extent to which the advantage of foreign countries relative to Malaysia is able to attract OFDI from Malaysia. However, variables with binary representations such as trade cost and communication language were excluded from using the relative approach as the ratios of binary values may generate indeterminate values.

The general model specification is as follows:

Malaysia's outward FDI stocks = f(relative market size of country, relative labour costs, relative natural resource-seeking, relative corporate tax rates, relative market openness, control of corruption in host country, transportation and trade costs, cultural proximity).[4]

The justifications for the variables are explained below.

i. Relative market size of country

According to Dunning and Narula (1996), in order to enjoy economies of scale, domestic firms need to seek larger foreign markets abroad. A large market size implies exploitation of economies of scale, efficient utilization of resources (Buckley et al. 2007) and higher potential investment returns. The positive relationship between foreign markets size (in comparison with Malaysia) with OFDI implies market-seeking investments in the host economies (Goh and Wong 2010; Kitchen and Syed Zamberi 2007). The greater the relative market size of foreign countries, the larger the amount of OFDI is expected to be attracted to these countries. Previous studies indicate that Malaysia invests abroad due to the limited size of its domestic market (Ariff and Lopez 2007; Ragayah 1999; Tham 2007). Therefore, the relative market size is expected to positively affect Malaysia's outward FDI stocks if OFDI is market-seeking in nature.

ii. Relative labour costs

Past studies also show that in vertical OFDI, an increase in domestic labour costs "pushes" Malaysia's labour-intensive activities to countries with relatively lower labour costs (Ariff and Lopez 2007; Ragayah 1999; Tham 2007). Tham (2007) argued that one of the main objectives of OFDI by Malaysia's manufacturing firms is to exploit lower wage costs in other developing countries. For example, Malaysia's investments in the textile and apparel industry in Laos, Cambodia, Indonesia, Vietnam and China are mostly labour cost-driven (Ariff and Lopez 2007). Therefore, relative labour cost indicates the extent to which it influences Malaysia's investment abroad. It is expected to be negatively related with efficiency-seeking OFDI. We are also interested to test whether Malaysia's OFDI into its top three host economies namely Singapore, Indonesia and Australia is significantly influenced by relatively cheaper labour costs. These countries, along with China,[5] therefore, are interacted with the relative labour costs indicator. Consequently, if Malaysia's OFDI in its top three hosts is driven by efficiency seeking, the relationship between relative labour costs and OFDI is expected to be negative.

iii. Natural resource-seeking
Malaysia's OFDI is also driven by natural resource-seeking motives (Ariff and Lopez 2007; Kitchen and Syed Zamberi 2007; Rasiah, Gammeltoft, and Yang 2010). Rosfadzimi, Abd Halim, and Abu Hassan (2012) argue that a diminishing supply of natural resources in Malaysia is one of the push factors for OFDI. In Ariff and Lopez (2007) and Kitchen and Syed Zamberi (2007), PETRONAS and plantation companies actively invest abroad to seek for natural resources (such as oil fields and arable land) due to the diminishing supply of these resources at home. If OFDI is motivated by natural resource-seeking, the relative natural resource-seeking indicator is expected to be positively related with OFDI. Investments in natural resource-abundant countries are motivated by the cheap and continuous supply of natural resources. As natural resource-seeking FDIs tend to be location specific, Malaysia's top three OFDI countries, namely Singapore, Indonesia and Australia (and China), are therefore included in the model as interaction terms to examine whether OFDI to these countries are significantly driven by natural resources.

iv. Relative corporate tax rates
Caves (1971) and Gordon and Hines (2002) argue that tax rates affect investments into host economies. A low tax rate is considered to be more competitive in attracting FDI because it yields a higher net return from

investments. "Tax haven" countries are therefore commonly sought by investors (Aminian, Fung and Lin 2008). Duanmu and Guney (2009) find supporting evidence that China and India's investments abroad are drawn to countries with low corporate tax rates. This may also be applicable to Malaysia. If foreign corporate tax rates are higher than Malaysia's (TAX_{ji}), a negative relation with OFDI is expected.

v. Relative market openness

The theory of internalization postulates that high trade costs (such as transport costs and tariffs) lead to a substitution relation between exports and FDI (Buckley and Casson 1981; Markusen 1995). The elimination of market restrictions such as tariff and non-tariff barriers[6] is therefore expected to attract more foreign investment. Market openness in the form of trade agreements also provide increased market access to large integrated markets. Empirical evidences show that market openness is one of the factors that motivate Malaysia's investment abroad (Ariff and Lopez 2007; Goh and Wong 2010; Kueh, Puah, and Apoi 2008). Given the above reasons, a relatively greater degree of market openness in other countries is expected to have a positive effect on Malaysia's OFDI.

vi. Control of corruption in host country

Corruption is deemed by investors as additional costs to investments. This is because higher corruption increases the cost of doing business, thus lowering the returns of investment as well as increasing uncertainty for FDI (Belgibayeva and Plekhanov 2015; Rahim 2014). Since corruption is not a new phenomenon, it has attracted great deal of attention from researchers who seek to ascertain the effect of corruption on FDI. Nevertheless, the overall empirical evidence is mixed. Several studies found a negative effect of corruption on FDI, thus lending support to the conjecture that high corruption level countries are less likely to attract FDI. Wei (2000) argued that corruption acts like a tax that drives away FDI while Habib and Zurawicki (2002) deemed corruption as morally wrong and may create operational inefficiencies. In short, various studies confirm that the level corruption level has an inverse effect on FDI (Belgibayeva and Plekhanov 2015; Castro and Nunes 2013; Chiappini 2014; Rahim 2014).

There are, however, some other studies that have found positive relationships between OFDI and the level of corruption. Belgibayeva and

Plekhanov (2015), for example, argue that corruption encourages FDI from the investors of similarly corrupt countries. This is because corruption is viewed as a "helping hand" or as "greasing the wheels" around rules and regulations, or red tapes by the investors. Thus, we hypothesize an ambiguous relationship between controls of corruption in host country with Malaysia's OFDI.

A caveat is that there may be joint influence of corruption and market attractiveness. Brouthers, Yan and McNicol (2008) argue that corruption and market attractiveness (or size) are both inter-related in affecting different types of OFDI. For example, their results show greater market attractiveness mitigates the negative effect of corruption on market-seeking FDI and not for resource-seeking FDI. Hence, there may be multi-collinearity between corruption and market size variable. To mitigate this problem, we adopt Brouthers, Yan, and McNicol's (2008) method by "centering"[7] the corruption indicator.

vii. Transportation and trade costs

Although the standard gravity model establishes a negative relation between trade costs and trade flows, the relationship between transportation costs and FDI hinges on whether the characteristics of FDI are vertical or horizontal (Duanmu and Guney 2009; Egger 2008; Fung, Garcia-Herrero and Siu 2009). Vertical FDI occurs when multinational enterprises (MNEs) disperses different production processes across borders to production facilities in different countries with the objective of minimizing production costs or increasing access to foreign capital and technology (Helpman, Melitz and Yeaple 2003; Wong 2005). Transportation and trade costs inversely affect vertical FDI because the cost of investing abroad needs to be lower than the cost of producing at home. Since vertical FDI operates in a production network setting, the movement of intermediate goods from one facility to another may require multiple border-crossing. Hence vertical FDI is more sensitive to transportation and trade costs. On the other hand, horizontal FDI occurs when MNEs conduct similar production activities in different countries. A decrease in trade costs renders horizontal FDI unattractive because the cost of exporting is relatively lower than setting up a new production facility abroad (Buckley and Casson 1981). To summarize, a negative relationship is expected for the vertical type of OFDI while a positive relationship is expected for horizontal type of investments.

viii. Cultural proximity

In initial stages of outward direct investment, the model of firm internationalization argues that firms tend to invest in countries with similar cultural backgrounds or in already well-established networking countries or trading partners to mitigate investment risks (Johanson and Vahlne 1977). Investing in a country with different cultural background may require additional costs as for example in translation of product specification manuals and language training for staff. Harzing (2003) finds that differences in national language can be a barrier to doing business abroad. Thus, it is hypothesized that the culture variable as proxied by the use of a common communication is expected to be positively related to OFDI.

Based on the explanation above, the formal model specification is presented below. Malaysia's outward FDI stock in country j is represented as:

$$
\begin{aligned}
\ln SOFDID_{ijt} = {} & \alpha + \beta_1 \ln GDPPC_{jit} + \beta_2 \ln ULCI_{jit} + \beta_3 DSG^* \ln ULCI_{jit} \\
& + \beta_4 DINDO^* \ln ULCI_{jit} + \beta_5 DAU^* \ln ULCI_{jit} \\
& + \beta_6 DCHN^* \ln ULCI_{jit} + \beta_7 \ln OIL_{jit} + \beta_8 DSG^* \ln OIL_{jit} \\
& + \beta_9 DINDO^* \ln OIL_{jit} + \beta_{10} DAU^* \ln OIL_{jit} \\
& + \beta_{11} DCHN^* \ln OIL_{jit} + \beta_{12} \ln TAX_{jit} + \beta_{13} \ln OPENN_{jit} \\
& + \beta_{14} CCONCRP_{jt} + \beta_{15} \ln DIST_{ijt} + \beta_{16} LANG_{ijt} + \varepsilon_i
\end{aligned}
\tag{1}
$$

where i, is Malaysia, and j is host country, t is year, and ε_i is the error term.

i. $GDPPC_{jit}$ – relative market size of country j to Malaysia i,

ii. $ULCI_{jit}$ – relative labour costs of the country j to Malaysia i,

iii. $DSG^* \ln ULCI_{jit}$ – interaction of Singapore country dummy with relative labour costs of the country j to Malaysia i,

iv. $DINDO^* \ln ULCI_{jit}$ – interaction of Indonesia country dummy with relative labour costs of the country j to Malaysia i,

v. $DAU^* \ln ULCI_{jit}$ – interaction of Australia country dummy with relative labour costs of the country j to Malaysia i,

vi. $DCHN^* \ln ULCI_{jit}$ – interaction of China country dummy with relative labour costs of the country j to Malaysia i,

vii. OIL_{jit} – relative crude oil proved reserves of the country j to Malaysia i,

viii. $DSG^* \ln OIL_{jit}$ – interaction of Singapore country dummy with relative crude oil proved reserves of the country j to Malaysia i,

ix. DINDO*lnOIL$_{jit}$ – interaction of Indonesia country dummy with relative crude oil proved reserves of the country j to Malaysia i,

x. DAU*lnOIL$_{jit}$ – interaction of Australia country dummy with relative crude oil proved reserves of the country j to Malaysia i,

xi. DCHN*lnOIL$_{jit}$ – interaction of China country dummy with relative crude oil proved reserves of the country j to Malaysia i,

xii. TAX$_{jit}$ – relative corporate tax rates of country j to Malaysia i,

xiii. OPENN$_{jit}$ – relative market openness of country j to Malaysia i,

xiv. CCONRP$_{jt}$ – corruption in country j,

xv. DIST$_{ijt}$ – distance from capital of Malaysia i to country j, and

xvi. LANG$_{ijt}$ – similar communication languages between Malaysia i and country j.

A description of the variables is shown in Table 5.1.

4. EMPIRICAL FINDINGS

This study uses a panel data of countries over time. The Hausman test (Prob>chi2 = 0.0000) indicates unique errors are correlated with the regressors; therefore, the fixed effect estimation method is selected. Also, since there are time invariant variables in the model, and the cross-section or panel groups are few, the Least Square Dummy Variable (LSDV) estimator is more appropriate for this study.

Results in Table 5.2 show that relative market size is significantly positive in influencing Malaysia's OFDI. A larger market has a higher potential demand, provides economies of scale, and has higher potential returns on investment. The result suggests Malaysia's OFDI is market-seeking. Goh and Wong (2010), Ragayah (1999) and Tham (2007) also share similar results whereby the expansion of existing market, diversifying risks and enhancing returns on investments are some of the reasons for Malaysia to invest abroad.

Our study shows that relative labour cost is an insignificant variable in its influence on OFDI from Malaysia. This is supported by detailed results, which show that only OFDI to Indonesia is driven by low labour-seeking. One plausible explanation is that due to the fact that major OFDI is concentrated in financial services and the oil and gas sector (see Figures 5.3 and 5.4) in Singapore and Australia, in which the activities are not unskilled labour-oriented. For China, it may be

TABLE 5.1
Description of Variables

Variables	Definitions	Sources	Expected Signs (+/−)
$SOFDID_{jit}$	Outward FDI stocks of Malaysia (i) in host country (j), (US$mil.)	Department of Statistics Malaysia (DOSM)	
$GDPPC_{jit}$	Relative market size is proxied by gross domestic product per capita of host country (j) to Malaysia (i), (US$ nominal)	EIU country data, https://eiu.bvdep.com/	(+)
$ULCI_{jit}$ ($DSG*lnULCI_{jit}$; $DINDO*lnULCI_{jit}$; $DAU*lnULCI_{jit}$; $DCHN*lnULCI_{jit}$)	Relative labour costs is proxied by ratio of unit labour costs index of host country (j) to Malaysia (i)	EIU country data, https://eiu.bvdep.com/	(−)
OIL_{jit} ($DSG*lnOIL_{jit}$; $DINDO*lnOIL_{jit}$; $DAU*lnOIL_{jit}$; $DCHN*lnOIL_{jit}$)	Relative abundance of natural resources is proxied by ratio of crude oil proved reserves of host country (j) to Malaysia (i), (billion barrels)	U.S. Energy Information Administration, http://www.eia.gov	(+)
TAX_{jit}	Relative taxes are proxied by ratio of corporate tax rates of host country (j) to Malaysia (i), (%)	KPMG, Corporate and Indirect Tax Survey 2011, http://www.gfmag.com	(−)
$OPENN_{jit}$	Relative openness is proxied by ratio of (total trade/ nominal GDP) of host country (j) to Malaysia (i), (US$ mil.)	EIU country data, https://eiu.bvdep.com/	(+)

Variable	Description	Source	Expected sign
$CCONCRP_{jt}$	Corruption in host country (j), (score), data centered by mean.	The Worldwide Governance Indicators; http://www.govindicators.org	(+)
$DIST_{ijt}$	Transportation costs is proxied by capital distance from Malaysia (i) to host country (j), (km)	http://www.globefeed.com/World_Distance_Calculator.asp	(+/−)
$LANG_{ijt}$	Cultural proximity is proxied by similar communication languages, dummy variable D=1 if English, Malay, Mandarin or Tamil/Hindu are official languages, D=0 if not.	Central Intelligence Agency, The World Factbook, https://www.cia.gov/library/publications/the-world-factbook/fields/2098.html	(+)

Notes:
i. DSG, DINDO, DAU and DCHN are respectively dummy variables for Singapore, Indonesia, Australia and China.
ii. DSG*lnULCI, DINDO*lnULCI, DAU*lnULCI and DCHN*lnULCI$_{jt}$ are respectively the interaction of j = Singapore, Indonesia, Australia and China country dummy with relative labour costs to Malaysia.
iii. DSG*lnOIL$_{jt}$, DINDO*lnOIL$_{jt}$, DAU*lnOIL$_{jt}$ and DCHN*lnOIL$_{jt}$ are the respective interaction of country dummy with relative natural resources to Malaysia.

TABLE 5.2
Regression Results

Number of observations: 128
R^2:0.8554

Stock of OFDI	Coefficient	$P > |t|$
Relative market size of country	1.817	0.002
Relative labour costs	1.356	0.106
Dummy Singapore*Relative labour costs	2.933	0.600
Dummy Indonesia*Relative labour costs	−4.340	0.096
Dummy Australia*Relative labour costs	1.735	0.102
Dummy China*Relative labour costs	−1.448	0.325
Natural resources seeking	−0.612	0.001
Dummy Singapore*Relative natural resources	−2.086	0.406
Dummy Indonesia*Relative natural resources	−2.280	0.056
Dummy Australia*Relative natural resources	0.661	0.035
Dummy China*Relative natural resources	0.240	0.744
Relative corporate tax rates	−1.736	0.023
Relative market openness	4.960	0.000
Control of corruption in host country	0.458	0.428
Transportation costs	17.160	0.038
Cultural proximity	22.989	0.002

Source: Authors' estimation.

due to the fact that OFDI to that country is market-driven rather than labour costs-seeking. This in part may be due to the increase in China's manufacturing labour costs.[8]

The results also show a negative and significant sign of the relative natural resources variable. There are two possible explanations for this. Recent findings by Poelhekke and Ploeg (2013) suggest that resource-seeking FDI crowds out non-resource-seeking FDI. This may be the case for our sample of countries which is more focussed on non-resource based activities. A discovery of relatively abundant natural resources in one of the resource-rich destination countries may "crowd-out" OFDI in non-resource based sectors to the extent that overall OFDI falls. Natural resource-seeking OFDI, however, tends to be location specific. Results from the country interaction terms show that only OFDI to Australia is significantly driven by this factor. The negative and significant coefficient from Indonesia may be due to the restrictive rules there that impede foreign investors from investing in the mining and quarrying sector.

At this current juncture, our findings suggest that the nature of Malaysia's OFDI is mostly market-seeking. To further support this, we examine the transportation and trade costs indicator. To reiterate, a negative relationship is expected for vertical OFDI (efficiency-seeking) while a positive relationship is expected for horizontal OFDI (market-seeking). The transportation and trade costs (proxied by distance) indicator shows a significant and positive sign. This is consistent with the findings of our previous variables and further solidifies our argument that Malaysia's investments are market-seeking in nature. Therefore, OFDI from Malaysia is considered horizontal in nature; which means that the main objective of Malaysian companies investing abroad is to seek new markets or to expand its existing markets.

Other control variables also show significant and expected coefficient signs. Our study finds a significant and negative relation between relative corporate tax rates and OFDI from Malaysia. This result implies that more competitive tax policies of foreign countries attracts more of Malaysia's investment abroad. The study is unable to ascertain the influence of corruption on OFDI. The relative importance of other variables, such as market size may have rendered the corruption variable insignificant. Since it has been established that OFDI from Malaysia is market-seeking in nature, considerations on market potential (or other variables) may have superseded the presence of corruption. Relative trade liberalization also has a positive impact on OFDI of Malaysia. Apart from the attractiveness of the size of the host economy, a higher degree of integration of the host country with the world (relative to Malaysia) will also allow Malaysian firms to use this country as an export platform to new international markets. Thus, the host country is more likely to receive more investment from Malaysia. Finally, cultural proximity affects stock of OFDI positively for similar reasons as explained in the previous section.

5. CONCLUSION

OFDI from Malaysia is increasing over time, especially after 2007, although the data shows a drop in 2013. These investments are led by GLCs and NRCCs in the earlier period from 1999 to 2004. RCCs are a minor player in these outward flows during this period. Moreover, these investments are focussed primarily in the services sector. As in the case of other developing countries, tax havens are also important destination countries. GLCs like PETRONAS invest where resources and markets are needed.

The main findings in this paper show that outward investment from Malaysia is driven mainly by horizontal, market-seeking type of investment while the literature indicates that its impact on trade is insignificant. This is not surprising as a complementary relation with trade is obtained mainly for vertical FDI, which is not the primary form of OFDI in the case of Malaysia. Repatriation of the returns on investment abroad is increasing over time, peaking in 2011 before dropping in 2012 and recovering in 2013.

Given that the findings on horizontal market-seeking investment, these investments are unlikely to generate exports from the home country as in the case of vertical OFDI. An important return from these investments will be the repatriation of profits back to the home country. Since a large chunk of the investments are from GLCs, to promote greater transparency, these companies need to report to the public: the returns on their investment abroad and whether these are repatriated back to the home country for Malaysia's further development. A second question is the necessity for investments in natural resources in other countries. Oil revenues in other resource-rich countries such as Norway are held in sovereign wealth funds that invest in countries and sectors that yield a high return for future generations. It is necessary to assess whether GLC investments should diversify from natural resources to other types of investments that may generate higher future earnings.

More disaggregated data is needed to further investigate the motivations for RCCs and NRCCs to invest abroad instead of locally. The future of OFDI from Malaysia depends on the local investment climate compared to that of other countries. Investments will be attracted to where returns are higher than the returns from investing in the domestic economy. Hence if the domestic investment climate deteriorates, then further OFDI is expected as there are no barriers to investing abroad, while the domestic market size is a limiting factor. Vertical OFDI can only emerge when Malaysian companies have the technology to enable them to go global on the basis of comparative technology advantage. Otherwise, outward investment will be driven more by efficiency gains. Finally, there need to be more studies on the impact of OFDI on the home economy. Again, more data is needed for that to be feasible.

Notes

1. An earlier version of this section of the paper was presented in the International Conference on Humanities and Social Sciences, at Kuala Lumpur Convention Centre, 3–5 June 2014 (Teo, Tham and Kam 2014).
2. As defined in Bank Negara Malaysia (2006), RCC refers to private companies in which residents have equity stake of more than 50 per cent.
3. Singapore, Indonesia, Australia, Mauritius, United Kingdom, Virgin Islands (British), Vietnam, Thailand, Cayman Islands, Hong Kong, China, Taiwan, Germany, the Netherlands and India. These countries account for approximately 64.5 per cent of Malaysia's total OFDI stock.
4. All indicators except distance from capital and communication languages represent the country of interest (in note 5) relative to Malaysia.
5. China is chosen as it is well known as a low labour cost country until recently. All four countries account for more than half of Malaysia's total OFDI during the period of this study.
6. Tariff includes duties and surcharges; non-tariff barriers include licensing regulations, quotas and other requirements.
7. "Centering" involves subtracting the independent variables with a certain value (in this study, the mean value is used) and re-estimated again so that the analysis is undertaken at the mean value.
8. Zhang (2012) reports that manufacturing sector labour costs in big cities doubled from US$1,534 per worker in 2003 to US$4,579 per worker in 2010. Chen and Estreicher (2011) also argued that the Shenzhen municipal government subsequently increased the city's minimum monthly wages by an average of 15.8 per cent to US$168 in 2010, and further increased to US$201 in April 2011.

References

Aminian, N., K.C. Fung, and C.C. Lin. "Outward FDI from East Asia: The Experience of Hong Kong and Taiwan". In *New Dimensions of Economic Globalization: Surge of Outward Foreign Direct Investment from Asia*, edited by R.S. Rajan, R. Kumar and N. Virgill. Singapore: World Scientific Publishing, 2008.

Ariff, M. and G.P. Lopez. "Outward Foreign Direct Investment: The Malaysian Experience". Paper presented at the International Workshop on Intra-Asian FDI Flows: Magnitude, Trends, Prospects and Policy Implications, New Delhi, India, 25–26 April 2007 <http://www.icrier.org/pdf/Mohamed%20Ariff%20 and%20Greg%20Lopez.pdf> (accessed 21 May 2012).

Bank Negara Malaysia. "Malaysia: Trends in Direct Investment Abroad". *Quarterly Economic Bulletin, Third Quarter 2006*. Kuala Lumpur: Bank Negara Malaysia, 2006.

———. "Monthly Statistical Bulletin September 2014" <http://www.bnm.gov.my/index.php?ch=statistic&lang=en> (accessed 31 October 2014).

Belgibayeva, A. and A. Plekhanov. "Does Corruption Matter for Sources of Foreign Direct Investment?" European Bank for Reconstruction and Development Working Paper no. 176, February 2015 <http://www.ebrd.com/news/publications/working-papers.html> (accessed 4 June 2015).

Brouthers, L.E., G. Yan, and J.P. McNicol. "Corruption and Market Attractiveness Influences on Different Types of FDI". *Strategic Management Journal* 29, no. 6 (2008): 673–80 <http://www.jstor.org/stable/20142047> (accessed 8 June 2015).

Buckley, P.J. and M. Casson. "The Optimal Timing of a Foreign Direct Investment". *Economic Journal* 91 (1981): 75–87.

Buckley, P.J., J.L. Clegg, A.R. Cross, X. Liu, H. Voss, and P. Zheng. "The Determinants of Chinese Outward Foreign Direct Investment". *Journal of International Business Studies* 38, no. 4 (2007): 499–518.

Castro, C. and P. Nunes. "Does Corruption Inhibit Foreign Direct Investment?". *Política/Revista de Ciencia Política* 51, no. 1 (2013): 61–83 <http://www.revistas.uchile.cl/index.php/RP/article/viewFile/27418/29062> (accessed 4 June 2015).

Caves, R.E. "International Corporations: The Industrial Economics of Foreign Investment". *Economica* 38, no. 149 (1971): 1–27 <http://www.jstor.org.www.ezplib.ukm.my/> (accessed 20 December 2012).

Central Intelligence Agency. "The World Factbook" <https://www.cia.gov/library/publications/the-world-factbook/fields/2098.html> (accessed 20 February 2014).

Chen, L. and S. Estreicher. "A New Labor Era: Higher Costs and Greater Pressures". In *China Business Review*, April 2011 <http://www.chinabusinessreview.com/a-new-labor-era-higher-costs-and-greater-pressures/> (accessed 10 March 2015).

Cheng, I.H. and H.J. Wall. "Controlling for Heterogeneity in Gravity Models of Trade and Integration". *Federal Reserve Bank of St. Louis Review* 87, no. 1 (2005): 49–63 <http://ir.nuk.edu.tw:8080/bitstream/310360000Q/11970/2/cheng-wall-Review.pdf> (accessed 20 December 2013).

Chiappini, R. "Institutionals Determinants of Japanese Outward FDI in the Manufacturing Industry". GREDEG Working Papers Series, 2014 <http://www.gredeg.cnrs.fr/working-papers/GREDEG-WP-2014-11.pdf> (accessed 4 June 2015).

Department of Statistics Malaysia (DOSM). "Outward FDI (Flows & Stocks) by Country and by Sector". Unpublished data, 2014.

Duanmu, J.L. and Y. Guney. "A Panel Data Analysis of Locational Determinants of Chinese and Indian Outward Foreign Direct Investment". *Journal of Asia Business Studies* 3, no. 2 (2009): 1–15.

Dunning, J.H. and R. Narula. "The Investment Development Path Revisited: Some Emerging Issues". In *Foreign Direct Investment and Governments*, edited by Dunning, J.H. and R. Narula. London: Routledge, 1996.

Economist Intelligence Unit. "EIU Country Data". <https://eiu.bvdep.com/> (accessed 23 May 2013).

Egger, P. "On the Role of Distance for Outward FDI". *Annals of Regional Science* 42, no. 2 (2008): 375–89.

Energy Information Administration. "U.S. Energy Information Administration". <http://www.eia.gov.> (accessed 22 May 2013).

EU Delegation to Malaysia. "An Overview of Malaysian Outward Foreign Direct Investment", January 2013 <http://www.ice.gov.it/paesi/asia/malaysia/upload/173/Malaysia%20OFDI%20review-Oct12.pdf.> (accessed 1 November 2014).

Fung, K.C., A. Garcia-Herrero, and A. Siu. "A Comparative Empirical Examination of Outward Foreign Direct Investment from Four Asian Economies: People's Republic of China; Japan; Republic of Korea and Taipei, China". *Asian Development Review* 26, no. 2 (2009): 86–101.

Goh, S.K. and K.N. Wong. "Malaysia's: The Effects of Foreign Market Size and Home Government Policy". Monash Economics Working Papers 33/10. Department of Economics, Monash University, 2010 <http://www.buseco.monash.edu.au/eco/research/papers/2010/3310malaysiagohwong.pdf> (accessed 2 January 2011).

Goh, S.K., K.N. Wong, and S.Y. Tham. "Trade Linkages of Inward and Outward FDI: Evidence from Malaysia". *Economic Modelling* 35 (2013): 225–30.

Gordon, R.H. and Jr. J.R. Hines. "International Taxation". NBER Working Paper, no. 8854. 2002 <http://www.nber.org/papers/w8854> (accessed 25 June 2013).

Habib, M. and Zurawicki. "Corruption and Foreign Direct Investment". *Journal of International Business Studies* 33, no. 2 (2002): 291–307. <http://www.jstor.org/stable/3069545> (accessed 8 June 2015).

Harzing, A.W.K. "The Role of Culture in Entry Mode Studies: From Negligence to Myopia?". *Advances in International Management* 15 (2003): 75–127.

Helpman, E., M. Melitz, and S.R. Yeaple. "Export Versus FDI". NBER Working Paper, no. 9439. Cambridge, MA: MIT Press, 2003.

Johanson, J. and J.E. Vahlne. "The Internationalization Process of the Firm: A Model of Knowledge Development and Increasing Foreign Market Commitment". *Journal of International Business Studies* 8, no. 1 (1977): 23–32.

Kitchen, P.J. and A. Syed Zamberi. "Overseas Investment by Developing Country Firms: The Case of Emerging Malaysian Corporations". *International Journal of Business and Management* 2, no. 4 (2007): 122–35 <http://www.ccsenet.org/journal/index.php/ijbm/article/viewFile/2235/3424> (accessed 13 January 2009).

KPMG. "Corporate and Indirect Tax Survey 2011" <http://www.gfmag.com> (accessed 22 May 2013).

Kueh, J.S.H., C.H. Puah and Albert Apoi. "Outward FDI of Malaysia: An Empirical Examination from Macroeconomic Perspective". *Economic Bulletin* 6, no. 28 (2008): 1–11 <http://economicsbulletin.vanderbilt.edu/2008/volume6/EB-07F20037A.pdf> (accessed 23 March 2013).

Markusen, J.R. "The Boundaries of Multinational Enterprises and the Theory of International Trade". *Journal of Economic Perspectives* 9 (1995): 169–89.

Menon, J. "Malaysia's Investment Malaise: What Happened and Can It Be Fixed?". In *Malaysia's Socio-Economic Transformation: Ideas for the Next Decade*, edited by B.D. Sanchita and P.O. Lee. Singapore: Institute of Southeast Asian Studies, 2014.

Poelhekke, S. and van der F. Ploeg. "Do Natural Resources Attract Non-resource FDI?". *The Review of Economics and Statistics* 95, no. 3 (2013): 1047–65.

Ragayah Haji Mat Zin. "Malaysia's Reverse Investments: Trends and Strategies". *Asia Pacific Journal of Management* 16 (1999): 469–96.

Rahim M. Quazi. "Corruption and Foreign Direct Investment in East Asia and South Asia: An Econometric Study". *International Journal of Economics and Financial Issues* 4, no. 2 (2014): 231–42 <http://www.researchgate.net/profile/Rahim_Quazi/publication/272564735_Corruption_and_Foreign_Direct_Investment_in_East_Asia_and_South_Asia_An_Econometric_Study/links/54e8de9e0cf2f7aa4d52e0d6.pdf> (accessed 4 June 2015).

Rasiah, S., P. Gammeltoft and J. Yang. "Home Government Policies for Outward FDI from Emerging Economies: Lessons from Asia". *International Journal of Emerging Markets* 5, no. 3/4 (2010): 333–57.

Rosfadzimi, M.S., M.N. Abd Halim, and S.M.N. Abu Hassan. "Outward Foreign Direct Investment (OFDI) Drivers in Developing Economies: A Case of Malaysia". *Business & Management Quarterly Review* 3, no. 1 (2012): 26–34.

Teo, Y.N., S.Y. Tham, and A.J.Y. Kam. "Re-Examining the Determinants of Malaysia's Outward FDI". Presented in the International Conference on Humanities and Social Sciences, Kuala Lumpur Convention Centre, 3–5 June 2014.

Tham, S.Y. "Outward Foreign Direct Investment from Malaysia: An Exploratory Study". *Südostasienaktuell* 5 (2007): 44–72 <http://www.giga-hamburg.de/openaccess/suedostasienaktuell/2007_5/giga_soa_2007_5_tham.pdf> (accessed 21 September 2010).

Tham, S.Y. and W.H. Loke. "Harnessing Services for Development in Malaysia". In *Malaysia's Socio-Economic Transformation: Ideas for the Next Decade*, edited by B.D. Sanchita and P.O. Lee. Singapore: Institute of Southeast Asian Studies, 2014.

UNCTAD. *World Investment Report 2006: FDI from Developing and Transition Economies: Implications for Development*. Geneva: UNCTAD, 2006a.

————. *Global Players from Emerging Markets: Strengthening Enterprise Competitiveness Through Outward Investment*. Geneva: UNCTAD, 2006*b*.

————. "UNCTADSTAT" <http://unctadstat.unctad.org/TableViewer/table View. aspx> (accessed 27 October 2014).

Wei, S. "How Taxing Is Corruption on International Investors?". *Review of Economics and Statistics* 82 (2000): 1–11.

Wong, H.T. "The Determinants of Foreign Direct Investment in the Manufacturing Industry of Malaysia". *Journal of Economic Cooperation* 26, no. 2 (2005): 91–110 <http://www.sesrtcic.org/files/article/89.pdf> (accessed 5 March 2014).

World Distance Calculator. <http://www.globefeed.com/World_Distance_ Calculator.asp> (accessed 4 January 2014).

Worldwide Governance Indicators. "Control of Corruption" <http://www. govindicators.org> (accessed 15 June 2015).

Zainal Aznam Yusof. "Outward Foreign Direct Investment by Enterprises from Malaysia". In *Global Players from Emerging Markets: Strengthening Enterprise Competitiveness through Outward Investment*. Geneva: UNCTAD, 2006.

Zhang, S. "China's Rising Costs". *China Business Review*, 1 July 2012 <http:// www.chinabusinessreview.com/chinas-rising-costs/> (accessed 10 March 2015).

6

INDONESIA'S OUTWARD FOREIGN DIRECT INVESTMENT

Maxensius Tri Sambodo

1. INTRODUCTION

Inward-looking policies brought Indonesia close to bankruptcy towards the end of Sukarno's government in the mid-1960s. In contrast, his successor, President Suharto, started to develop a new development strategy by pursuing an outward-looking policy with more liberal trade and foreign investment regime (Thee 2012). The Foreign Investment Law was enacted in 1967 and the Domestic Investment Law was issued in the following year. The "open door" policy succeeded in attracting new foreign investment flows in the oil sector, other mining projects and the mining sector (Hill 1988, p. 81).

As seen from Figure 6.1, inward foreign direct investment (IFDI) flow increased gradually from about US$145 million in 1970 to about US$1.3 billion in 1975. Then between 1976 and 1989, the average IFDI flow was about US$349 million. IFDI flow gradually increased after 1989 and it reached a peak at US$6.2 billion in 1996, then it declined to US$4.7 billion in 1997 (before the economic crisis in 1997–98). On the other hand, the movement of outward foreign direct investment (OFDI) flow was not as

FIGURE 6.1
Inward and Outward Foreign Direct Investment of Indonesia

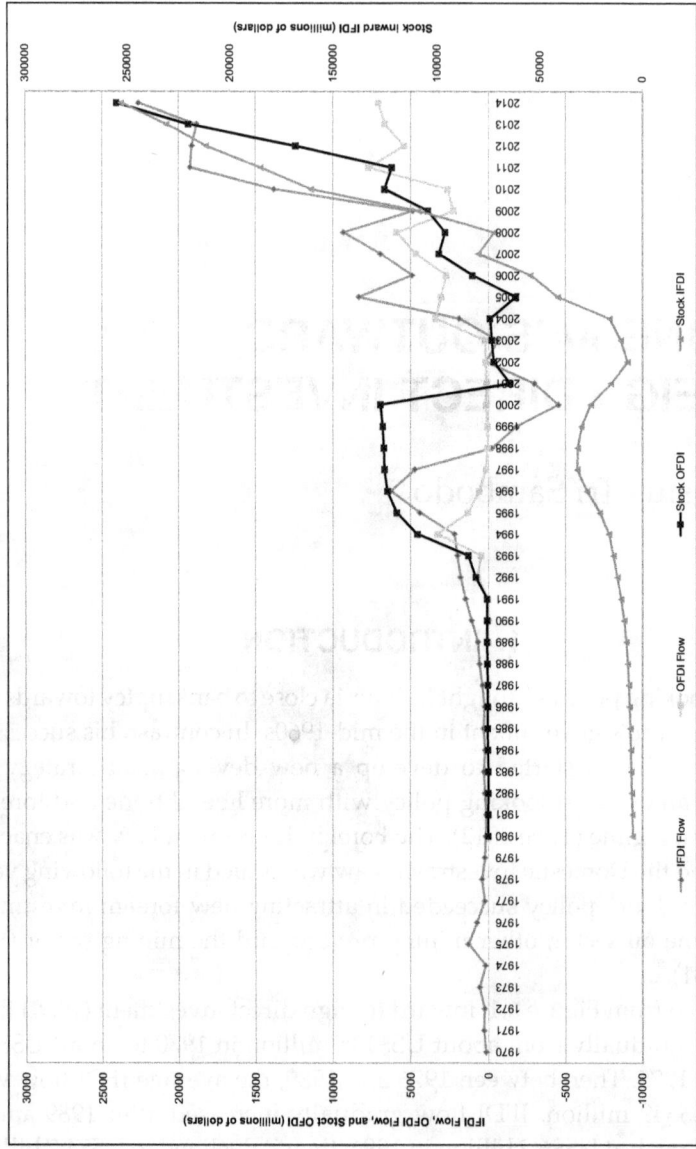

Note: IFDI (Inward Foreign Direct Investment); OFDI (Outward Foreign Direct Investment); IFDI consists of three components: equity capital, reinvested earnings, and intra-company loans. FDI-outward is defined as assets, while FDI-inward is called as liabilities. FDI-outward is recorded with a negative sign in the balance of payments.
Source: UNCTAD (2015).

quick as IFDI. However, in 1994, the ODFI flow was higher than IFDI. Even, for seven consecutive years (1998 to 2004), the flow of ODFI was higher than IFDI. In 2014, the flow of ODFI was about US$7.1 billion. The ODFI flow has increased more than double compared to its level in 2005. This indicates that IFDI and ODFI flows have increased in the same direction. By 2014, the IFDI stock in Indonesia was about US$253.1 billion, while the OFDI was about US$24 billion (UNCTAD 2015). This indicates that the share of OFDI stocks to inward FDI stock was about 9.5 per cent.

Today, Indonesia lags in the promotion of OFDI. According to the Central Intelligence Agency (CIA), in term of OFDI stock, Indonesia was ranked 48 out of 93 countries. In the ASEAN region, Indonesia lags behind Singapore (rank 18), Malaysia (rank 27), and Thailand (rank 34).[1] As seen from Figure 6.2, in 2012, there were no Indonesian firms in the list of top-100 non-financial Transnational Corporations (TNCs) from developing and transition economies. In the list, about 50 per cent of the top non-financial TNCs came from China and Singapore. Thus, Indonesia's companies lack in internationalization record compared to other developing countries.

Some have argued that OFDI is a form of capital flight and reflects an un-nationalistic attitude because OFDI aims to maximize tax benefits offered by foreign countries. Under such presumptions and conditions, Carney and Dieleman (2011) have argued that OFDI is underreported under official statistics.

This chapter aims to develop an understanding of the status of Indonesia's OFDI. This chapter is organized into six sections. After the introduction, we investigate the pattern of investment development path (IDP) in the case of Indonesia and discuss how this framework can explain the trend and trajectory of OFDI. Section 3 focuses on the motives and strategies of Indonesia's OFDI. Section 4 examines Indonesia's OFDI in Singapore. Section 5 provides an analysis of Indonesia's Multinational Enterprises (MNEs) overseas. Finally, Section 6 provides a discussion of policies to promote Indonesia's OFDI.

2. INVESTMENT DEVELOPMENT PATH (IDP)

Narula and Dunning (2010) developed a framework on investment development path (IDP) to understand the interaction between investment

FIGURE 6.2
Number of Companies in Top 100 Non-financial TNCs from Developing and Transition Economies, Ranked by Foreign Assets, 2012

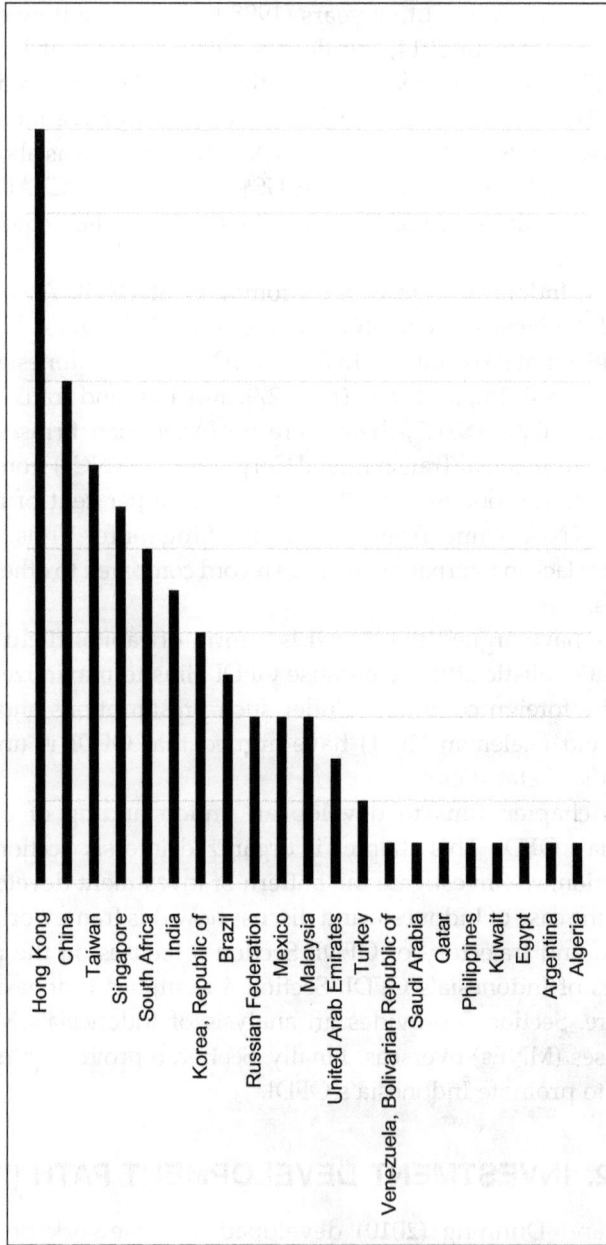

Source: UNCTAD (database).

and development. The IDP has five stages: (i) natural resource based; (ii) investment driven; (iii) innovation driven; and (iv & v) increasing knowledge and service intensity; knowledge economy. In addition, domestic capabilities to assimilate and to adopt the knowledge flow from MNEs activity depends on industrial policy that may vary depending on the stage of IDP and the focus of MNEs-related development strategies (Narula and Dunning 2010). The IDP framework covers the transformation of investment intensity from low level of technology capability to high level of technology capability. In terms of five enabling factors that can transform developing economies to advanced ones, Abramovitz (1986) and Dowrick (1992) have listed five factors, namely — physical infrastructure, educational attainment, market institutions and the size, competence, and freedom of action of its entrepreneurial classes.

In the case of Indonesia, Thee (2012, p. 128) has argued that, due to the lack involvement of TNCs in the economy, the country has not participated in a major way in the regional product fragmentation trade, the cross-border dispersion of parts and components production within vertically integrated production processes. The major reason for Indonesia's poor performance was its ambiguous attitude towards foreign direct investment (FDI) which made the country a relatively unattractive place to invest for foreign investors (Thee 2012, p. 128).

For example, since 1967, industrial policy in Indonesia has moved like a pendulum from a protectionist regime to a liberal one and back again. The history of industrial policy in Indonesia can be divided into three sub-phases (Hill 1994, pp. 78–80 in Thee 2012). In the *first sub-phase*, trade and investment were the main drivers of rapid industrial growth from 1967 to 1973. The government promoted export-promotion strategy and also provided investment incentives such as tax holidays, and liberalized the capital account which allowed foreign investors to transfer their profits and dividends freely to their headquarters overseas (Thee 2012). Initially, foreign investors were interested in the extractive sectors (forestry and mining), then they moved to manufacturing projects such as a labour-intensive industry and a capital-intensive industry (Thee 2012).

In the *second sub-phase* (1974–81), industrial policy became more inward-looking. At that time, the nominal and effective rates of protection for consumer goods were among the highest among Southeast Asian countries (Thee 2012). The government became more restrictive in providing incentives to the manufacturing sector, and Indonesia moved towards implementing an import-substitution policy. As seen from Figure 6.3, in the first sub-phase, inward FDI flow increased substantially from about US$145 million to about US$581 million. However, in the second sub-phase, the country's inward FDI declined from about US$1,293 million in 1975 to about US$133 million in 1981. Thus, industrial policy is an important determinant of the flow of IFDI. However, there is no information on OFDI both in the first and second sub-phase.

The *third sub-phase* of industrial development covers the period 1982–96. During that period, efficiency-minded economists attempted to shift the government's industrial policy from import substitution to export-promotion (Thee 2012). Serious effort to open the country's economy began in 1986 when the price of oil was very low. The government attempted to improve investment climate and to promote investments that could directly boost exports. Duty exemptions and a drawback scheme were introduced in May 1986 and further trade reforms were undertaken to eliminate "anti-export bias" (Thee 2012).

Figure 6.4 depicts the increase in inward FDI flows after the mid-1980s. IFDI flow reached a peak in 1996 (before the economic crisis). Similarly,

FIGURE 6.3
Inward FDI Flow (in US$ million)

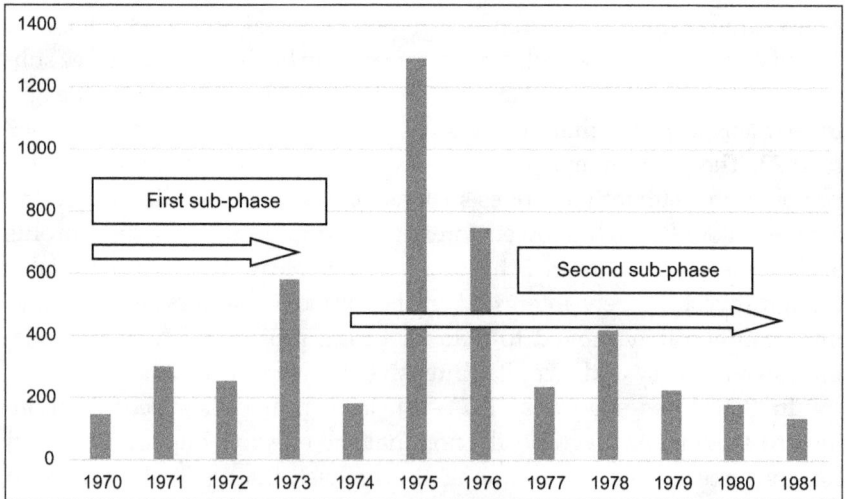

Source: UNCTAD (database).

FIGURE 6.4
Indonesia's Investment Development Path

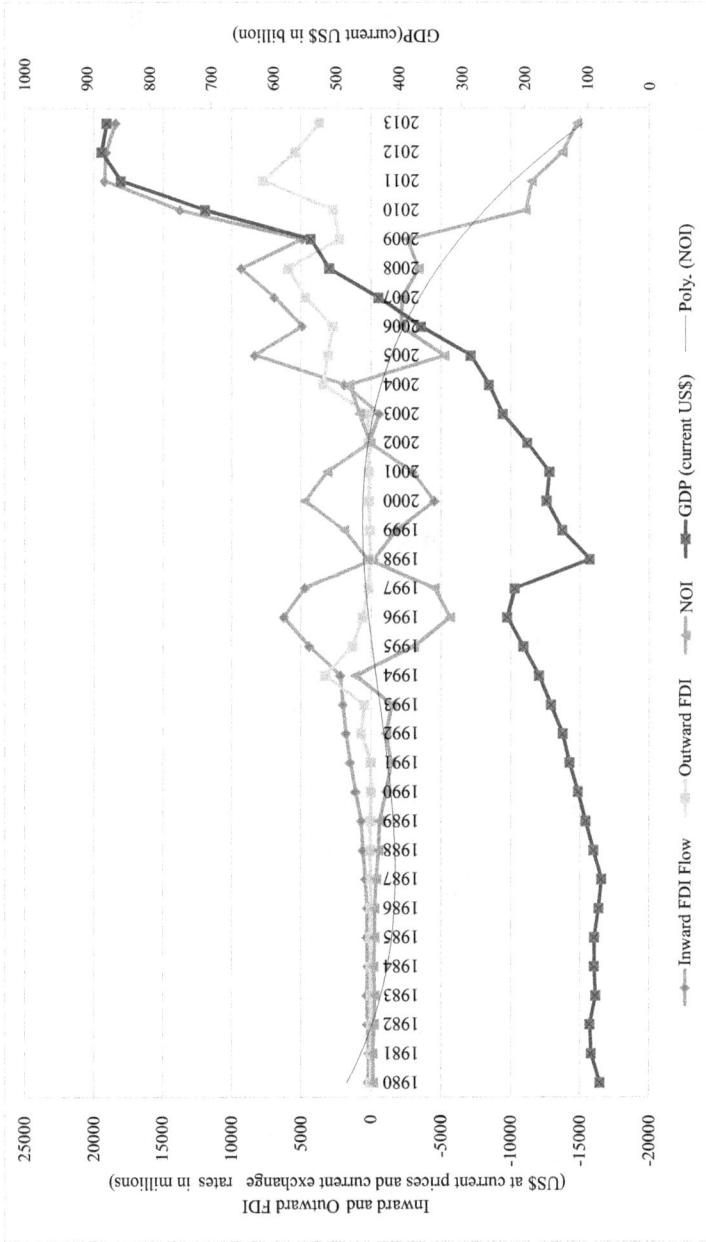

Note: The arrow signs indicate spike of OFDI.
Source: UNCTAD (data base) and World Development Indicators.

the OFDI flow started to increase in the early 1990s and it reached a peak before the economic crisis. Figure 6.4 indicates that the flow of inward FDI has moved in a similar direction as the GDP. Thus, there appears to be a positive correlation between inward FDI, outward FDI and GDP. The coefficient correlation is quite high around 0.8. As seen from Figure 6.4, before the Asian financial crisis in 1997–98, the amount of inward FDI was larger than the OFDI except for 1994. Before the crisis, the level of inward FDI flow peaked at US$6,245 million in 1996.

Post-Asian Financial Crisis of 1997–98

During the period 1998–2001, the inward FDI flow was negative and the highest capital outflow was recorded in 2000 with total capital flight exceeding US$4.5 billion (Figure 6.4). OFDI did not increase substantially during the crisis. However, the figure showed that between 1998 and 2004, the amount of OFDI was larger than the inward FDI. The pre-crisis value of inward FDI was reached in 2005. This indicates that it took more than eight years to restore investors' confidence. When the level of FDI inflows started to increase, OFDI flows also increased gradually. The previous highest record of OFDI attained in 1994 was surpassed in 2004. As seen from Figure 6.4, after the 1997–98 crisis, OFDI showed an increasing trend with three distinguishable leaps in the years 2004, 2008 and 2011. Most of Indonesia's OFDI jumps were contributed by rapid increase of OFDI to countries such as China, Japan, Singapore, Thailand and the United States. The OFDI flows from Indonesia to those countries were substantial.

The global financial crisis (GFC) hit Indonesia in the fourth quarter of 2008 through the trade channel as export-oriented industries contracted sharply (Thee 2012). The global financial crisis also affected OFDI in the U.S. and EU countries. Between 2008 and 2009, the IFDI decreased from US$9,318 million to about US$4,877 million. Similarly, OFDI decreased from US$5,900 million to about US$2,249 million. However, IFDI increased significantly after 2009, while OFDI moved slowly. Between 2007 and 2008, OFDI to the U.S. decreased from US$106 million to US$88 million. In the Netherlands, it decreased from US$330 million to US$120 million, while in France it increased from US$75 million to US$99 million. Thus, the impact of the GFC on Indonesia's OFDI showed mixed results.

Indonesia was mildly affected by the GFC compared to its Southeast Asian neighbours for three reasons (Thee 2012). First, the share of manufactures to total exports was relatively low. Second, the share Indonesia in inter-regional trade was low. Third, Indonesia had a relatively low degree of "export-led" growth. Basri and Patunru (2012) have also argued that Indonesia could survive due to its huge domestic market. Reflecting on the GFC, Basri and Patunru (2012) pointed out that it is necessary to maintain a balance between export-oriented and inward-looking strategies. Similarly, Hill (2012) also mentioned other factors that ease the impact of the GFC on Indonesia such as better regulations in the financial and fiscal sector, increase in commodity prices, and strong economic growth in China. Although there are some fluctuations in OFDI flows between 2004 and 2013, it showed an upward trend. This is because inward FDI grew substantially after 2003. The net outward investment, NOI (outward minus inward flows) tended to decline between 2000 and 2013 (Figure 6.4). However, between 2004 and 2013, the average yearly growth of inward FDI and OFDI flows increased by 7 per cent and 18 per cent, respectively.

Indonesia's OFDI

Indonesia's OFDI can be tracked using data from the World Investment Report which publishes data on two modes of FDI: (i) mergers and acquisitions (M&As); and (ii) greenfield investment.[2] In 2005, Indonesia was listed amongst the top 15 developing and transition economies in terms of stock of OFDI that was about US$13,735 million (UNCTAD 2006). A number of Indonesian companies were also included in the top 10 cross-border M&A deal in the oil and gas industry. These include Bumi Modern which acquired the Gallo Oil Limited (United States) with value of sales about US$1.3 billion. Similarly, Central Asia Petroleum acquired Mangistau Oil and Gas from Kazakhstan with value of sales US$592 million. Conoco Phillips's sold of its affiliates in Algeria to an Indonesian state-owned company, Pertamina for US$1.8 billion (UNCTAD 2014). Asia Petroleum Limited (Pakistan) set up a joint venture with CPL (Nigeria), Korean Electric Corporation, and Medco (Indonesia) to invest US$5 billion in Nigeria.

Further, as seen from Figure 6.5, most of Indonesia's OFDI is dominated by equity capital and reinvested earnings. This type of OFDI has increased gradually since 2005. The figure also indicates that the ratio of OFDI stock to FDI has increased from about –9 per cent in 2001, to 2 per cent

FIGURE 6.5
Stock of Direct Investment Abroad from Indonesia

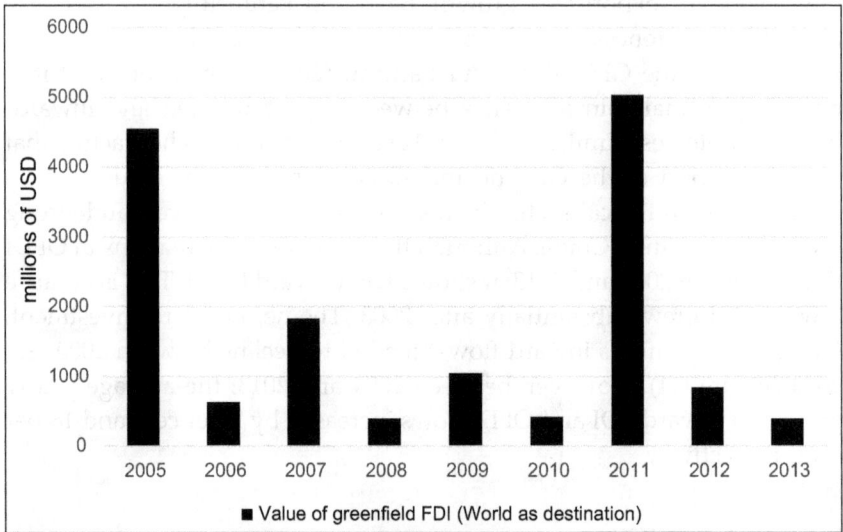

Source: Indonesia Financial Statistics, Central Bank (data base).

in 2006, and reaching more than 7 per cent in 2013. Thus, increase in equity capital and reinvested earnings have made positive contributions to Indonesia's OFDI.

Greenfield project is also an important component of OFDI. In 2005, Indonesia was listed in the top 15 list of developing and transition economies in terms of OFDI stock (UNCTAD 2006). However, as seen from Figure 6.6, the value of greenfield OFDI was less than US$5,000 million or its share of total OFDI was about one-third. This situation differs from the global OFDI composition in which the value of greenfield is higher than M&A. Between 2006 and 2010, greenfield investment decreased substantially, but in 2011, TNCs greenfield investment reached about US$5,000 million.

However, by investigating the longer time period and in comparison with other indicators, the data showed that the role of Indonesia's OFDI becomes less important in comparison with domestic capital formation. UNCTAD (2014) showed that the share of OFDI's stock as percentage of gross fixed capital formation declined from 2.7 per cent in 1995 to about

FIGURE 6.6
Indonesia's Greenfield OFDI

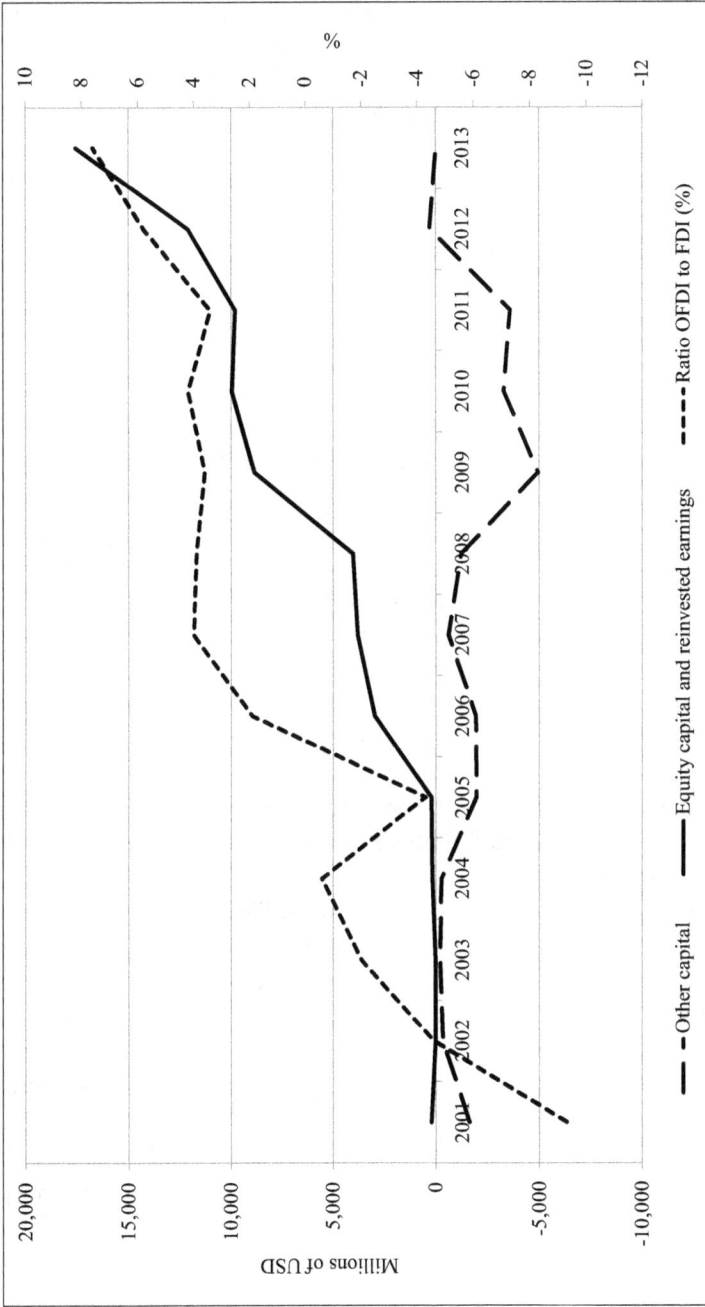

Source: UNCTAD (data base).

1.8 per cent in 2013. Even for the shorter time period, the share of OFDI's flow as percentage of gross fixed capital formation declined from 4.0 per cent (in 2005–07) to about 1.3 per cent in 2013. For comparison, the stock of China's OFDI as a percentage of gross domestic product increased from 2.3 per cent to 6.7 per cent between 1995 and 2013. Similarly, the share of OFDI's flow as a percentage of gross fixed capital formation increased from 1.8 per cent in 2005–07 to about 2.4 per cent in 2013. This indicates that the "going out" strategy that has been proposed since 2000 in China, is more successful compared to Indonesia.

3. MOTIVES AND STRATEGIES

Figure 6.7 shows Indonesia's FDI stock abroad. Most of OFDI from Indonesia is accumulated in Asian countries especially China and Singapore. The FDI stock abroad in these countries has showed an increasing trend in the past ten years. For example in China, OFDI increased from US$997 million in 2001 to about US$2,103 million in 2012. Indonesian OFDI in Singapore increased from about US$871 to about US$1,920 million. The share of OFDI stock in China and Singapore reached 73.5 per cent of total OFDI stock in 2012. Carnery and Dieleman (2011) argued that China is on the top list of OFDI because of the huge size of Chinese economy and its rapid economic growth. Furthermore, Chinese Indonesians may be inclined to invest in their ancestral country. European countries that bare important destinations for Indonesian OFDI include Belgium, France, and Netherlands. The United States is also on the list of top five Indonesian OFDI destination.

The sum of OFDI stock, as seen from Figure 6.7, covers about 47 per cent of total estimated OFDI's figure (UNCTAD 2013). Thus, Figure 6.4 may not capture the total OFDI's stock from Indonesia. Data from Figure 6.7 is obtained from UNCTAD's bilateral FDI Statistics that are based on national data sources, and it is possible that many countries do not provide report on OFDI due to poor records or for reasons such as protection of investors' information.

Table 6.1 presents statistics on the share of OFDI stock and the stock of investment from selected countries in Indonesia. There are two patterns from Table 6.1. First, there is unbalanced (in terms of value) FDI between inward and outward. Where Indonesia has relatively high investment in countries such as in Singapore, Thailand, United States, Netherlands, and

FIGURE 6.7
Indonesia's FDI Stock Abroad, by Geographical Destination (in 2012)

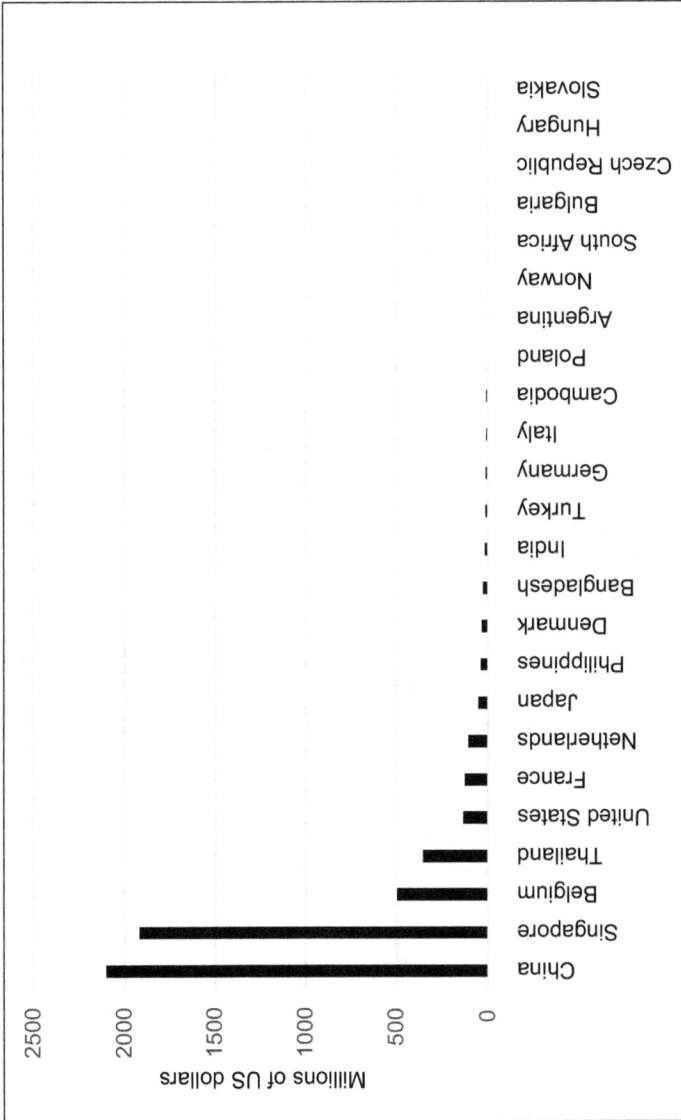

Note: This figure is obtained from <http://unctad.org/en/Pages/DIAE/FDI%20Statistics/FDI-Statistics-Bilateral.aspx>, for Indonesia.
Source: UNCTAD FDI/TNC (database).

TABLE 6.1
Inward and Outward FDI Stock for Selected Countries
(in 2012, US$ million)

	Country	Inward	Outward
1	Singapore	37,013	1,920
2	China	4,772	2,103
3	Belgium	164	496
4	Thailand	2,917	355
5	United States	10,160	136
6	France	3,239	128
7	Netherlands	13,636	108
8	Japan	11,574	55
9	Philippines	11	40
10	Denmark	5	35
11	India	408	17
12	Germany	2,104	12
13	Italy	35	10
14	Norway	7	3

Note: For example in the case of Singapore, inward indicates Singapore's investment in Indonesia; while outward shows Indonesia's investment in Singapore.
Source: UNCTAD FDI/TNC (data base).

Japan, those countries do not necessarily have relatively high investment in Indonesia. Second, Indonesia has dominant share of OFDI stock for several countries such as Belgium, Philippines, and Denmark.

The Indonesian government does not have any report or publication on Indonesia's OFDI. There are a number of studies on Indonesian OFDI despite such limitations. These include: (i) Carney and Dielman (2011) who have analysed OFDI from 25 domestic private owned business group; (ii) Aminullah (2013) who conducted a case study for three firms in the natural resource-based sector; and (iii) Lecraw (1993) who studied 24 industries that contained at least one Indonesian multinational. Thus, understanding the OFDI need to be approached by investigating the Indonesia FDI for each countries. Due to this limitation, the next section mainly focused on Indonesia's OFDI in Singapore for five reasons: (i) data is more reliable; (ii) Singapore is the second most important destination for Indonesian OFDI after China; (iii) Singapore's investment in Indonesia is substantial; (iv) it has been a public knowledge that many wealthy Indonesians invest their money in Singapore; and (v) Singapore is geographically very close to Indonesia.

4. INDONESIA'S OFDI IN SINGAPORE

Singapore is the second most important destination for Indonesian OFDI (stock) after China. As seen from Table 6.2, Indonesia's investment in Singapore is mostly concentrated in the financial and insurance services sector. The financial services sector consists of three main sub-sectors, namely, banks, investment holding companies, and other financial services. In the banking sector, there are two Indonesian's state banks that have operations in Singapore, namely Bank Mandiri and Bank BNI. Singapore offers lucrative business prospects not only for business people but also migrant workers.[3] As seen from Table 6.3, the number of Indonesian migrant workers in Singapore was about 145,000 people in 2013. The total remittance from Singapore was estimated to be around US$93 million, or about 6 per cent of net profits of one the largest state-owned bank in Indonesia (Bank Mandiri).[4] The reciprocity principle has become a key reason for Indonesian banks to operate in Singapore. Trade financing and remittances are lucrative business for Indonesia's banks operating in Singapore.[5]

TABLE 6.2
OFDI from Indonesia in Singapore by Major Industry
(stock as Year-End, in S$ million)

Major Industry	2008	2009	2010	2011	2012	2013
Manufacturing	19	22	7	–49	(s)	(s)
Construction	(s)	(s)	–	–	–	–
Wholesale & Retail Trade	315	243	–96	–683	–625	173.7
Accommodation & Food Service Activities	(s)	–2	(s)	–	(s)	(s)
Transport & Storage	513	652	304	384	460	545.0
Information & Communications	1	11	(s)	(s)	(s)	(s)
Financial & Insurance Services	1,895	1,977	522	1,401	1,884	2,370
Real Estate Activities	16	57	51	45	50	97.7
Professional, Scientific & Technical Administrative & Support Services	215	894	–150	–83	–110	–58.3
Others	–4	(s)	(s)	(s)	1	(s)
Total	2,962	3,894	1,483	963	1,662	3,173.8
Share of financial sector (%)	64	51	35	145	113	74.7
Share of transport & storage (%)	17.3	16.7	20.5	39.9	27.7	17.2

Note: – nil or negligible; (s) suppressed to avoid disclosure of data of individual companies.
Source: Department of Statistics Singapore.

TABLE 6.3
Remittance and Number of Indonesian Migrants in 2013

Country	Remittances of foreign workers by country of origin (US$ million)	Number of Indonesian Migrant Workers by host country (Thousands of People)	The average remittance per worker (US$)
ASEAN	472.00	2,134.00	221
Malaysia	158.00	1,941.00	81
Singapore	93.00	145.00	641
Asia excluding ASEAN	1,455.00	475.00	3,063
Hong Kong SAR	6.00	192.00	31
Japan	290.00	30.00	9,667
Taiwan	95.00	189.00	503
South Korea	222.00	43.00	5,163
Australia	74.00	4.00	18,500
Netherlands	19.00	3.00	6,333
France	47.00	1.00	47,000
Germany	3.00	3.00	1,000
United Kingdom	37.00	2.00	18,500
Italy	31.00	8.00	3,875
Total Foreign Workers' Remittances	2,613.00	4,016.00	651

Source: Central Bank of Indonesia (database).

Singapore's insurance sector has a high degree of openness (Claessens and Glaessner 1998). Singapore has increased its commitment to allow the extension of branches in the insurance industry and subsidiaries to set up companies in the country (Setiawan 2012). An example mentioned in Setiawan (2012) is ACA (Asuransi Central Asia) from Indonesia. The company has established business networks in Cambodia, Philippines, Vietnam, and Singapore. In Cambodia, ACA has developed joint ventures with local companies such as Asia Insurance Cambodia and Cambodia Reassurance with capital ownership 80 per cent and 20 per cent, respectively (Setiawan 2012).

Another important sector for Indonesian OFDI in Singapore is transport and storage. This is because about 90 per cent of international trade is transported by sea and Singapore has become an important hub for Indonesia's trade shipment (USAID 2008). Dick (2008) has argued that governments cannot decouple transportation policy from trade policy. Shipping laws have substantial impacts on cabotage, logistics, marine safety, and development of the shipping industries (Dick 2008). Dick (2008) has opined that the attractiveness of Singapore as a world's great financial and maritime centres with conducive business, legal and regulatory environment is the reason why shipping companies have Singaporean flag instead of Indonesian flag. Even since 1968, Singapore had implemented a tax waiver on shipping company profits (Dick 2008). Further, in 2006, the head of the Indonesian Seamen's Union had claimed that 70 per cent of the foreign-flag ships operating in Indonesian waters were actually owned by Indonesians (Dick 2008). This is partly due to the avoidance of government regulations such as those on the age limit for Indonesian ships and those related to saving crewing costs (Oktaveri 2006, as cited by Dick 2008). Carney and Dieleman (2011) called this situation as "institutional escape".

5. LESSON LEARNED FROM INDONESIA'S MNEs

By observing fourteen export-enhancing Indonesian multinationals, Lecraw (1993) indicated that OFDI can enhance competition advantages by gaining access to technology, distribution, and management. Similarly, Aminullah et al. (2013) investigated three Indonesia's MNEs that focus on natural resource based products, namely, (i) instant noodles, wheat flour, cooking oil and margarine,[6] (ii) peanuts, jelly, snack, biscuits, and beverages; and (iii) branded cosmetics and herbal medicine products using traditional ingredients. Aminullah et al. (2013) concluded that there are three major motives of internationalization of these companies: (i) to ensure supply of raw materials for the firms and to have a better position in controlling the market; (ii) to make the production centre closer to the market in order to get wider access to the international market; and (iii) to develop a brand image in the foreign market. The objectives of Indonesia's OFDI is similar with China's — to promote domestic productivity and strengthen domestic production. However, Wang, Mao and Guo (2014) has argued that for large Chinese OFDI, the main motivation is technology seeking.

Very few Indonesian businessmen aim to benefit from OFDI. Most of them are still domestic-oriented entrepreneurs. Most are well connected to the natural resource sector such as pulp and paper, palm oil, rubber, coal, mining, oil and coal. Thus, their wealth depends on international commodity prices. During the commodity booming price, they can create substantial wealth, but this is not sustainable. Some invest in real estate, buildings and towers, and holding franchise but most of the businesses attempt to serve the high-income segment and lack in promoting inclusive growth. Carney and Dieleman (2011) used the archival analysis methodology to examine Indonesia's top-25 domestic privately-owned business group. They found that only two business groups — the Salim group and the Lippo group — can be classified as emerging market MNEs. They argued that Indonesia business groups have little appetite for international activity or they focus substantially on the domestic market.

Further, in Forbes' list of 2,000 global leading companies, only nine were from Indonesia.[7] These were from five main sectors: (i) *banks*: Bank Mandiri Indonesia, Bank Rakyat Indonesia, Bank Central Asia, Bank Negara Indonesia, and Bank Danamon Indonesia; (ii) *telecommunication*: Telekom Indonesia; (iii) *gas*: Perusahaan Gas Negara (PGN); (iv) *cigarette*: Gudang Garam; and (v) *cement*: Semen Indonesia. The asset value of these companies are estimated to be about 29.6 per cent of Indonesia's GDP. The internationalization experiences of three non-bank companies are discussed next. They are Telekom Indonesia, Perusahaan Gas Negara, and Semen Indonesia.

Telekom Indonesia

Telekom Indonesia has developed business alliances by setting up subsidiaries with indirect ownership under the "Telin" brand such as Telin Singapore, Telin Hong Kong, Telin Timor Leste, Telkom Australia, and Telin Myanmar. Other subsidiaries include Telkom Macao Limited, Telkom Taiwan Limited, and Telekomunikasi Indonesia Internasional (USA) Inc. The Telin group has developed an undersea cable system that connects Thailand-Indonesia-Singapore and with satellite support. Telin also had joined Asia America Getaway (AAG) since April 2007. With the help of a consortium, Telin has developed the Batam-Singapore Cable System (BSCS). It has also developed a cable network that connects to the South East Asian Japan Cable System (SJC). Up to December 2013, Telin has signed international telecommunication agreements involving 79 international operators in 26 countries.

Perusahaan Gas Negara

Perusahaan Gas Negara (PGN) is a state-owned company involved in the transportation and distribution of natural gas. The company developed transmission pipeline crosses the sea to carry gas from the ConocoPhillips and Petro China fields to Singapore (Gas Supply Pte Ltd) via a 468-km pipeline via Batam.[8] PT. Transportasi Gas Indonesia (Transgasindo), a subsidiary of PGN, signed a strategic partnership agreement in September 2002. About 40 per cent of Transgasindo's shares is owned by a joint venture company namely Transasia Pipeline Company Pvt. Ltd (Transasia). Transasia is owned by Petroliam Nasional Berhad (PETRONAS), ConocoPhillips, Talisman Energy Inc (Talisman), and Singapore Petroleum Company Limited (SPC). SPC is a subsidiary of Keppel Oil and Gas Service Pte Ltd, a wholly-owned subsidiary of Keppel Corporation Limited. Thus, Transgasindo is treated as foreign investment, and SPC is tasked to assist in the financing of the Singapore pipeline.[9] This indicates that internationalization of Transgasindo developed through strategic partnership under the flag of Share Sale and Purchase Agreement (SSPA).

Semen Indonesia

Semen Indonesia is a state-owned company that produces cement. The company's shares are owned by the Indonesian government (51 per cent) and public (49 per cent). On 18 December 2012, Semen Indonesia acquired the Thang Long Cement Joint Stock Company (TLCC) in Vietnam by buying 70 per cent of the company's shares (PT. Semen Indonesia 2013). There are four main reasons for acquisition (PT. Semen Indonesia 2013): (i) Vietnam can be a hub for regional market because it has a long coastline; (ii) Vietnam needs foreign investment due to declining economic performance; (iii) TLCC is a reputable cement company in Vietnam with technology from Europe and well-established infrastructure; (iv) TLCC has a very efficient and effective business infrastructure. TLCC has a cement factory in Quang Ninh province that is located near the Cai Lan Port. It also owns a milling factory that is located near Ho Chi Minh (Saigon) that is connected to the Mekong River.

After the acquisition, PT. Semen Indonesia claimed that TLCC's performance had gradually improved in terms of profits, product quality and market expansion. In 2013, TLCC exported cement to Peru, Singapore, and Indonesia. TLCC has also obtained permission from the Vietnamese government to expand its cement production capacity from 2.7 million ton per year to about 6.4 million ton per year.

6. OFDI POLICIES AND ASEAN INTEGRATION

The Indonesia Investment Coordinating Board (BKPM) has representative offices in eight countries: Abu Dhabi (UEA), London (UK), New York (US), Seoul (South Korea), Singapore, Sydney (Australia), Taipei (China), and Tokyo (Japan). The tasks of the representative office in Singapore is mainly to facilitate investment in Indonesia rather than promoting investment from Indonesia to Singapore. On the other side, there is a well-established business network in Singapore, namely the Indonesian Business Centre (IBC) that aims to optimize the diaspora linkages. The IBC was established in year 2000 with a membership of about 5,000 people that comprises businessmen, entrepreneurs, and professionals. There are three main IBC programmes, namely, business forum, business lunch, and business and cultural trip to Indonesia. IBC not only aims to connect medium and large firms between the two countries but also among small and medium enterprises (SMEs). For example, there is a Memorandum of Understanding between the West Java Centre Board of Indonesia SMEs and IBC. However, there is a need to develop more strategic alliance between BKPM's representative offices and the overseas business organizations such as IBC. The network aims to promote more Indonesia's investments in other countries.

Further, Indonesia also currently has 64 Bilateral Investment Treaties (BITs) and 14 International Investment Agreements (IIAs) (UNCTAD 2014). BITs can help investors to reduce their overseas risks. However, it seems that the government plans to terminate the BITs because foreign investors have used it to stop government policies that are aimed at protecting national interests. This intention was announced in July 2015.[10] The Indonesian government has claimed that this decision was taken in order to synchronize and to equalize between international law and national laws.[11] However, Indonesia needs to consider this proposal carefully, especially from the perspective of protecting Indonesian investors overseas.

However, Indonesia needs to implement the ASEAN Comprehensive Investment Agreement (ACIA).[12] ACIA was signed in March 2012. ACIA aims to create a liberal, facilitative, transparent, and competitive investment

environment in the ASEAN region. Between 2006 and 2013, the FDI inflows
in ASEAN increased from US$63.9 billion to about US$122.4 billion.[13]
Although the share of intra-ASEAN investment increased from US$8,694
million to US$21,426 million between 2006 and 2013, the proportion of
intra-ASEAN's FDI to the total FDI in ASEAN increased in the small
proportion from 13.6 per cent to 17.5 per cent for the same period.[14] Thus,
it is expected that ACIA can boost intra-ASEAN investment.

In 2006, the total FDI flow from Indonesia to ASEAN was US$604
million (the third largest after Singapore and Malaysia).[15] By 2013, the flow
reached US$2,648 million (the second largest after Singapore). However,
Indonesia received a much higher FDI flows from ASEAN countries.
In 2006, Indonesia received US$1,354 million and in 2013 this reached
US$8,721 million.[16]

TABLE 6.4
Incentives for ASEAN Countries — Presidential Regulation No. 39 Year 2014

Investment Sector	ASEAN	Other countries
Survey consultancy	Max 50%	Domestic capital 100%
Accommodation	Max 70%	Foreign capital ownership and location max 51%
Recreation, art, and entertainment	100% in Java/Bali 70% outside Java/Bali	Foreign capital ownership and location max 51%
Promotion	Max 51%	Domestic capital 100%
Foreign transportation (not include cabotage)	Max 60%	Foreign capital ownership max 49%
Marine cargo handling services with CPC 7412	Max 60%	Foreign capital ownership max 49%
Hospital services/specialist	Max 70% in City of provinces	Foreign capital ownership and location max 67%
Clinic specialist-Medical services	Max 70% in city of provinces except Makassar and Manado	Foreign capital ownership and location max 67%
Clinic specialized dental services	Max 70%	Foreign capital ownership and location max 67%
Nursing service with CPC (Clinical Practice Council) 93191	Max 51 for Makassar and Manado Max 70% for all cities	Foreign capital ownership and location max 49%

ACIA has promoted progressive liberalization for five sectors: manufacturing and related services; agriculture and related services; fisheries and related services; forestry and related services; mining and quarrying and related services. Indonesia can optimize this opportunity by enhancing investment in ASEAN. Indonesia has offered an "ASEAN Premium" for greater access and ownership by ASEAN investors. As seen from Table 6.4, in the case of the accommodation sector, the Indonesia government allows for 70 per cent foreign ownership for ASEAN investors and 51 per cent for investors from other countries. Other ASEAN countries have also implemented similar policies. For example, in the healthcare sector, Lao PDR, Cambodia, Singapore, and Vietnam have allowed for full foreign ownership. In the telecommunications industry, Cambodia, Lao PDR, and Myanmar have allowed for 100 per cent foreign equity. This implies that Indonesia can expand its services sector to these other countries. However, Nikomborirak and Jitdumrong (2013) pointed out that aside from foreign equity, others issues also have to be considered such as land, professional workers, business permits, monopoly power and the role of state enterprises.

Notes

1. Stock of direct foreign investment abroad compares the cumulative US dollar value of all investments in foreign countries made directly by residents — primarily companies — of the home country, as of the end of the time period indicated. Direct investment excludes investment through purchase of shares <https://www.cia.gov/library/publications/the-world-factbook/rankorder/2199rank.html?countryname=Indonesia&countrycode=id&regionCode=eas&rank=48#id> (accessed 30 October 2014).
2. According to WRI-Methodological Note, there are three types of M&As: (i) selling a domestic company to a foreign company; (ii) selling of a foreign affiliate to a domestic company; and (iii) purchasing a foreign company of another foreign company operating in a host economy. Further, greenfield consist of new investment projects and expansion of existing projects. Joint ventures are included if it consists of new physical operation.
3. <http://www.thejakartapost.com/news/2013/04/09/singapore-central-bank-getting-softer-ri-expansion-says-bri.html> (accessed 30 October 2014).
4. The net profit of Mandiri Bank was about 18.8 trillion rupiah and the middle exchange rate 12,189 rupiah/US$1.
5. <http://www.infobanknews.com/2013/03/bri-ajukan-izin-pembukaan-cabang-di-singapura/> (accessed 30 October 2014).
6. This company has Joint Venture company in Nigeria, Saudi Arabia, Syria, Egypt, and Malaysia.

7. <http://www.forbes.com/global2000/list/> (accessed 29 October 2014).
8. <http://www.kepcorp.com/en/news_item.aspx?sid=513> (accessed 30 October 2014).
9. Ibid.
10. <http://www.ft.com/cms/s/0/3755c1b2-b4e2-11e3-af92-00144feabdc0.html# axzz3I9ZhLHFv> (accessed 5 November 2014).
11. Ibid.
12. Refer to <http://www.oecd.org/investment/investmentfordevelopment/ 46485529.pdf>.
13. Refer to ASEAN Statistical Yearbook 2014.
14. Ibid.
15. Ibid.
16. Ibid.

References

Abramovitz, M. "Catching Up, Forging Ahead and Falling Behind". *Journal of Economic History* 46, no. 2 (1986): 385–406.

Aminullah, E., T. Fizzanty, K. Kusnandar and R. Wijayanti. "Technology transfer through OFDI: the case of Indonesian natural resource-based MNEs". *Asian Journal of Technology Innovation* 21, no. S1 (2013): 104–18.

Basri, M.C. and A.A. Patunru. "How to keep trade policy open: the case of Indonesia". *Bulletin of Indonesian Economic Studies* 48, no. 2 (2012): 191–208.

Carney, M. and M. Dieleman. "Indonesia's missing multinationals: business group and outward direct investment". *Bulletin of Indonesian Economic Studies* 47, no. 1 (2011): 105–26.

Claessens, S. and T. Glaessner. *Internationalization of Financial Services in Asia.* World Bank, 1998.

Dick, H. "The 2008 Shipping Law: Deregulation or Re-regulation?". *Bulletin of Indonesian Economic Studies* 44, no. 3 (2008): 383–406.

Dowrick, S. "Technological Catch Up and Diverging Incomes: Patterns of Economic Growth 1960–88". *Economic Journal* 82 (1992): 600–10.

Hill, Hal. "The Best of Times and the Worst of Times: Indonesia and Economic Crisis". In *Working Paper*, March 2012 <https://crawford.anu.edu.au/acde/ publications/publish/papers/wp2012/wp_econ_2012_03.pdf> (accessed 29 October 2014).

———. *Foreign Investment and Industrialisation in Indonesia.* Singapore: Oxford University Press, 1988.

———. *Indonesia's New Order: The Dynamics of Socio-Economic Transformation.* Crows Nest, NSW: Allen and Unwin, 1994.

Lecraw, D.J. "Outward Direct Investment by Indonesia Firms: Motivation and Effects". *Journal of International Business Studies* 24, no. 3 (1993): 589–600.

Narula, R. and J.H. Dunning. "Multinational Enterprises, Development and Globalization: Some Clarifications and a Research Agenda". *Oxford Development Studies* 38, no. 3 (September 2010): 263–87.

Nikomborirak, D. and S. Jitdumrong. "ASEAN Trade in Services". In *The ASEAN Economic Community: A Work in Progress*, edited by Sanchita Basu Das, Jayant Menon, Rodolfo Severino, and Omkar Lal Shrestha. Singapore: Institute of Southeast Asian Studies, 2013.

PT. Semen Indonesia. *Annual Report 2013*. Jakarta, 2013.

Setiawan, S. "Analisis Keterbukaandan Daya Saing Sektor Perasuransian Indonesia di ASEAN" [Analysing the openness and competitiveness of Indonesia's insurance in ASEAN]. Policy Paper Kebijakan Fiskal, Seri 1, 2014.

Thee Kian Wie. *Indonesia's Economy Since Independence*. Singapore: Institute of Southeast Asian Studies, 2012.

UNCTAD. *World Investment Report 2006*. New York: United Nations.

———. *World Investment Report 2013*. New York: United Nations.

———. *World Investment Report 2014*. New York: United Nations.

———. *World Investment Report 2015*. New York: United Nations.

USAID. "Indonesia Port Sector Reform and The 2008 Shipping Law". August 2008 <http://pdf.usaid.gov/pdf_docs/PNADN188.pdf> (accessed 28 October 2014).

Wang, B., Mao, R., and Q. Gou. "Overseas Impact of China's Outward Direct Investment". *Asian Economic Policy Review* 9 (2014): 227–49.

7

FACTORS INFLUENCING THAILAND'S OUTWARD FDI[1]

Kornkarun Cheewatrakoolpong and
Panutat Satchachai

1. INTRODUCTION

Inward foreign direct investment (FDI) has been one of the important driving forces for Thailand's economic growth during the last few decades. Thailand is an important production and assembly base in Southeast Asia for many industries such as automobiles and hard disk drives. The country has attracted tremendous investments from multinational enterprises based in developed countries such as Japan, the European Union, and the United States. FDI was a crucial factor behind the miraculous economic growth in Thailand and East Asian countries during the 1990s (Jansen 1995; Chen and De Lombaerde 2009). The more recent study by Cheewatrakoolpong and Sabhasri (2012) showed that FDI from developed countries leads to technology transfers and knowledge spillovers as well as promoting employment, productivity and international trade in Thailand.

Given Thailand's status as a middle-income country with significant inward FDI, what explains outward FDI (OFDI) from Thailand? The goal of this study is to examine the factors influencing Thailand's OFDI. It analyses the determinants of Thailand's OFDI in ASEAN-5 and

CLMV countries.[2] In addition, this study also investigates the opportunities and effects of adopting ACIA on Thai economy. Finally, this study will consider two case study sectors, namely food processing, and textile and garments. Both are among the prioritized sectors for Thailand's OFDI.

2. OFDI AND THE FLYING GEESE THEORY

Kojima (1975) proposed the "Flying Geese Theory" to explain Japan's OFDI in the region. The theory attempts to explain Japan's OFDI into the newly industrialized countries such as Singapore, Hong Kong, South Korea and Taiwan in the 1960s. In the more recent study, Aminian, Foong and Hitomi (2007) have argued that the cost of production has increased in Singapore, Hong Kong, South Korea and Taiwan. This has led to a loss of competitive advantage which could have resulted in investment being relocated to countries with lower cost of production such as Malaysia, Thailand and Indonesia. Hiratsuka (2006) has argued that the flying geese theory can be used to explain the recent OFDI in Malaysia, Thailand and Indonesia.

Why has the flying geese phenomenon occurred in Thailand? Thailand has experienced a lack of operational workers for several years. This problem arises from a mismatch between demand and supply in the labour market. While the demand for workers who graduate from vocational school has been increasing because of the rise in manufacturing bases in Thailand, a larger proportion of the new generation chooses to pursue a Bachelor's or higher degree instead. Part of the trend is due to the national policy to increase the minimum salary of workers with a Bachelor's degree to THB15,000 per month (approximately US$500) in 2011.[3] This policy dissuades students from pursuing vocational studies. According to the World Bank (2012), Thailand faces the severe problem of shortage in operational workers and skilled labour compared to other ASEAN countries.

Furthermore, wages rose sharply in 2013 due to the national uniform minimum wage law which mandates a daily rate of nearly US$10 (around US$9.86 per day). The minimum wage rate was around US$7.17 in Bangkok and US$5.40 in provincial areas in 2011. The increase in the national minimum wage has severely affected labour-intensive industries such as textiles, garments, electronics, and leather wares.

Additionally, Thailand is becoming an ageing society. Compared to other ASEAN countries, with the exception of Singapore, the population ageing problem in Thailand is more severe. This problem has caused a further decline in labour force and intensified the shortage of operational workers.

The mismatch in demand and supply in the labour market, the lack of operational workers, the increase in wage levels and production cost, and the ageing society discussed above can be classified as "push factors" for OFDI. "Pull factors" of outward FDI are external factors that pulls or attracts an investment from the home country to the host country. Major pull factors include low wage, large domestic market, market access and attractive investment incentives. These are major factors behind the increase in the foreign direct investment to the CLMV countries. The relatively lower wages in Cambodia, Laos PDR, Myanmar, and Vietnam have attracted foreign investment from Japan, Korea, China as well as Thailand. Another factor is the investment incentives given by the host country's government, for example, corporate tax exemption, lower income tax rate, or infrastructure. According to the OLI theory proposed by Dunning (1993), firms will exploit their ownership advantages such as patents, knowledge, technology and skills together with locational advantages of the recipient countries such as resources, lower labour costs, tariff privileges and market sizes to invest abroad. Also, firms also have internationalization motives such as reducing trade costs, control over production and management, and prevention of product or technology imitation to transit from international trade to outbound investment.

UNCTAD (2006) highlights domestic factors of source countries as determinants of outward FDI, the so-called "push factors", including market conditions from small domestic markets or market saturation, trade costs from trade barriers such as export quotas, costs of production, local business conditions such as high competition in a domestic market and home government policies that promote outward investment.

3. THAILAND'S OUTWARD FDI TRENDS

Thailand's outward FDI stock has increased sharply especially between 2008 and 2012 (Figure 7.1). Even though OFDI remains lower than IFDI, this pattern reveals an important change in the structure of the Thai economy, namely, the increasing importance of Thailand as an investor.

In terms of sectoral distribution of OFDI, Table 7.1 shows that, after 2012, manufacturing, and mining and quarrying are the two largest sectors that Thai investors invest abroad. Although the overall patterns of

FIGURE 7.1
Thailand's FDI Stocks, 2001–13

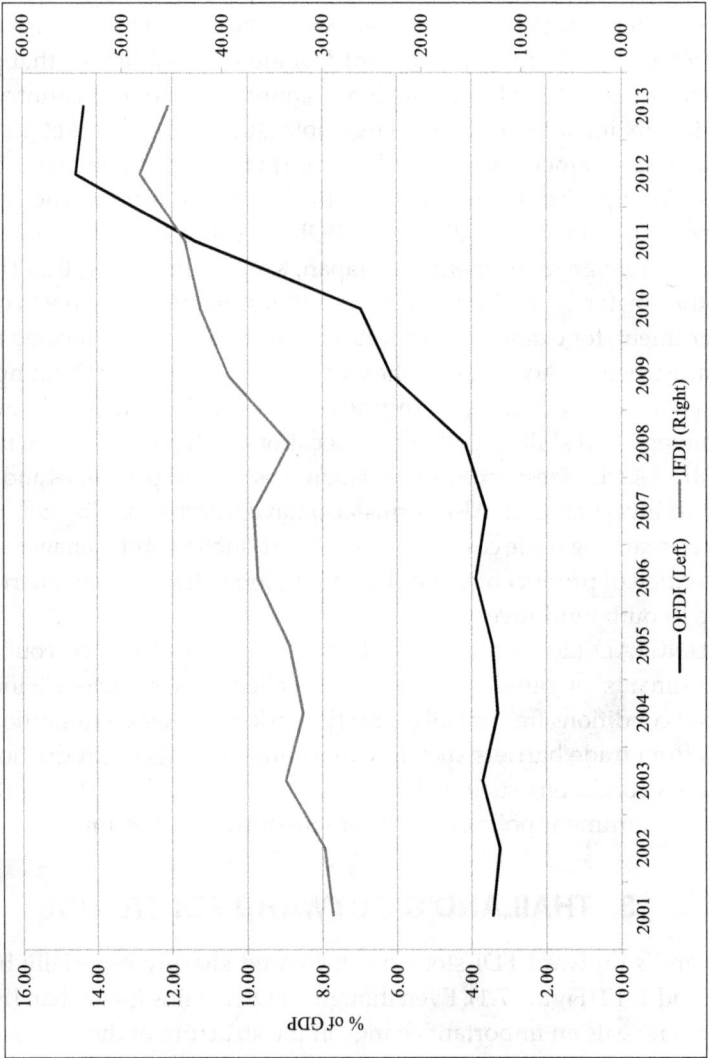

Source: UNCTAD.

TABLE 7.1
Thailand's Outward FDI Flows during 2009–14, by Sectors (US$ million)

	2005	2006	2007	2008	2009	2010	2011	2012p	2013p	2014p
Agriculture, Forestry and Fishing	0.00	12.21	0.00	-4.25	0.00	18.36	0.00	0.00	10.41	-0.57
Mining and Quarrying	65.66	-350.72	-947.04	-979.67	1,324.37	2,778.05	4,164.32	3,125.18	2,152.01	-2,171.88
Manufacturing	-401.33	-543.66	983.85	-1,443.94	803.55	1,017.13	1,898.94	4,589.73	2,905.50	-273.83
Electricity, Gas, Steam and Air Conditioning Supply	66.06	-106.82	4.17	-289.33	68.91	142.21	13.59	4.19	0.72	0.49
Construction	4.39	-29.98	-72.84	-44.20	36.23	-20.96	-38.38	-0.78	-37.63	-75.71
Wholesale and Retail Trade; Repair of Motor Vehicles and Motorcycles	229.57	133.13	-162.29	-936.55	-24.56	744.39	-192.25	1,014.82	1,075.07	-538.83
Transportation and Storage	-89.32	4.96	-127.98	-96.68	169.47	129.93	-17.86	6.48	34.57	17.47
Accommodation and Food Service Activities	-9.96	-14.68	57.08	-60.42	-51.10	-19.97	-14.80	-1.71	48.21	-188.66
Financial and Insurance Activities	-231.93	-154.06	-2,337.52	-1,790.53	1,755.14	-454.49	1,390.63	1,341.26	793.62	-1,595.31
Real Estate Activities	-7.50	-14.75	-272.90	335.77	51.24	269.86	93.19	116.68	96.65	-92.16
Others	-128.67	91.87	-141.94	1,211.92	19.52	11.77	-659.71	2,702.28	-349.83	-1,866.99
Total	-503.03	-972.50	-3,017.41	-4,097.88	4,152.77	4,616.26	6,637.67	12,898.12	6,729.30	-6,785.97

Source: Bank of Thailand.

outward FDI are reversed in 2014, food products and computer, electronic and optical products are two of the sub-sectors in manufacturing with the highest outward FDI flows (Table 7.2).

Apart from the change in the domestic economic structure, several changes in regional policies that are aimed at promoting connectivity within ASEAN community are an important driving forces for Thailand. These include trade liberalization and economic reforms in the Greater-Mekong Subregional (GMS) countries and trade and economic cooperation in the region such as ASEAN Economic Community (AEC).

In addition, the nature of vertical specialization and the formation of the co-production base among ASEAN countries is also a reason for the increase in outward FDI. Baldwin and Okubo (2012) also considers the nature of Japanese MNEs and examines whether Japanese FDI is "networked FDI" or not.[4] The study finds that many sectors can be categorized as networked FDI such as machinery and electronics sectors. Hiratsuka (2008) also shows that outward FDI from Japanese MNCs in East Asian and ASEAN countries results in the formation of co-production bases in this region. The stages of production are divided among different suppliers that are located in different countries. As a result, when Japanese MNCs establish their production bases in emerging markets such as Vietnam and Cambodia, the Thai suppliers need to relocate their production bases to support their lead firms as well.

The driving forces from both changes in domestic economic structure and regional policies have highlighted outward FDI to policymakers in Thailand. The Board of Investment of Thailand (BOI) has started to pay attention to outward FDI. This is related to the point made by Ohno (2009) that outward FDI is an important factor that could help the newly industrialized economies (NIEs) exit the middle-income trap.[5] Thus, in the BOI's current five-year strategic plan (2013–17), BOI has changed its mission from "promoting inbound investment" to "promoting both inbound and outbound investment". According to the BOI's strategic plan, Thai overseas investment is necessary to enhance industrial competitiveness, to overcome domestic resource limitations and to seek new business opportunities. As a result, the BOI has set up Thailand Overseas Investment Support Center (TOISC) and Thai Overseas Investment (TOI) Plan: 2013–2017 in 2012.

According to the BOI, the prioritized sectors for Thailand's outward FDI promotion are composed of food processing, textile and garments, and

TABLE 7.2
Thailand's Outward FDI Flows in Manufacturing Sub-Sectors during 2009–14

	2005	2006	2007	2008	2009	2010	2011	2012p	2013p	2014p
Food Products	-115.99	-198.37	1,375.83	-347.54	41.98	682.34	155.86	933.26	1,139.40	730.98
Beverages	10.15	10.97	3.79	-101.93	-35.97	-89.37	332.75	618.44	395.49	-293.23
Textiles	-4.04	-8.54	-21.50	-156.35	92.20	39.99	192.02	35.46	69.63	-16.57
Chemicals and Chemical Products	-21.86	-36.56	-72.52	-287.68	39.53	253.92	560.12	382.65	225.97	-43.58
Computer, Electronic and Optical Products	-14.49	-138.92	-98.04	-68.69	111.02	136.04	172.26	1,562.28	-13.64	982.86
Electrical Equipment	-20.25	-31.64	-89.57	-64.92	151.46	2.04	-29.09	49.08	121.00	-30.64
Machinery and Equipment n.e.c.	0.00	-0.99	4.59	1.19	16.50	30.58	83.11	200.17	148.46	-91.35

Source: Bank of Thailand.

parts and components. And the prioritized destination countries consist of CLMV countries and Indonesia.

This study analyses the determinants of Thailand's outward FDI in ASEAN-5 and CLMV countries.[6] In addition, we also investigate the opportunities and effects of adopting ACIA on Thai economy. Finally, we consider two case study sectors, namely food processing, and textile and garments. Both are among the prioritized sectors for Thailand's outward FDI. We also evaluate the impact of ACIA on these industries. The results of this study can give insights about the way Thailand should set up its outward FDI promotion policy.

Our study consists of two parts. First we adopt panel regression to analyse the factors influencing Thailand's outward FDI into the ASEAN-5[7] and CLMV countries. Next we review ACIA and provide the qualitative results from evaluating the impact of ACIA on Thai's selected industries in the last section.

4. METHODOLOGY

The empirical part of this study consists of two parts. First, a panel regression is used to analyse the factors influencing Thailand's outward FDI into the ASEAN-5 and CLMV countries. Next, the ACIA is reviewed and qualitative results are used to evaluate the impact of ACIA on the Thai's selected industries.

In this study, we consider only the country-level determinants of outward FDI. Gao (2005), Buckley et al. (2007), Zhang and Daly (2011), Bhasin and Jain (2013) have suggested the following country-level factors influencing outward FDI:

(i) Market related factors such as market size (using GDP) and income level (using GDP per capita);
(ii) Macroeconomic factors such as inflation rate, real exchange rate, and real interest rate;
(iii) Policy and institutional factors in FDI recipient countries such as trade openness, FDI openness, governance, political risks, and corruption;
(iv) Production related factors such as capital, technology, and human capital.

In this study, we consider the factors determining outward FDI of Thailand
into ASEAN-5 countries during the 2001–10 period, and into CLMV
countries during the 2005–11 period.[8] Both cases are analysed using the
same fixed-effect panel regression model. Our regression is given in the
following equation.

$$
\begin{aligned}
\log(OFDI_{it}) = \ &\alpha_0 + \beta_1\log(GDP_{it}) + \beta_2(GDPPC_{it}) \\
&+ \beta_3\log(FDI_{it}) + \beta_4\log(TradeOpen_{it}) \\
&+ \beta_5\log(FinOpen_{it}) + \beta_6\log(REER_{it}) + \beta_7Inflation_{it} \\
&+ \beta_8LFP_{it} + \beta_9TFP_{it} + \beta_{10}z_{it} + u_{it}
\end{aligned}
\tag{1}
$$

where $OFDI_{it}$ is the outward FDI flows from Thailand to country i at
time t.

GDP_{it} is the gross domestic product of country i at time t.

$GDPPC_{it}$ is the per capita gross domestic product of country i at
time t.

FDI_{it} is the total stock of inward FDI per GDP of country i at
time t.

$TradeOpen_{it}$ is the level of trade openness of country i at time t.

$FinOpen_{it}$ is the level of financial openness of country i at time t.

$REER_{it}$ is the level of real effective exchange rate of country i at
time t.

$Inflation_{it}$ is the level of inflation rate of country i at time t.

LPF_{it} is the labour force participate rate of country i at time t.

TFP_{it} is the total factor productivity level of country i at time t.

z_{it} is other related factors.

Due to data limitation in CLMV countries, we separate the estimation
of equation (1) for ASEAN-5 and CLMV countries. Production-related
factors such as TFP and LPF are not included in the regression for CLMV
countries since there is no available data for these countries.

Also, due to the nature of bilateral OFDI flows that possibly contains
a number of zeros or negative values that are not random, we employ a
Heckman-type two-stage estimation procedure in comparison with the
normal fixed-effect regression model. We consider outward FDI decision
as a two-stage procedure. The first stage is the selection of OFDI and the
second stage is determining OFDI flows.

Our estimation methodology for the first stage is to estimate OFDI
participation using a probit model to find the probability of OFDI flows

being positive. This stage will determine whether or not the home country will decide to invest or not to invest abroad. All determinants according to equation (1) are included in this equation. The second stage is to estimate OFDI flows using augmented gravity model. We include the inverse Mills ratio into the gravity regression of OFDI in the second stage to capture sample selection bias.

We follow Garrett (2011) and use the institution variables only in the first stage and as the exclusion restrictions in the second stage. In addition, we also follow Helpman et al. (2008) and drop the determinants concerning FDI recipient countries' policies such as trade and financial openness, and corruption from the gravity estimation. This is because although the country-policy determinants are significant for the investment decision, they are less important in determining the magnitude of flows once investors have made investment decision. Hence, we drop them in the second stage.

5. DATA SOURCES

In the first part of the empirical analysis in this study, we consider five ASEAN countries, or ASEAN-5, which include Indonesia, Malaysia, Philippines, Singapore and Thailand. Thailand is treated as the "home" country, while the remaining four ASEAN countries are the destinations or the "host" countries for Thailand's OFDI. The host countries are labelled by i, $i = 1, 2, 3, 4$. The time period, t, in this study cover ten years from 2001 to 2010. The data are collected from various sources, which are summarized in Table 7.3.

We also consider the possible country-specific effects and time-specific effect by including dummy variables and time trend.

Table 7.4 shows the descriptive statistics of the data used in this study. Due to the nature of outward FDI flows, there are missing values in OFDI (8 missing values from our sample). The average size of Thailand's outward FDI during this period and over five countries are US$127.96 million, with the maximum of US$2,009 million and minimum of US$–511 million (drawing back investment).

In the ASEAN-5 data used, Indonesia is the biggest economy in our sample in terms of GDP, while Singapore has the highest GDP per capita and is the most active country in terms of its openness to trade and investment.

The second part of the empirical analysis in this study consider the outward FDI flows from Thailand into CLMV countries between 2005 and

TABLE 7.3
Summarized Data Sources

Variable	Definition	Unit	Source
OFDI	Bilateral outward foreign direct investment flows from Thailand to host countries at time t	US$ million	United Nations Conference on Trade and Development (UNCTAD)
GDPHost	Host country i's GDP at time t	US$ million	
GDPPCHost	Host country i's GDP per capita at time t	US$	
Imports	Value of host country's imports	US$ million	
Exports	Value of host country's exports	US$ million	
REER	Real effective exchange rate index		International Monetary Fund (IMF)
Inflation	% Change in consumer price index	%	World Bank
TFP	(Estimated) Total factor productivity		United Nations Industrial Development Organization (UNIDO)
LFP	% of labour force to total population	%	International Labour Organization (ILO)
CPI	Corruption Perception Index	Scale from 1 to 10	Transparency International (TI)
FDIOpen	Ratio of host country's inward foreign direct investment to host country's GDP	%	Computed by Authors (based on data from UNCTAD)
TradeOpen	Ratio of host country's total value of trade to host country's GDP	%	Computed by Authors (based on data from UNCTAD)

2011. Due to data limitation, we have to drop some variables and there are only the maximum number of 28 observations. Table 7.5 summarizes descriptive statistics for the case of CLMV.

In this dataset, the major destination for Thai direct investment is Vietnam, which has the highest level or per capita income and level of trade openness in the CLMV. Cambodia has the highest level of financial openness.

TABLE 7.4
Descriptive Statistics for the Case of ASEAN-5

Variable	Obs	Mean	Std. Dev.	Min	Max
OFDI	48	127.9612	333.026	−511.9148	2009.247
GDPHost	56	241463.1	193296.3	76262	878043
GDPPCHost	56	11409.23	15154.81	756.0595	52604.48
REER	56	93.95268	9.142231	67.16417	113.1908
Inflation	56	4.055895	3.042672	−.3916769	13.10942
OFDIHost	56	7414.228	8834.931	−250.0293	36897.15
IFDIHost	56	11781.78	15997.37	−4550	63772.32
FDIOpenness	56	9.67673	12.43953	−2.659031	47.58099
TradeOpenness	56	179.0181	135.0652	45.36226	444.1567
TFP	44	.4896818	.2172994	.257	.873
LFP	56	64.82143	2.899323	59.1	68.1
CPI	48	4.745833	2.84313	1.7	9.4

Source: Authors.

TABLE 7.5
Descriptive Statistics for the Case of CLMV

Variable	Obs	Mean	Std. Dev.	Min	Max
OFDI	28	266.3845	445.4022	2.119509	2171.072
GDPPCHost	21	846.9514	268.5158	471.1625	1408.006
REER	28	7612.281	6601.068	5.44145	20509.75
Inflation	28	10.02742	8.575046	−.6613076	35.0246
FDIOpenness	28	37.15301	11.08807	17.47496	53.39318
TradeOpenness	21	122.0717	36.31829	70.97261	178.1327
Imports	28	1.19e+09	1.07e+09	3.14e+07	3.49e+09
Exports	28	2.36e+09	1.61e+09	6.97e+08	6.99e+09

Source: Authors.

6. RESULTS

ASEAN-5

Table 7.6 summarizes the results for ASEAN-5 countries using benchmark models (columns 1, 2, 6 and 7) based on traditional augmented gravity estimations. The benchmark is estimated by using the least squares dummy variables (LSDV) or equivalent to the fixed-effects estimation.

TABLE 7.6
Estimation Results for ASEAN-5

Dependent Variable: log(OFDI)	Benchmark		Heckman			Benchmark		Heckman		
Variable	(1) LSDV#1	(2) LSDV#2	(3) First Stage	(4) Second Stage	(5) Second Stage	(6) LSDV#3	(7) LSDV#4	(8) First Stage	(9) Second Stage	(10) Second Stage
log(GDPHost)	14.867 (8.936)	12.885** (3.815)	197.980 (233.376)	13.783 (8.749)	12.410** (4.659)					
log(GDPPCHost)						14.959* (8.148)	12.886*** (4.447)	115.918* (68.929)	13.911* (7.778)	12.373*** (4.222)
REER	-0.188* (0.103)	-0.146* (0.059)	-3.241 (3.703)	-0.158 (0.103)	-0.141** (0.058)	-0.195* (0.099)	-0.156** (0.058)	-1.942* (1.106)	-0.155 (0.097)	-0.147** (0.056)
Inflation	-0.083 (0.160)	-0.095 (0.135)	3.279 (4.257)	-0.118 (0.159)	-0.103 (0.131)	-0.064 (0.161)	-0.075 (0.135)	1.821 (1.197)	-0.119 (0.160)	-0.094 (0.134)
TFP	-25.167 (17.814)	-26.098** (11.063)	-13.466 (95.389)	-24.669 (17.965)	-24.978** (11.081)	-25.993 (17.299)	-28.216** (10.889)	-58.461 (50.753)	-25.302 (17.115)	-26.865** (10.801)
LFP	-0.178 (0.297)	-0.207 (0.314)	0.021 (1.363)	-0.159 (0.302)	-0.139 (0.305)	-0.091 (0.289)	-0.147 (0.293)	-0.177 (0.732)	-0.061 (0.292)	-0.059 (0.274)
dIND	-34.837 (25.197)	-25.659*** (6.396)	-790.469 (993.495)	-29.721 (25.186)	-24.656*** (6.278)	20.892 (13.669)	23.334 (15.062)	13.476 (56.927)	22.691 (13.895)	22.479 (14.434)
dMYS	-13.818 (10.013)	-10.101*** (2.855)	-293.319 (371.286)	-12.194 (9.956)	-9.442*** (2.869)	11.199 (7.013)	12.140 (7.732)	40.906 (32.344)	11.214 (6.822)	12.035 (7.494)
dPHL	-21.245 (14.465)	-14.935** (6.149)	-498.937 (626.946)	-17.897 (14.715)	-14.131** (6.221)	20.384 (15.105)	21.752 (15.481)	61.424 (52.849)	21.354 (14.954)	21.259 (14.921)
time	-1.308 (1.128)	-1.063 (0.631)	-23.172 (27.011)	-1.181 (1.107)	-1.029 (0.617)	-1.007 (0.869)	-0.798** (0.498)	-11.053* (6.549)	-0.910 (0.829)	-0.778 (0.481)
CPI	-0.551 (2.689)		-37.413 (53.593)	-0.536 (2.711)		-0.915 (2.687)		-18.511 (15.032)	-0.937 (2.691)	
log(FDIOpen)	-0.206 (0.219)		-1.655 (3.405)	-0.178 (0.213)		-0.186 (0.218)		-0.906 (1.871)	-0.152 (0.203)	
log(TradeOpen)	-1.634 (3.543)		-152.074 (195.335)	0.039 (3.925)		-1.313 (3.349)		-77.155 (204.951)	0.792 (3.696)	
IMR				-0.136 (0.095)	-0.145* (0.078)				-0.289 (0.225)	-0.283 (0.186)

Note: (1) Country-specific and year-specific are included. (2) Standard errors are reported in parentheses. (3) * indicates significance level where *** p<0.01, ** p<0.05, * p<0.1

The differences between these four columns are in terms of the use of different market-related factors (GDP and GDP per capita) and host country's institution (Corruption Perception Index, FDI Openness, and Trade Openness).

The results show that market demand of the host country (measured by GDP per capita) and real effective exchange rate are the most influential determinants of Thailand's outward FDI in ASEAN-5 countries. Larger demand in the host country seems to be the main factor driving the Thais to invest more in those countries (market-seeking). However, the negative sign of the real effective exchange rate shows that the appreciation of the Thai baht does not increase the competitive advantage (cheaper to invest abroad) and induce more outward investment.

Although the signs of other factors, such as host country's GDP, inflation, TFP, or LFP are mostly consistent with theory and findings from the previous literature, they are statistically insignificant in most cases. These can imply that the resource-seeking (abundance labour supply) or efficiency-seeking (higher productivity) are not the main drivers of Thai outward FDI in these countries.

However, we find that the trade openness and FDI openness have the contradicted signs, but both are not statistically different from zero. The possible explanation is that these countries have already been open, both commercially and financially, and an additional increase in openness would not benefit Thailand much when compared to other destination or host countries. Thus, they have no impact on the level of outward investment.

Since there were negative or zero values of outward FDI in our sample, dropping or treating them as zero might induce the so called "sample selection bias" problem in our estimations if the occurrence of zeros is not random. To take into account the possibility of this problem, we re-estimate the models using the Heckman two-stage estimation. The first stage is to estimate the probit model to determine the country's decision to invest abroad, and we use the institutional variables to represent the fixed cost of outward investment. The inverse Mills ratio, IMR, is then computed and is used in the second stage as the addition variable to control for the sample selection problem in the augmented gravity model.

The results from Heckman two-stage estimation are shown in columns 3–5 and 8–10 in Table 7.6. The first stage is the results from probit estimation, while in the second stage, we consider the augmented gravity adding the inverse Mills ratio as additional regressor. The institution variables are also served as the exclusion restrictions in the second stage, but we also report the cases where all variables were included.

In this case, the results are more consistent with the previous literature in the sense that both GDP and GDP per capital are the most influential determinants of the Thai's outward FDI. That is, the size and demand of host country's economy are the major reasons for Thai to invest abroad. Real exchange rate and total factor productivity are both statistically significance, but are of the opposite signs. This can be similarly explained that Thailand's outward investment is not driven by the appreciation of the currency or efficiency-seeking. And we still find that resource-seeking does not determine the level of Thailand's outward FDI in ASEAN-5.

As for the sample selection bias problems, we find mixed results. When we control for the host country's market size, measured by GDP, the inverse Mills ratio is statistically significant at the 10 per cent level, which indicates that the sample selection bias is presence. However, when we control for the host country's demand, measured by GDP per capita, the sample selection does not seem to be the trouble. In either case, the sizes and signs of coefficients do not change much in magnitude compared to the benchmark models. The only differences are in country-specific effects, in which the signs switched.

In sum, we find that the main purpose of Thai outward FDI in ASEAN-5 is the market-seeking or is driven by the demand in the host country. When compared to the outward investment of other medium developing or developed countries, efficiency-seeking or resource-seeking are neither the causes of Thailand's outward investment.

CLMV

For Thai OFDI in CLMV countries, the results from our estimation of equation (1) using fixed effect panel regression are shown in Table 7.7. We can see that GDP per capita, which indicates market demands of recipient countries, is the most influential factor determining outward FDI flows of Thailand in CLMV countries. Moreover, FDI openness significantly explains outward FDI of Thailand to CLMV countries. It is also important to note that trade openness variables have an opposite sign compared to findings in the existing literature. This is due to the fact that CLMV countries, have a very low level of trade, with the exception of Vietnam. However, Thailand has high investment in Myanmar due to its proximity and natural resource abundance. As a result, the sign of coefficients for

TABLE 7.7
Panel Regression of Equation (1) in case of CLMV[a]

Dependent Variables	Model 1	Model 2	Model 3	Model 4
log(Imports)	−0.0116			−0.797*
	(0.589)			(0.379)
log(Exports)	0.0456			−38.27**
	(2.419)			(12.98)
log(GDPPCHost)	21.19***	21.22***	16.49***	2.887**
	(5.391)	(4.862)	(3.277)	(1.133)
log(REER)	3.007	2.991		0.0822
	(1.825)	(2.204)		(0.0779)
Inflation	0.0116	0.0115	0.0152	−0.0222
	(0.054)	(0.0376)	(0.0434)	(0.0116)
log(FDIOpen)	10.30*	10.32**	7.641**	2.450**
	(5.226)	(3.984)	(2.787)	(871.9)
log(TradeOpen)	−20.29*	−20.21*	−15.47**	
	(9.753)	(8.284)	(6.147)	
country	−4.372*	−4.364*	−1.614**	1.304
	(2.147)	(2.103)	(0.451)	(0.845)
Constant	−152.3***	−151.8**	−98.63***	−1,926**
	(40.05)	(44.04)	(19.39)	(706.1)
Observations	21	21	21	28
R-squared	0.867	0.867	0.839	0.672

Notes: a. Due to high correlation between GDP and GDP per capita, we remain only GDP per capita in our estimation.
– parentheses denote standard errors.
*** $p < 0.01$, ** $p < 0.05$, * $p < 0.1$

openness variables in our panel regression contradicts a hypothesis that trade openness of host countries bring about higher outward FDI. Finally, economic-related factors of host countries including real effective exchange rate and inflation rate do not significantly determine outward FDI from Thailand to CLMV countries.

Comparing with the regression results of ASEAN-5, we can see that while market-seeking is the main explanation of Thailand's OFDI to the ASEAN-5 countries, the recipient countries' policies including trade openness and FDI openness are the most important explanatory variables in case of CLMV countries.

Due to the limitation of data, we cannot include technology-related variables in CLMV regression. Also, we cannot employ the Heckman two-stage estimation in case of CLMV due to data limitations.

7. CASE STUDY OF TEXTILE AND GARMENT, AND FOOD AND FOOD PROCESSING INDUSTRY

The above econometric analysis is supplemented by two case studies based on interviews with firms in two industries, namely, textile and garment and food and food processing.[9]

Textile and Garment Industry

Due to its high gross product and export values, textile and garment industry is one of the most important industries in Thailand. This sector is also an important source of employment. Unlike the automobile industry, which is owned by foreigners, a large proportion of owners in the textile and garment industry is Thais. Figure 7.2 shows that Thai owners have been investing in neighboring countries for quite some time. But the number has only increased recently. (Note that the value of Thailand's outward FDI to CLMV is as of 2012 and is only an estimate.) The popular OFDI destinations for textile and garment industry are Vietnam and Cambodia.

We choose garment industry as the representative of the textile and garment industry since its structure is suitable for outward FDI. Due to its high labour-intensive structure, the rapid increase in minimum wage (300-Baht-Minimum-Wage Law) is the main reason why firms in the textile and garment industry have moved their investment abroad. Together with the lack of unskilled labour to supply the production process, Thai investors need to relocate part of their production to a country with more abundant and cheaper labour.

Thus, we find that it was the inward factors — higher wage costs, scarcity of unskilled labour, and the expiring of the Thai's Generalized System of Preferences (GSP) — that pushed Thai owners to go out and invest in the neighbouring countries. These factors are all important for the future competitiveness of Thai textile and garment industry since the Thai economy has relied on these industries for high economic growth in the past.

There are only four attractive countries for outward FDI in the textile and garment industry, i.e., Indonesia, Vietnam Cambodia, and Myanmar (in order of increasing attractiveness). The attractive features of those countries include low wage (resource-seeking), high domestic growth and the growing textile and garment industry within the host country

FIGURE 7.2
Thailand's Outward FDI in Textile Industry in ASEAN and CLMV

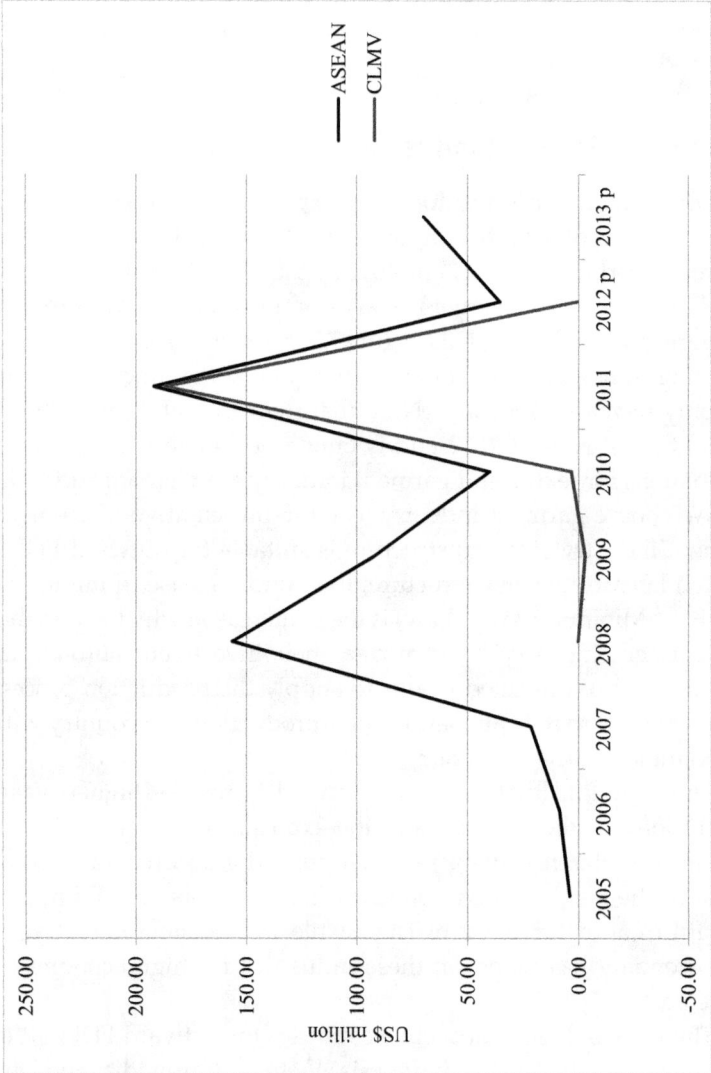

Source: Bank of Thailand.

(market-seeking), and the incentive (both tax and non-tax) given by the host country's government. The effects of Thai outward FDI in the textile and garment industry are beneficial both in terms of expanding the conventional trade and creating the production network/base for exports, especially for Vietnam, Cambodia, and Myanmar. These are countries still receiving the GSP (Cambodia and Myanmar) or expect to benefit from the TPP (for Vietnam).

However, the main obstacles that currently hinder the outward FDI in the textile and garment industry are the frequently uninformed changing of the local laws and regulations, lack of the host's infrastructure needed, lack of reliable investment-related information, and lack of Thai government's incentive and clear outward FDI policy.

For the Thai textile and garment industry, ACIA would be beneficial to SMEs and investors who are less likely to qualify for the special investment incentive (both in terms of tax and non-tax) from the host country's government.[10] It also provides investment protection in case of any dispute between state and small investors. However, from the in-depth interview, we find that the benefit of ACIA in this sector would still be limited due to the lack of knowledge on the agreement of Thai investors, especially those of small and medium firm size.

Food and Food Processing Industry

Food and food processing industry is an important industry in Thailand. Food and food processing products are major exports of Thailand. Wee (1997) has pointed out that the food industry is one of the major Thai industries that has invested abroad after the Asian financial crisis in 1997. Today, Thailand has become an important investor of food processing industry in ASEAN. According to Indonesia's statistics, Thailand is the most important ASEAN investor in food processing industry, accounting for 34.4 per cent of total ASEAN investment in this industry.

The food and food processing industry has several major Thai MNEs such as the Charoen Pokphand Group (CP), Thai Union Frozen, and Berli Jucker Thailand. The main drivers of outward FDI in this industry include seeking for labour and agricultural/fishery resources abroad, utilizing the GSP granted to least developed countries by the U.S. and EU, and seeking for emerging markets in the recipient countries.

The rise in wage levels in Thailand is also an important driver for the companies in food and food processing industries to invest abroad. Wage increase affects small and medium enterprises especially in processing fishery and meats. In addition, Thailand has been experiencing shortages in materials and resources due to the early mortality syndrome (EMS) disease in Whiteleg (Vannamei) shrimps as well as excess demand in other fishery products. The increase in land prices in Thailand is also another factor that has driven Thai companies in this industry to invest abroad.

As for frozen and processing chicken, most of the enterprises in this industry are large enterprises or MNEs. The main purpose of investing abroad in this industry is to seek markets with high growth and potential. In the sugar-processing industry, the enterprises in this industry have invested abroad, mainly in Lao PDR and Cambodia, in order to gain the GSP privileges from the U.S. and EU (Thailand no longer has GSP for this product).

However, investing abroad in food and food-processing industry still face several barriers due to lack of skilled labour, inconsistent law and regulation in home countries, poor law enforcement, differences in environment between Thailand and home countries which cause disease in the agricultural products such as sugar cane, lack of necessary infrastructure and utilities such as electricity.

Impact of ACIA

Considering the impact of the ACIA, many ASEAN countries still include fishery and agricultural activities in the exclusion or sensitive lists of ACIA. According to the submitted negative list under ACIA, we can conclude the items related to food processing industry as follows:

- Lao PDR
  The following sectors are reserved to Laos or are required to form joint-venture with Laos:
  o Fish Processing and Storing
  o Animal and Vegetable oil
  o Fruit and Vegetable Process
  o Ice Cream and Ice Manufacturing
  o Flour and Flour Product
  o Bakery Product
  o Non-alcoholic Beverage

- Myanmar
  The following sectors are reserved for Burmese firms:
  o Bakery Product

- ○ Non-alcoholic Beverage
- ○ Alcoholic Beverage

- Vietnam
  The following sectors are reserved for Vietnamese firms:
  - ○ Non-alcoholic Beverage
  - ○ Alcoholic Beverage
  - ○ Cane Sugar Production

- Indonesia
  The following sectors are reserved for Indonesian firms:
  - ○ salting/drying fish and other waters biota industry and smoked fish industry
  - ○ Palm Sugar
  - ○ processed food from seeds and roots, sago, gnetum gnemon nut and copra industry, soya sauce, tempe, tofu industry, cracker, chips, peanut cracker, and the like

Due to several restrictions on investing in food processing industry contained in ACIA, the benefit of ACIA for this sector might be limited. Also, even in the sectors which allow for foreign investment from ASEAN investors, there might be a requirement for a minimum capital size in order to receive investment promotion from the host countries.

Furthermore, there is a concern in Thailand over the future impact of ACIA on three sectors, namely aquaculture, forestry, and plant improvement. These three sectors are listed in the temporary exclusion list of Thailand under ACIA but they were scheduled to be opened gradually in 2010, 2012 and 2014. As of today, only Thai lobster aquaculture, tuna cultured in net cages, and onion improvement are open for ASEAN investors under ACIA. These sectors are not economically significant for Thailand. However, there is concern that if these sectors are more liberalized, foreign investors may bring about higher land use competition and agricultural knowledge spillovers.

8. CONCLUSION

Several internal and external factors, including increases in wage levels, lack of operational workers, regional economic cooperation between Thailand and other countries, ageing society, labour scarcity, and the increase in the costs of production, have driven Thailand and other middle-income countries in ASEAN to invest abroad.

This study analyses the factors influencing outward investment decision of Thailand in ASEAN-5 and CLMV countries. It also considers case studies of two specific industries, namely, textile and garment and food processing as well as evaluate the impact of ACIA on these industries.

Using panel regression, we find that market seeking is the most important motivation of the Thai investors to invest in ASEAN-5 countries. As for CLMV countries, their FDI openness policies and their trade openness policies influence the level of outward FDI of Thailand the most.

Regarding the impact of ACIA on Thailand's OFDI, ACIA still has limited benefits for investors since all countries agree upon investment liberalization at the extent allowed by domestic law. However, Thailand should be cautious if further investment liberalization in fishery and agricultural sectors are considered.

As for textile and garment industry, ACIA would be beneficial to SMEs and investors who may not obtain investment promotion packages from the host countries. It also provides investment protection in case of any dispute between state and small investors. However, the benefit of ACIA might be limited due to the investors' lack of knowledge.

Thailand plays a vital role in the food processing industry in ASEAN. However, the impact of ACIA on outward FDI in food processing is limited since many sub-sectors are listed in the countries' negative lists. There are some concerns over liberalization in aquaculture and agricultural sectors in Thailand. Finally, as the main benefit of ACIA comes from investor protection, the ACIA negotiation in the review round should improve dispute settlement mechanisms.

APPENDIX 1

List of Interviewees

1. Chiangrai Chamber of Commerce
2. Mae Sod Chamber of Commerce
3. Tak Chamber of Commerce
4. Mukdahan Chamber of Commerce
5. The Federation of Thai Industries
6. The Federation of Thai Industries, Chiang Rai Province
7. The Federation of Thai Industries, Tak Province
8. The Federation of Thai Industries, Mukdahan Province
9. Thai Garment Manufacturers Association
10. Thailand Textile Institute
11. Chiangmai Frozen Foods Public Co, Ltd.
12. Narathip Agriculture Co, Ltd.
13. Betagro Public Co, Ltd.
14. Mitr Phol Co, Ltd.
15. Mitr Lao Co, Ltd.
16. TK Garment Co, Ltd.
17. Thai Union Frozen Public Co, Ltd.

APPENDIX 2

ASEAN Comprehensive Investment Agreement: ACIA

ASEAN Comprehensive Investment Agreement (ACIA) is an agreement between the 10 ASEAN Member States, namely, Brunei Darussalam, Cambodia, Indonesia, Laos, Malaysia, Myanmar, the Philippines, Singapore, Thailand and Vietnam.

The main objective of ACIA is to create an open and free investment regime in the Southeast Asian region, which in turn should complement the regional integration efforts among the Member States, particularly the ASEAN Economic Community (AEC) in the year 2015.

On 26 February 2009, Economic Ministers of the Member States signed ACIA during the 14th ASEAN Summit held in Thailand, and it has entered into force since 29 March 2012.

ACIA is composed of 49 articles, 2 Annexes and Reservation Lists of the 10 ASEAN Member States. The Agreement covers all 4 main pillars of investment, namely, Liberalization, Protection, Promotion, and Facilitation. Despite the fact that ASEAN Investment Area (AIA)[11] and ASEAN Investment Guarantee Agreement (IGA)[12] form the foundation of ACIA, ASEAN Member States intend to make this Agreement to be more modern and comprehensive than its predecessors.

In respect of investment liberalization, ACIA covers Agriculture, Fishery, Forestry, Mining, Manufacturing and Services Incidental to these sectors (and other sectors which the ASEAN Member States may agree in the future). The liberalization approach adopted therein is a "negative-list" approach, whereby the Member States are presumed to fully liberalize these sectors with only limitations stated in each Member State's Reservation List.

In respect of investment protection, ACIA contains provisions on national treatment, most-favoured nation treatment, fair and equitable treatment, expropriation, transfers, subrogation and investor-state dispute settlement, all of which are fundamental to a good investment protection regime.

Since ACIA has superseded AIA and IGA, it is now the main agreement on investment between the 10 ASEAN Member States. With its modernized provisions and wide coverage, ACIA will expand the market, and create more competitive and safer business environment for both large and small investors. This agreement, hence, will inarguably increase intra-ASEAN direct investments as well as those from outside the region. In addition, it will also help strengthen the growing of ASEAN production network and supply chain; hence, the long-term prosperity of ASEAN. According to the AEC blueprint, this, in the end, would be the stepping stone for the regional financial integration.

However, the impact of ACIA will be limited, at least, in the aspect of liberalization. This comes from the fact that almost all ASEAN member countries have their own investment promotion policies which offer both tax and non-tax incentives for foreign investors. Also, under the "negative-list approach" of ACIA negotiation, the scopes of investment liberalization under ACIA is similar to those are allowed by ASEAN countries' domestic laws.

The true benefits of ACIA will be investment protection especially in less developed countries such as Myanmar, and protection for the small and medium enterprises. Myanmar is the only country in ASEAN that does not participate in the New York Arbitration Convention.[13] As a result, ACIA will provide state-to-investor dispute settlement protocols for investors in such country.

Notes

1. Parts of this paper are revised from the research projects organized and funded by International Institute for Trade and Development (Public Organization), Thailand, and the Thailand Research Fund.
2. CLMV stands for Cambodia, Lao PDR, Myanmar and Vietnam. We consider CLMV countries here since the BOI's strategic plan prioritizes these countries as the most important outward FDI recipients of Thailand (the first cluster).
3. The policy came from previous Prime Minister Yingluck Shinawatra.
4. Networked FDI occurs when affiliate firms operate as nodes in regional production networks. These firms tend to import a substantial share of intermediate goods and export a substantial share of final outputs. These are accompanied by low levels of both local sales and local sourcing.
5. NIEs include South Korea, Hong Kong, Singapore and Taiwan.
6. See note 2 above.
7. ASEAN-5 includes Malaysia, Indonesia, the Philippines, Singapore and Thailand.
8. Both time fixed effect and country fixed effect are employed.
9. See Appendix 1 for list of companies interviewed.
10. See Appendix 2 for explanation of ACIA.
11. AIA was signed on 7 October 1998, and covered investment liberalization among ASEAN Member States.
12. IGA was signed on 15 December 1987, and covered investment protection among ASEAN Member States.
13. Convention on the Recognition and Enforcement of Foreign Arbitral Awards, also known as "the New York Convention" provides common legislative standards for the recognition of arbitration agreements and court recognition and enforcement of foreign and non-domestic arbitral awards. The Convention's principal aim is that foreign and non-domestic arbitral awards will not be discriminated against and it obliges Parties to ensure such awards are recognized and generally capable of enforcement in their jurisdiction in the same way as domestic awards. An ancillary aim of the Convention is to require courts of Parties to give full effect to arbitration agreements by requiring courts to deny the parties access to court in contravention of their agreement to refer the matter to an arbitral tribunal. For more information, see <http://www.newyorkconvention.org>.

References

Aminian, N., K.C. Fung, and I. Hitomi. "Foreign Direct Investment, Intra-regional Trade and Production Sharing in East Asia". RIETI Discussion Paper Series 07-E-064, 2007.

ASEAN Secretariat. *ASEAN Investment Report 2012: The Changing FDI Landscape*. Jakarta: ASEAN Secretariat, 2013.

————. *ASEAN Statistical Yearbook 2013*. Jakarta: ASEAN Secretariat, 2014.

ASEAN Secretariat and UNCTAD. *ASEAN Investment Report 2013–2014: FDI Development and Regional Value Chains*. Jakarta, 2014.

Banga, R. "Impact of government policies and investment agreements on FDI inflows". Working Paper No. 116, Indian Council for Research in International Economic Relations, 2007.

Bhasin, N. and V. Jain. "Home Country Determinants of Outward FDI: A Study of Select Asian Economies". 2013 <SSRN: http://ssrn.com/abstract=2206739> or <http://dx.doi.org/10.2139/ssrn.2206739>.

Buckley, P.J., L. Jeremy Clegg, A.R. Cross, X. Liu, H. Voss, and P. Zheng. "The Determinants of Chinese Outward Foreign Direct Investment". *Journal of International Business Studies* 38, no. 4 (2007): 499–518.

Cheewatrakoolpong, K. and C. Sabhasri. "The role of Japan's FDI on economic development in the GMS and its impact on the Thai economy". Thailand Research Fund, 2012.

Chen, L. and P. De Lombaerde. "Regional Production Sharing Networks and Hubness in Latin America and East Asia: A Long-term Perspective". *Integration & Trade* 15, no. 32 (2011): 17–34.

Dunning, J.H. *Multinational Enterprise and the Global Economy*. Wokingham: Addison Wesley, 1993.

Gao, T. "Foreign direct investment from developing Asia: Some distinctive features". *Economics Letters* 86, no. 1 (2005): 29–35.

Garrett, J.Z. "Asymmetries in Bilateral FDI Flows between Country-pairs Explained: Heterogeneous Firm Productivities". Working Paper, 2011.

Helpman, E., M. Melitz and Y. Rubinstein. "Estimating trade flows: trading partners and trading volumes". *Quarterly Journal of Economics* 123, no. 2 (2008): 441–87.

Hiratsuka, D. "Outward FDI from and Interregional FDI in ASEAN: Trends and Drivers". Institute of Developing Economies, Discussion Paper No. 77, 2006.

Jansen, K. "The macroeconomic effects of direct foreign investment: The Case of Thailand". *World Development* 23, no. 2 (1995): 193–210.

Kojima, K. "International Trade and Foreign Direct Investment: Substitutes or Complements". *Hitotsubashi Journal of Economics* 16 (1975): 1–12.

Ohno, K. "Dynamic Capacity Development: What Africa can learn from Industrial Policy formulation in East Asia". In *The Middle Income Trap: Implications for Industrialization Strategies in East Asia and Africa*, Chapter 2. GRIPS Development Forum: Tokyo, 2009.

Porter and Bryden. *International Cluster Competitiveness Project*. Institute for Strategy and Competitiveness, Harvard Business School, 2010.

UNCTAD. *World Development Report 2006 FDI from developing and transition economies: Implications for Development*. United Nations, 2006.

Wee, K. "Outward Foreign Direct Investment by Enterprises from Thailand". *Transnational Corporations* 16 (2007): 89–116.

Wei, W. "China and India: Any difference in their FDI performances?". *Journal of Asian Economics* 16, no. 4 (2005): 719–36.

World Bank. "Thailand Economic Monitor". December 2012.

Zhang, X. and K. Daly. "The determinants of China's outward foreign direct investment". *Emerging Markets Review* 12 (2011): 389–98.

8

OUTWARD FOREIGN INVESTMENT
The Case of Vietnam

Hoang Thi Thu

1. INTRODUCTION

Since the launch of market-oriented economic reforms in 1986, Vietnam has become one of the fastest growing countries in Southeast Asia. During this period, the Vietnamese government has quickly joined the competition for inward foreign direct investment by restructuring the domestic economy and by opening its economy to the external trade and investment.

Foreign direct investment (FDI) is one of the most significant features of Vietnam's movement from a planned economy to a market economy. Since Vietnam's government regulations on foreign investment abroad were signed in 1999, the number of outward FDI (OFDI) projects as well as registered capital has increased steadily. In 2013, the registered capital of Vietnam's outward FDI was more than 157 times of that in 2003 and 789 times of that in 1999. The average registered capital of Vietnam's FDI outflow annually amounted to US$887.5 million. The average value of a project is about US$23.9 million. Although Vietnam's outward direct investment is still small relative to its huge inward FDI, it increased dramatically in Vietnam over time. So how has Vietnam's OFDI performed since economic reforms were carried out in 1986? What are the prospects for the country's OFDI? What policies has the country implemented to increase its direct investment overseas in the long run? This study intends to address these specific questions.

The structure of this chapter is organized as follows. Section 2 presents an overview of the Vietnamese economy's performance. Section 3 briefly shows the development of outward FDI policies in Vietnam. The next section presents the current state of OFDI in Vietnam. Section 5 explains the prospects of Vietnam's FDI outflows. The final section deals with conclusions and policy implications.

2. THE PERFORMANCE OF VIETNAM'S ECONOMY

After Vietnam gained independence in 1975, the country adopted a centrally planned economic regime. This economic model under this regime was based on the classic Soviet-type command economy with strong governmental control over all economic decisions. At this time, all of economic decisions were taken by the State, not by the market. The State not only assumed management functions such as issuing policies, laws, regulations, monitoring and inspecting foreign trade activities, it also fulfilled the functions of guiding business decisions such as fixing the list of trade products, trade markets, and export-import prices. Non-state companies cannot directly carry out trade activities as only some permitted State-owned companies and enterprises are permitted to undertake such activities. Domestic prices were isolated from the influence of international prices through a complex system of multiple exchange rates and trade subsidies. Exports were discouraged through overvalued exchange rates and low procurement prices, while imports were impeded by an extensive system of quotas and licences.

The centrally planned economy was presented as an irrational economic structure with serious imbalances at the macroeconomic level. The economy — its agriculture and industry sectors — could not keep up with the needs of national economic development. The average economic growth rate reached only 3.4 per cent with the agriculture-forestry sector and industry sector growing at only 3.64 per cent and 4.1 per cent, respectively (GSO 1995). The size of Vietnam's imports and exports were quite low. Exports slumped and the value of imports were nearly four times greater than that of exports. The enveloping system of subsidies in foreign trade led to the large trade deficit. The inflation rate increased from 21.2 per cent in 1975–80 up to 74.2 per cent in the 1981–85 period. The low economic efficiency had led to a decline in the Vietnamese living standard. During the time, the living standard of Vietnamese decreased from US$101 in 1976 to US$91 in 1980.

Vietnam has been in transition from a centrally planned economy to a market-oriented economy since December 1986. From that time up to the present, Vietnam has witnessed amazing economic achievements in terms of the growth of gross domestic product (GDP), GDP per capita, and foreign direct investment. Important trade and economic agreements were signed with major trading partners.

The GDP of Vietnam has increased dramatically since 1986 (Figure 8.1). In 2013, the GDP value was nearly six times of that in 1986. From a low economic growth rate of 2.8 per cent in 1986, the annual growth rate of Vietnam has increased to over 9 per cent in both 1995 and 1996. However, due to the Asian financial crises in 1997–98 and the global economic crises since 2008, the country's GDP growth rates fluctuated over the first decade of the 21st century. The economy successfully recovered and grew at the average annual growth rate of 6.4 per cent over the 2000–13 period. This helped the country increase its national income per capita over time, from US$97.15 in 1988 up to over US$1908.6 in 2013 (GSO 2013). These achievements showed that the reforms initiated by Vietnamese leaders were going in the right way.

Besides the increase in GDP growth rates, the Vietnamese economic structure has also shifted in the direction of industrialization and modernization. Vietnam's economy transformed itself from being a primary sector dependent economy to a more industry and services sector oriented one (Table 8.1). During 1986–90, agriculture, forestry and fishing factor accounted for 41 per cent of total GDP output, and it decreased to 19.38 per cent in 2011–13. Industry and services sectors have higher shares of GDP — 38.28 per cent and 42.34 per cent, respectively — in the first decade of the twenty-first century. The change in the economic structure was in the right direction and suitable with the industrialization and modernization policy announced by the government.

With an objective to develop a socialist-oriented market economy under the State's management, the Vietnamese government kept the central leading role of the state sector while facilitating the development of

FIGURE 8.1
Economic Growths in Vietnam, 1986–2013

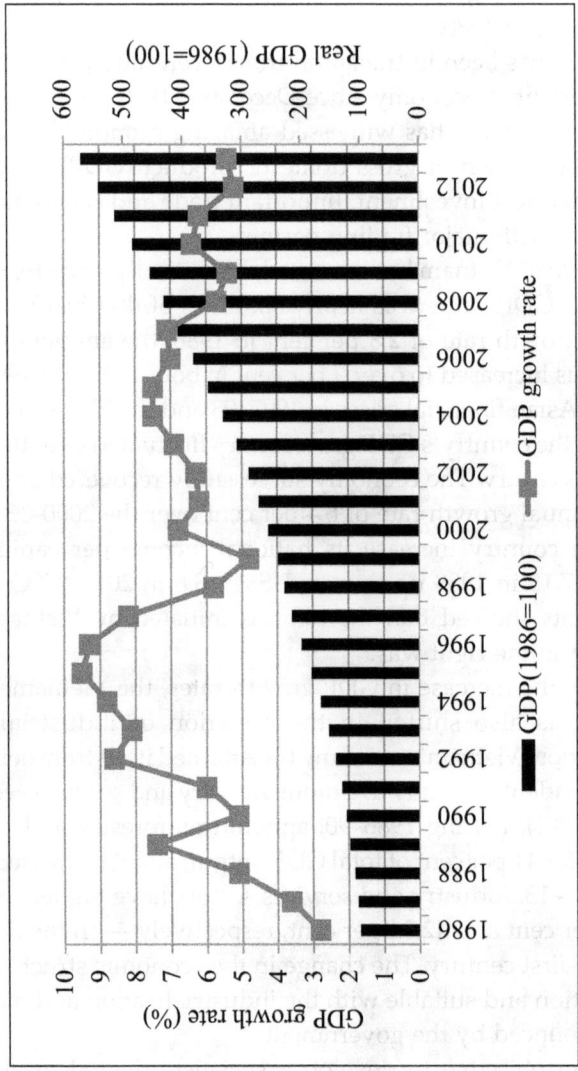

Source: Own calculations based on data obtained from the WB website, 2015.

TABLE 8.1
Structure of GDP in Vietnam

Period	Share of GDP by sector (%)				Share of GDP by ownership (%)			
	Total	Agriculture, Forestry and Fishery	Industry	Services	Total	State	Non-State	Foreign investment
1986–1990	100	41.15	25.36	33.49	100	35.26	63.60	1.14
1991–1995	100	31.78	27.52	40.70	100	33.78	57.54	5.68
1996–2000	100	25.85	33.10	41.05	100	39.54	49.82	10.40
2001–2005	100	22.29	39.44	38.27	100	38.68	46.54	14.60
2006–2010	100	20.55	40.27	39.18	100	35.48	46.64	17.89
2011–2013	100	19.38	38.28	42.34	100	32.48	48.95	18.56
1986–2013	100	26.83	33.99	39.17	100	35.87	52.18	11.38

Source: Own calculations based on data obtained from Vietnam statistical year book 2013.

other economic sectors. As a result, the number of state-owned enterprise declined,[1] while the GDP's shares of the state sector did not change much over time. The number of the foreign-owned and non-state enterprises has been growing. However, the foreign investment sector share of the GDP has also increased, from 1.14 per cent in 1986–90 to 18.56 per cent in 2011–13. In contrast, the non-state sector's share of in GDP decreased from 63.6 per cent in 1986–90 to 48.95 per cent in 2011–13 (Table 8.1).

The Sixth Party Congress in December 1986 was a turning point in Vietnam's economic policies. Market-oriented and opening the economy were the two important policies to help Vietnam embrace trade liberalization and external investment.

The total volume of Vietnam's trade in 1986–2013 was US$1,733.67 billion. As a result of Vietnam's strategy of increasing export growth to boost the country's economic development, export has been playing a more and more important role in the country's economy. The annual average value of export and the shares of export in GDP have increased significantly. While the annual average export value in 1986–1990 was US$1.4 billion, the value in 2011–13 increased up to US$114.5 billion, more than 81 times of that in 1986–90. Export accounted for 74.25 per cent of the GDP in 2011–13 (Table 8.2). The increase in exports was due to the diversification and development of export products as well as changes in the country's export structure that fit market demands.

TABLE 8.2
Annual Average Value and Ratio per GDP of Major Factors

Period	Annual average Value (US$ million)			Ratio per GDP (%)			
	Exports	Imports	Inward FDI	Outward FDI	Exports/GDP	Imports/GDP	Inward FDI/GDP	Outward FDI/GDP
1986–1990	1406.3	2537.0	320.7	0.1	6.95	12.54	1.58	0.00
1991–1995	3431.0	4556.8	3675.8	2.2	24.62	32.70	26.37	0.02
1996–2000	10365.0	12322.8	5101.9	2.4	36.75	43.69	18.09	0.01
2001–2005	22163.4	26033.3	4161.2	111.5	49.69	58.37	9.33	0.25
2006–2010	56081.1	68631.4	29614.9	2089.4	60.32	73.82	31.85	2.25
2011–2013	114489.3	117520.9	18106.3	2832.6	74.25	76.22	11.74	1.84

Source: Own calculations based on data obtained from the WB website 2015 and Vietnam statistical year book 2013.

Vietnam's imports mainly comprises inputs in the form of machines, raw materials and technologies for domestic productions as well as for consumption. Table 8.2 shows that the annual average value of imports increased quickly over time. The annual export value in 2011–13 was US$117.5 billion, more than 46 times of that in 1986–90. Imports' share of GDP has increased significantly to 76.2 per cent of GDP in 2011–15 and to 63.1 per cent for the whole period.

Since the economic renovation in 1986, FDI has been seen as a crucial factor in the growth of the Vietnamese economy. Since the implementation of the first law on Foreign Investment in the late 1987, which granted legal status for FDI inflows, Vietnam has attracted the attention of foreign investors. FDI inflows into Vietnam increased rapidly during the 1990s and in the first decade of the 2000s. From 1988 to 2013, there are 17,379 inward FDI projects with a total registered capital amounting to US$268.7 billion. Since Vietnam issued the foreign investment law in 2005 and joined the WTO in 2006, the annual average registered capital of inward FDI peaked in the 2006–10 period at US$29.6 billion. The country's inward FDI accounted for 31.85 per cent of GDP in 2006–10. Although Vietnam's outward FDI is still relatively small compared to inward FDI, it increased dramatically in Vietnam over time. At the end of the 2013, Vietnam had 818 investment projects in 63 countries and territories around the world with a total registered capital of over US$19.5 billion. Since the Law on Investment (2005) and Decree No. 78/2006/ND-CP[2] of Vietnamese government took effect, the average registered capital of Vietnam's FDI outflow annually increased from US$0.1 million in 1991–95 period to US$2368.1 million in 2006–13 period.

In short, after nearly thirty years of renovation in 1986, Vietnam has recorded relatively high growth rates with the annual average GDP growth rate of 5.5 per cent in 2011–13, satisfying the planned targets. The country's economic structure has gradually shifted along the lines of industrialization and modernization, closely tied to the market for better efficiency. Vietnam significantly increased the volume of its exports and imports, while at the same time registering positive flows of IFDI and OFDI during the transition period.

3. EVOLUTION OF VIETNAM'S OUTWARD FDI POLICY

Direct investments abroad from Vietnam has taken place since 1989. During these early years of OFDI, pioneering private enterprises in provinces that share borders with Laos and Cambodia started investing in these countries on the basis of bilateral cooperation agreements between local governments of Vietnam with those in the two countries. During this period, investments abroad received less legal guidance. This situation stemmed from the slow and late liberalization of the Vietnamese economy, the shortage of investment capital as well as the government policy which was more focused on encouraging domestic investment. On 14 April 1999, the Vietnamese Government issued Decree No. 22/1999/ND-CP which prescribed and guide how outward foreign direct investment of Vietnam enterprises should be managed. This was the country's first legal provision on overseas investment by Vietnamese enterprises, more than ten years of the implementation of *Doi Moi*.

According to Article 1 of Decree No. 22/1999/ND-CP, Vietnamese enterprises investing abroad is defined as enterprises that place their capital in cash and other assets abroad to invest in countries overseas. However, the decree also stated that Vietnamese enterprises that wish to invest abroad have to meet a number of conditions, namely: (i) that investment project abroad is feasible; and (ii) the enterprise has the financial capacity and owes no taxes to the state. When state-owned and other enterprises are interested to invest US$1 million or more abroad, they are required to obtain approval in the form of an investment licence from the Ministry of Planning and Investment (Article 6, Decree No. 22/1999/ND-CP).

In implementing Decree No. 22/1999/ND-CP, the ministries concerned have issued specific guidelines for Vietnamese enterprises investing abroad. The introduction of direct regulations on outward FDI has created a legal framework for the investment activities of enterprises in Vietnam, while at the same time creating a stable and clear environment to encourage Vietnamese enterprises to invest abroad.

Subsequently, a number of official guidelines and decisions dealing with various aspects of OFDI have been issued in Vietnam. One of these is Circular No. 01/2001/TT-NHNN dated 19 January 2001 which provides guidance by the State Bank of Vietnam to Vietnamese enterprises in foreign exchange management for direct investments abroad. According to the circular, enterprises that are interested in investing in projects abroad must open a foreign currency deposit accounts at authorized banks' foreign exchange operations (hereinafter referred to as authorized banks). All transfers of money abroad and in Vietnam related to such investment activities abroad must be made through these accounts.

Another important official decision on OFDI is the decision No. 116/2001/QD-TTg from the Prime Minister dated 2 August 2001 which provides a number of incentives to encourage outward FDI in the oil and gas sector. These incentives were aimed at encouraging investments in search, exploration, development and mining in the oil and gas sector. In addition, when determining the corporate income tax payable in Vietnam for investments in oil and gas projects abroad, enterprises may deduct tax paid in foreign countries.

The regulation on Vietnamese investment abroad was significantly liberalized with Circular No. 05/2001/TT-BKH dated 30 August 2001 of the Ministry of Planning and Investment. Under the new regulations on the investment projects abroad, written official approval of investments, contracts and agreements with foreign investors (involving investment projects) were no longer required. This is considered a step forward in terms of removal of barriers that were created by previous law on investments abroad.

A number of incentives to encourage enterprises to invest abroad were created under Circular No. 97/2002/TT-BTC. The Circular states that machinery, equipment and parts that are exported to foreign countries (to create fixed assets of investment projects abroad) and liquidated or at the end of the project lifespan and imported back into Vietnam, can be imported duty free and not subjected to value added tax. In addition, in the assessment of income tax payable in Vietnam, Vietnam enterprises that have invested abroad may deduct tax paid in the foreign countries from income tax payable in Vietnam. However the amount of deducted tax cannot exceed the income tax under the provisions of the Law of corporate income tax in Vietnam.

Overall, the promulgation of Decree No. 22/1999/ND-CP and various guidance documents have created the legal framework for the operation of direct investment abroad for Vietnam. These have generated favourable conditions for the launch of OFDI projects. However, the Decree on OFDI is still confusing, difficult to implement and reveals some limitations. Other problems include the lack specific, comprehensive, and consistent regulations. The administrative procedures for the licensing of outward FDI are relatively complex and the procedural adjustments for investment certificates are not clear. During this period, businesses faced many difficulties in transferring capital abroad for investment as well as transferring profits home. There was no regulation on loans in foreign currency for enterprises to invest abroad. According to Decree No. 22/1999/ND-CP, only Vietnamese enterprises are allowed to invest abroad.

The Vietnamese National Assembly approved the Investment Law in 2005, to take effect on 1 July 2006. The Investment Law has devoted a chapter on the regulation of overseas investment by enterprises in Vietnam. According to the Investment Law, outward FDI investors are defined as organizations and individuals that carry out investment activities in accordance with the laws of Vietnam. They may invest abroad, as stipulated by the laws of Vietnam and the country receiving the investment. The Vietnamese government encourages economic enterprises in Vietnam to invest abroad in the export sectors (which uses more labour and promote efficiency) and traditional trades of the country. To invest abroad, enterprises that fulfil all financial obligations to the State of Vietnam will be issued investment certificates. The Law also provides the procedures for registration and verification of the outward investments.

On 9 August 2009, Decree No. 78/2006/ND-CP on outward FDI by the Government of Vietnam was issued, replacing Decree No. 22/1999/ND-CP. This Decree was introduced to overcome some of the shortcomings in the current legislation on outward investment. The Decree has a number of objectives:

(1) to enable enterprises to invest abroad;
(2) to provide clear, specific and transparent investment procedures in a direction which reduces state intervention and increase the autonomy of enterprises;
(3) to increase the efficiency of state management and clearly define the responsibilities of state agencies in supporting and enabling enterprises to invest overseas; and
(4) to simplify administrative procedures.

Decree No. 78/2006/ND-CP stipulates that investors and enterprises in all economic sectors, including foreign-invested enterprises, are entitled to invest overseas, have autonomy and are solely responsible for the results of the business. In addition, it also specifies the relationship between the state agency and investors, their responsibilities, and the sanctions if both investors and state agency do not follow properly the provisions of law.

After the Vietnamese Government issued Decree No. 78/2006/ND-CP, the State Bank of Vietnam issued Circular No. 10/2006/TT-NHNN to guide commercial banks supporting the enterprises to invest directly abroad. The Government also issued Decree No. 121/2007/ND-CP dated 25 July 2006 on direct investment abroad in oil and gas activities which enables the Prime Minister to approve investments in oil and gas projects using state funds from US$1,000 billion or more of capital or other economic sectors from US$3,000 billion or more.

In consequence, the legal framework of outward FDI of Vietnam has gradually been improved. Decree No. 22/1999/ND-CP with a number of documents provided the legal framework for outward direct investment of Vietnamese enterprises before promulgating the investment law. Through the Investment Law 2005 and Decree No. 78/2006/ND-CP, the provisions on procedures for foreign investment in Vietnam has become more specific and clearer.

4. OUTWARD FDI FROM VIETNAM

4.1 Trends

Vietnam has undergone transition from a centrally planned economy to a market-oriented one since December 1986. There has been a surge in outward FDI from Vietnam especially since 2006. Starting from nearly zero in the early nineties, FDI outflows from Vietnam exceeded US$4.4 billion in 2013. At the end of the 2013, Vietnam has 818 investment projects in 63 countries and territories around the world with a total registered capital of over US$19.5 billion.[3] The average registered capital of Vietnam's FDI outflow annually amounted to US$887.5 million. The average capital of a project is about US$23.9 million.

The history of Vietnam's outward FDI can be divided into three stages based on the development of the country's outward FDI policies (Table 8.3).

Stage 1 (1989–98): The FDI outflow in this period is small and fragmented due to lack of the government regulations on investments abroad. In 1989, Vietnam began conducting its direct investment abroad with only one project which is a Vietnamese–Japanese project with a registered capital of US$0.6 million. Vietnamese enterprises have invested in 17 projects abroad with a total registered capital reached US$13.6 million; the average size of each project achieves US$0.8 million. The investments abroad by Vietnamese enterprises during this period are mainly exploratory in nature and comes from the intrinsic demands of the

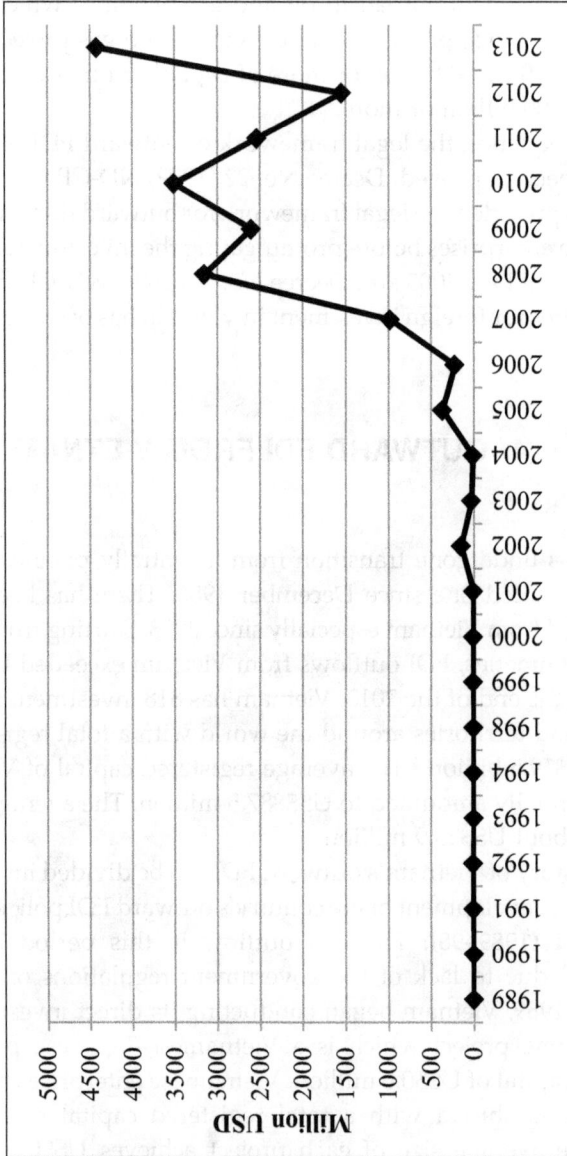

FIGURE 8.2
Trend of Vietnam's Outward FDI, 1989–2013

Data source: Vietnam Statistical Yearbook 2013.

TABLE 8.3
Vietnam's Outward FDI

| Period | Project | | Registered Capital | | Registered |
	No. of Project	Percent (%)	Value (US$ million)	Percent (%)	Capital/Project (US$ million)
1989–1998	17	2.08	13.6	0.07	0.80
1999–2005	127	15.52	567.7	2.91	4.47
2006–2013	674	82.40	18,944.7	97.02	28.11
1989–2013	818	100	19,526	100	23.87

Data source: Vietnam statistical Yearbook, various issues.

business. Vietnamese investors are likely to seek profitable opportunities in neighbouring countries such as Laos and Cambodia on the basis of bilateral agreements between two local governments.

Stage 2 (1999–2005): This stage shows a major change in terms of both the quality and quantity of Vietnam's outward FDI. It is marked by the introduction of Decree No. 22/1999/ND-CP and the guidance documents for implementation. These established a legal basis for the operations of investment abroad by enterprises in Vietnam. The total number of projects in this period amounted to 127 projects with a total registered capital of US$567.7 million, more than 7.5 times of the number of projects and 41.7 times of the total registered capital over the 1989–98 period.

Stage 3 (2006–13): This is the boom stage of Vietnam's outward FDI and begins with the enactment of the Investment Law in 2005 and Decree No. 78/2006/ND-CP. During this period, there were 674 Vietnamese outward FDI projects. The total registered capital reached US$18.9 billion which was about 33.4 times the size of registered investment in the period 1999–2005. The average invested capital reached US$28.11 million per project which was much higher than recorded in the previous period. Aside from factors such as financial resources, capacity and project management experiences, this boom was partly the result of the completion of the legal framework for investment activities abroad. Another factor was the role of the "Promoting Vietnam's Investment Abroad" project approved on February 2009 by the Prime Minister, which listed the priority areas of investment and provided instant support solutions that helped Vietnamese investors to conduct their investment activities abroad.

4.2 Sectoral Composition of the Outward FDI of Vietnam

Vietnamese outward FDI structure has also shifted in the direction of industrialization and modernization. Table 8.4 shows the amount invested (in terms of registered capital) in the agriculture, forestry and fishery sector accounted for 11 per cent of the total outward FDI during 1989–2005. There were 107 projects invested in the agriculture, forestry and fishery sector over 1989–2013 with the average capital per project around US$25.6 million. The service sector contributed the highest number of invested projects overseas with a 55 per cent share of the total number of project in 1989–2013. However, the average size of capital per project is small, only about US$10 million. Even though the share of the industry and construction sector decreased during 1989–2013, this sector still played an important role. It accounted for 60 per cent of the registered capital in the Vietnamese's outward FDI. The average size of capital was US$46.6 million over the 1989–2013 period. This accelerated the industrialization of the country.

Table 8.5 shows the Vietnam's investment abroad by economic activities. Up to 31 December 2013, Vietnamese enterprises have invested in 713 projects abroad with a total registered capital investment of US$16.6 billion. These investments are most concentrated in the mining and quarrying sector with 63 projects and US$7.3 billion, accounting for

TABLE 8.4
Structure of Outward FDI of Vietnam by Sector, 1989–2013 (%)
(Only effective projects)

Sector	1989–2005		1989–2010		1989–2013	
	No. of Project	Registered Capital	No. of Project	Registered Capital	No. of Project	Registered Capital
Agriculture, forestry and fishery	5.8	11.0	10.6	13.5	15.0	16.5
Industry and construction	48.1	83.2	39.7	61.6	30.0	60.0
Services	46.1	5.8	49.7	24.9	55.0	23.5
Total	100.0	100.0	100.0	100.0	100.0	100.0

Source: Calculated from Vietnam statistical year book, various issues.

TABLE 8.5
Vietnam's Outward FDI by Economic Activity, 1989–2013
(Only effective projects)

Economic activity	1989–2005		1989–2010		1989–2013	
	No. of Project	Registered Capital (US$ million)	No. of Project	Registered Capital (US$ million)	No. of Project	Registered Capital (US$ million)
Total	154	621.8	559	8,782.4	713	16,624.0
Agriculture, forestry and fishing	9	68.5	59	1,183.2	107	2,739.7
Agriculture, forestry and fishing	9	68.5	59	1,183.2	107	2,739.7
Industry and Construction	74	517.1	222	5,412.7	214	9,977.7
Mining and quarrying	12	168.9	87	4,294.2	63	7,341.9
Manufacturing	57	68.0	107	428.7	113	424.3
Electricity, gas, stream and air conditioning supply	1	273.1	4	653.7	9	2,124.4
Water supply, sewerage, waste management and remediation activities			2	7.9	3	9.4
Construction	4	7.1	22	28.2	26	77.7
Service	71	36.2	278	2,186.5	392	3,906.6
Wholesale and retail trade; Repair of motor vehicles and motorcycles	19	8.7	95	148.8	148	113.1
Transportation and storage	10	3.4	11	17.1	16	53.6
Accommodation and food service activities	7	2.6	18	31.3	24	113.9
Information and communication			27	507.1	38	1,296.1
Financial, banking and insurance activities			15	202.6	26	503.3
Real estate activities	34	21.3	28	162.0	29	509.7
Professional, scientific and technical activities			59	36.6	58	79.0
Administrative and support service activities			9	9.7	14	82.6
Education and training			3	2.1	6	3.5
Human health and social work activities			3	31.6	7	20.9
Arts, entertainment and recreation			3	1,034.5	4	1,125.1
Other activities	1	0.2	7	3.1	22	5.8

Data source: Vietnam Statistical Yearbook, various issues.

8.8 per cent of total projects and 44.16 per cent of the total registered capital in 1989–2013. This is followed by agriculture, forestry and fisheries (107 projects and invested US$2.7 billion, accounting for 15 per cent of projects and 16.5 per cent of total investment).[4] These are sectors in which Vietnam is competitive compared to other countries in the world. However, since 2010, Vietnamese enterprises have invested into other sectors such as electricity, gas, stream and air conditioning supply (12.78 per cent of the total registered capital);[5] information and communication (7.8 per cent);[6] arts, entertainment and recreation (6.77 per cent); real estate activities (3.07 per cent); financial, banking and insurance activities (3.03 per cent) and manufacturing (2.55 per cent). Even though the number of implemented projects are not large, the average values of these investments are large, leading to a new direction in Vietnamese OFDI.

4.3 Geographical Distribution of Vietnamese Outward FDI

After nearly 30 years of overseas investment, Vietnamese enterprises have invested abroad in 63 countries and territories around the world. Over the 1989–2013 period, Asia, particularly Southeast Asia, is still the main target region of Vietnamese outward FDI with a total of 513 invested projects (about 73.4 per cent of the projects) and more than US$9 billion registered capital (or 55.1 per cent of the total registered capital). Since 2010, the investment area targeted has expanded to many countries and regions. The second most important region is Latin America with 132 projects and a total registered capital which accounted for 22.6 per cent of total projects. This is followed by Africa at 11.1 per cent, Europe 10 per cent and Oceania 1.1 per cent (Table 8.6).

By the end of 2013, Laos was the top destination of Vietnam's outward FDI, with investments in 230 projects amounting to US$4.6 billion of invested capital. Other important countries include Cambodia, Russia, Malaysia, Myanmar and Algeria which are traditional markets for Vietnamese investors in the fields of petroleum, hydropower, industrial crops (rubber), telecommunications and insurance.[7]

Besides promoting and maintaining business operations in Vietnam's traditional markets such Laos, Cambodia, Russia and Algeria, Vietnamese enterprises have successfully explored a number of new markets which required high levels of competition and technology such as the United States, Japan, Australia, Hong Kong, Singapore as well as long-distance markets such as Venezuela, Peru, Haiti, Mozambique and Madagascar.

TABLE 8.6
Structure of Outward FDI of Vietnam by Region (in %)
(Only effective projects)

Region	1989–2005 No. of Project	1989–2005 Registered Capital	1989–2010 No. of Project	1989–2010 Registered Capital	1989–2013 No. of Project	1989–2013 Registered Capital
Total	100	100	100	100	100	100
ASIA	72.73	85.22	75.3	54.02	73.42	55.11
Eastern Asia	7.79	1.06	8.94	0.37	7.01	0.24
Southeast Asia	62.34	67.36	65.46	51.02	65.85	54.57
South Central Asia	1.30	0.56	0.72	1.49	0.56	0.30
Western Asia	1.30	16.24	0.18	1.14		
LATIN AMERICA	10.39	1.19	14.85	27.15	18.59	22.57
Northern America	10.39	1.19	12.52	2.87	15.99	2.49
Caribbean			1.61	2.50	1.40	1.06
South America			0.72	21.78	1.20	19.02
EUROPE	15.58	7.80	5.37	9.02	3.65	10.04
Eastern Europe	12.99	7.03	3.58	8.87	1.40	9.57
Western Europe	2.60	0.77	1.79	0.15	2.24	0.48
OCEANIA			2.15	1.25	2.24	1.14
AFRICA	1.30	5.79	2.33	8.56	2.10	11.14
Eastern Africa			0.36	5.27	0.14	2.08
Middle Africa			1.61	0.35	1.4	1.42
Northern Africa	0.65	5.63	0.36	2.94	0.28	7.59
Southern Africa	0.65	0.16				
Western Africa					0.28	0.04

Data source: Vietnam Statistical Yearbook, various issues.

In these new places, even though Vietnamese enterprises have only invested in a few projects, each project required high technology and large amount of capital.

Briefly, Vietnam's outward FDI has increased rapidly in both quantity and quality since 1989. There has been a shift in the country's OFDI from small-scale projects to large-scale projects. The industry focus of the country's OFDI has shifted over time from services, tea products, coffee, transport, and hotels to industries requiring high technology and large capital as the exploration and exploitation of petroleum, power production, construction materials and rubber plantations. Although the number of projects and the scale of capital investment enterprises abroad are small, the financial strength, technological level, techniques

TABLE 8.7
Top 10 Destination of Outward FDI of Vietnam, 1989–2013
(Only effective projects)

Country		No. of Project	Registered capital	
			Value (US$ million)	Percent (%)
	TOTAL	713	16624.0	100.0
	Total 10 top countries	538	15612.7	93.92
1	Laos	230	4601.8	27.68
2	Cambodia	150	3046.3	18.32
3	Venezuela	2	1825.4	10.98
4	Russia	10	1590.1	9.57
5	Peru	6	1336.9	8.04
6	Algeria	2	1261.5	7.59
7	Malaysia	11	747.9	4.50
8	Myanmar	12	442.9	2.66
9	United States	114	414.2	2.49
10	Mozambique	1	345.7	2.08

Data source: Vietnam Statistical Yearbook 2013.

and investment management experiences of Vietnamese enterprises are improving. Vietnam's OFDI has increased investment capital, expanded production and opened markets for export as well as develop greater economic cooperation between Vietnam and other countries around the world. This success is created by both the efforts of investors and the favourable support from Vietnam's State which includes improvements in the legal framework for OFDI.

5. PROSPECTS FOR OUTWARD FDI

On 20 February 2009, the Prime Minister of Vietnam approved the project named "Promoting Vietnam's Investment Abroad". The project's objectives are:

- Promoting further investments abroad by enterprises that are established and operating in Vietnam to ensure active participation in international economic integration.
- Strengthening of measures and creating favourable conditions to promote Vietnam's investments abroad.

- Managing effectively the outward FDI of enterprises, especially state-owned enterprises.

Under the project, the enterprises are expected to continue to exploit and strengthen Vietnamese enterprises by investing in traditional markets such as Laos, Cambodia, the Russian Federation and other countries in the region; and gradually expand investments to countries and new markets such as Latin America, Eastern Europe and Africa. The project supports investments abroad in the fields of energy, electricity production and exploitation of natural resources, especially the exploitation of oil, gas and other minerals, and plantation sector. It supports investment projects abroad to meet domestic requirements of raw materials for production.

In the future, as an international investor, Vietnam will follow the general trend in global FDI flows in which intra-regional investments between developing countries will continue to increase with new investments or M&A remaining the main form of investments. The areas that will receive the attention of Vietnamese investors include mining and extraction, agriculture, forestry, fishing, manufacturing, telecommunications, banking, hotel services, wholesale and retail services. This is driven by market demand in the form of firms seeking new and additional input sources as well as competition from competitors and higher labour costs. Another reason for Vietnamese investment abroad is the continuous depreciation of domestic assets that yield low returns in the country.

The traditional destinations for Vietnam's OFDI such as Laos, Cambodia, Russia, Malaysia and Algeria will expand in the future. Besides investing in the mining sector, forest industry, hydropower, telecommunications, and infrastructure construction in these countries, Vietnam enterprises are interested to invest in aviation, banks, and insurance activities.[8] Laos remains the most important destination for Vietnamese investors. Many Vietnamese enterprises have put in large amount of investments in long-term projects in Laos in the form of commercial centres, apartments, office buildings; wood-processing plants, rubber plantations; hydropower stations, and iron and copper mining projects. According to the Foreign Investment Agency, Vietnamese enterprises' investments abroad is projected to continue to boom in next five years with an estimated average amount increasing by up to US$500 million each year. Major players will include the State of Petroleum Corporation, the Coal-Minerals Corporation,

Viettel Telecom Group, Vietnam Electricity Group, Investment Bank and Development of Vietnam.

Beside the traditional destinations for Vietnam's OFDI, Vietnamese enterprises today invest abroad in developed markets such as Japan, the United States, Korea, Australia, Germany and Singapore. This reflects the confidence and maturity of Vietnamese enterprises. Other new potential markets include other developing countries in Asia, Africa and Latin America. The construction and development needs of these countries are large. In addition, there are few foreign companies invested in these countries which makes them relatively easy for foreign investors to enter these markets. Regional economic integration in Africa lowers taxes on the exchange of goods thus enlarging this market. The market potential is large for goods from Vietnam such as motorcycles, electronics, refrigeration, beverage and garments. It is profitable for Vietnamese enterprises to invest in these markets.

6. CONCLUSIONS AND POLICY IMPLICATIONS

Vietnam's outward FDI has increased dramatically since the launch of its renovation policy (*Doi Moi*) in 1986. This study aims to provide an overview of the country's OFDI in terms of policy development, current situation and prospects. The legal framework in the country for outward FDI has gradually been improved, creating a more liberal legal framework and enabling Vietnamese enterprises to put themselves in the region and world market. Vietnamese outward FDI structure has also shifted in the direction of industrialization and modernization with 60 per cent of the registered capital invested abroad in the industry and construction sectors. Vietnamese OFDI is moving beyond traditional destinations by moving into developed countries or new developing countries where Vietnamese enterprises could get higher profits.

To promote Vietnam's outward FDI in the future, the government should continue to do the following. First, it should develop and perfect the legal framework and policies on foreign investment in order to create more favourable conditions and orientation for entrepreneurs and enterprises to invest abroad safely and effectively. Second, it should improve administrative procedures for investment abroad towards more simple and convenient system by reducing the interference by administrative measures even for projects using state capital, and by increasing the autonomy and self-responsibility of business enterprises. Third, it should provide regular measures to encourage and support investments abroad, with particular focus on supporting measures that provide information about the environment and investment opportunities abroad as well as protect the interests of enterprises investing abroad in the course of conducting business overseas.

Notes

1. Numbers of state-owned enterprises were reduced from 12,000 in 1990 to 4,086 by 2005 and to 3,189 enterprises at the end of 2013 (GSO 2013).
2. In 2005, the Congress government has legislated investment activities abroad and take effect on 7 January 2006. Decree No. 78/2006/ND-CP dated 9 September 2006, replaced Decree No. 22/1999/ND-CP, permits investors and enterprises of all economic sectors (including enterprises with foreign investment capital) to invest abroad.
3. Capital of Vietnamese investors only; including supplementary capital to licensed projects in previous years.
4. The largest project of Vietnamese outward FDI is in agriculture, forestry and fishery sector. This is the US$600 million project; collaboration between PetroVietnam fertilizer and Chemicals Corporation with Cherifie Phosphates Corporation in Casablanca, Morocco to establish manufacturing plants DAP and ammonia to provide the Vietnam market and region. In addition, there are many small- and medium-scale investment projects in rubber and industrial plants in Laos and Cambodia: the US$32 million project of planting rubber of Vietnam Rubber Group in Laos, the US$24 million project of planting rubber of Daklak Rubber Limited Company in Laos.
5. There are a number of large-scale capital projects over US$100 million such as the Sekaman 1 and Sekaman 3 hydropower projects in Laos with the total invested capital of US$441.6 million and US$275 million respectively; the project of oil and gas exploration in Algeria of Vietnam Oil and Gas group with the total invested capital of US$243 million and in Madagascar with the total invested capital of US$117 million.
6. Some large projects in telecommunications and mobile communication networks in Cambodia with total registered capital of US$29 million and US$16 million in Laos of Viettel Group.
7. See notes 4, 5 and 6.
8. In 2009, the contractual joint venture established the national airline of Cambodia (Cambodia Angkor Air-CAA) has been signed between Vietnam Airline and its partners in Cambodia. Bank for Investment and Development of Vietnam has officially announced the presence of its trade and investment with the creation

of a new legal entity in Cambodia. Moreover, the Insurance Corporation of Cambodia-Vietnam was established and tries to become reputable insurance company in Cambodia's insurance market.

References

General Statistical Office. *Vietnamese Statistical Yearbook*, several issues. Statistical Publishing House, Hanoi, 1995–2013.

Ministry of Finance. *Circular No. 97/2002/TT-BTC dated 24 October 2002 guiding the implementation of tax obligations for Vietnam enterprises to invest abroad.* 2002.

Ministry of Planning and Investment of Vietnam <www.mpi.gov.vn>.

National Assembly Chairman. *Law on Foreign Investment in Vietnam.* 2005.

Prime Minister. *Decree No. 22/1999/ND-CP dated 14 April 1999 of the Prime Minister on regulation of direct investment abroad of Vietnamese enterprises.* 1999.

——. *Decision No. 116/2001/QD-TTg dated 2 August 2001 of the Prime Minister on a number of incentives to encourage foreign investment in oil and gas activities.* 2001.

——. *Circular No. 05/2001/TT-BKH dated 30 August 2001 of the Ministry of Planning and Investment guiding investment abroad activities of Vietnam businesses.* 2001.

——. *Decree 78/2006/ND-CP dated 9 September 2006 of the Prime Minister on regulation of investment abroad of Vietnamese enterprises.* 2006.

——. *Decree 121/2007/ND-CP dated 25 July 2007 of the Prime Minister on Regulations on direct investment abroad in oil and gas activities.* 2007.

State Bank of Vietnam. *Circular No. 01/2001/TT-NHNN dated 19 January 2001 of the State Bank of Vietnam on guiding foreign exchange management for direct investments abroad by Vietnam enterprise.* 2001.

World Bank. <http://www.worldbank.org> (accessed August 2015).

9

MYANMAR AS A DESTINATION FOR OFDI
A New ASEAN Foreign Investment Frontier

Jean-Pierre A. Verbiest and Tin Htoo Naing

1. INTRODUCTION

The wide-ranging economic and institutional reforms undertaken by the government of Myanmar over the past four years has made the resource-rich country a major new investment frontier in Asia. However, the policy challenges that the country faces remain formidable, in particular, in view of the weak capacity of key policy-making institutions and the low level of human resources development. Infrastructure including transport and power is underdeveloped after decades of neglect. Myanmar's economic and institutional challenges today are similar to those faced by Vietnam after *Doi Moi* in the late 1980s and early 1990s. Myanmar can thus learn not only from the experience of Vietnam, but also from that of many other ASEAN countries such as resource-rich Malaysia and Indonesia, as well as the experience of Cambodia in the 1990s and even Thailand in the 1980s (Lim and Yamada 2013).

Compared to earlier development experiences in Asia, the big difference working to Myanmar's advantage today is the much more advanced stage of integration in Asia in general, and in ASEAN in particular — the latter with the ASEAN Economic Community (AEC) becoming effective at the end of 2015. A more integrated Asia has become the economic power-house of the world. The reason for this is succinctly expressed in ADB (2014): "Regional cooperation and integration provides a great opportunity to secure access to regional and global markets, technology, as well as finance and management expertise." The development of regional production networks and intra-industry trade in parts and components offers great opportunities for Myanmar to jumpstart its economic development. Geographical location, low labour cost, abundant natural resources and the growing size of its domestic market all work to the advantage of Myanmar in an integrated ASEAN. For ASEAN investors, the political and economic reforms ongoing in the country offer vast and unique opportunities to enhance competitiveness and expand the scale of their operations. There is no doubt that Myanmar will become a major destination for outward foreign direct investment (FDI) from ASEAN countries over the next decades.

ASEAN has been the external economic and political lifeline of Myanmar, particularly during the time of the trade sanctions in the 1990s and the year 2000s. After the collapse of its socialist economic system in 1988 and the market-oriented reforms that followed during the first half of the 1990s (including the adoption of the first FDI Law in November 1988) Myanmar joined ASEAN with the aim of attracting FDI from ASEAN countries. However, Myanmar joined ASEAN in July 1997, the month the Asian financial crisis started in Thailand and FDI from ASEAN collapsed. In the past decade and a half, FDI inflows were further limited due to the imposition of Western economic sanctions. ASEAN and China became the main source of FDI and also Myanmar's main trading partners.

Section 2 of this chapter provides a brief overview of Myanmar's economic potential. Section 3 analyses the main FDI trends in Myanmar over the past two decades. FDI opportunities for ASEAN countries by the 2030 horizon are presented in Section 4 and the most attractive sectors for ASEAN FDI are summarized in the last section of the paper.

2. MYANMAR: A BRIEF ECONOMIC HISTORY

Compared to other countries in Asia, up to the early 1960s, Myanmar, then called Burma, was a prosperous and advanced country. It was indeed widely considered as one of the few Asian countries which could emulate Japan's rapid development experience. Burma was the world's largest rice exporter; it had rich natural resources including forestry, minerals and petroleum; literacy rates were among the highest in developing countries at the time (Ginsburg 1961). Per capita income in 1960 was three times that of Indonesia and twice that of Thailand.

However, starting in the mid-1960s, political and economic mis-management progressively led to a prolonged decline in the development level of the country (Myat Thein 2004). As a result, economic and social indicators, and infrastructure deteriorated dramatically over the past five decades. During two decades in the 1990s and 2000s, the country was further affected by economic sanctions which effectively isolated it and crippled its external trade.

Following the adoption of a new constitution in 2008, national election in 2010 — the first in twenty years — and the formation of a new government in March 2011 led by President Thein Sein, a remarkable programme of political, economic and social reforms was pursued, effectively opening the economy to trade and investment and enabling the country to reintegrate into the international community (ADB 2012).

For Asia as a whole but in particular for ASEAN, the political and economic reforms in Myanmar and the opening of the country are a major development, a historical event. Indeed, in spite of its low per capita income of about US$1,221 in 2014 (IMF 2014), its depleted infrastructure, and low level of human development, Myanmar is a country with enormous economic potential. In terms of land area, it is the second largest ASEAN country — a quarter larger than Thailand and twice the size of Vietnam — and its geographical location is unique as a land bridge between China, India and the rest of ASEAN. The population is estimated by a 2014 population census at about 52 million, sizeable but relatively small in relation to land area. Resources in forestry and fisheries remain abundant. Agriculture benefits from diverse topography and ecosystems, and from vast water resources in four major river systems — fresh water per capita is 9 times that of China, 16 times that of India and 5 times that of Vietnam (Wong 2014). Exploitable hydropower potential is estimated at about 50,000 MW. The country has also large mineral resources including various minerals and oil and gas. While Myanmar's current proven natural gas reserves are relatively small, it is highly likely that new discoveries will be done in the many unexplored offshore and onshore areas. Some estimates put likely natural gas reserves at about 90 trillion cubic feet, higher than Malaysia today and just below those of Indonesia (Verbiest 2014). Tourism has a unique potential with numerous historical, cultural, religious and scenic sites. The country also has a well-known and rich handicraft industry and is the source of many gemstones and semi-precious stones. Tourism arrivals in 2014 soared to over 3 million, compared to only 300,000 in 2010. By 2020, arrivals have been estimated at over 7.5 million (ADB 2014; Jamieson and Schipani 2015).

In sum, Myanmar is a country of vast economic potential located strategically in ASEAN (ADB 2014). In the decades to come, the country is bound to play a major role in the development of ASEAN, particularly in offering major opportunities for ASEAN outward FDI.

3. FOREIGN DIRECT INVESTMENT IN MYANMAR: RECENT TRENDS

Although historically Myanmar benefitted substantially from what would now be called foreign direct investment (FDI) after independence in 1948 until the end of the 1950s — in sectors such banking, the oil industry, extractive industries and shipping — the economy was largely closed to trade and investment from the early 1960s up to 1988 (Myat Thein 2004). It is only at the end of 1988 that the country reopened to FDI with the adoption in November 1988 of the first Foreign Investment Law. At the same time, from 1988 to the mid-1990s, Myanmar introduced a wide range of market-oriented reforms, similar to the *Doi Moi* reforms in Vietnam. It also joined ASEAN in 1997 (Findlay, Park and Verbiest 2015).

However, as Asia recovered from the 1997 financial crisis and intra-Asian FDI resumed, progressively stronger economic sanctions from the United States and the European Union started affecting Myanmar's trade and economy in general. Partly as a result, FDI flows to Myanmar up to 2005 were insignificant — less than one tenth of a per cent of GDP, with approvals totalling a mere US$662 million from 1998 to 2004, much lower than in other ASEAN countries. From 2005, the situation changed as several large investments, mainly by China and Thailand, were approved (Figure 9.1). On an approval basis, FDI fluctuated widely from US$6,065.7 million in 2005 — 43 per cent of GDP — to US$19,998.9 million in 2010 — about 33 per cent of GDP — while from 2006 to 2009, approvals totalled only US$2,239 million. The large fluctuations in approvals reflect bulky

FIGURE 9.1
Approved Foreign Direct Investment, Annual Foreign Direct Investment Inflows and Total Investment (per cent of GDP)

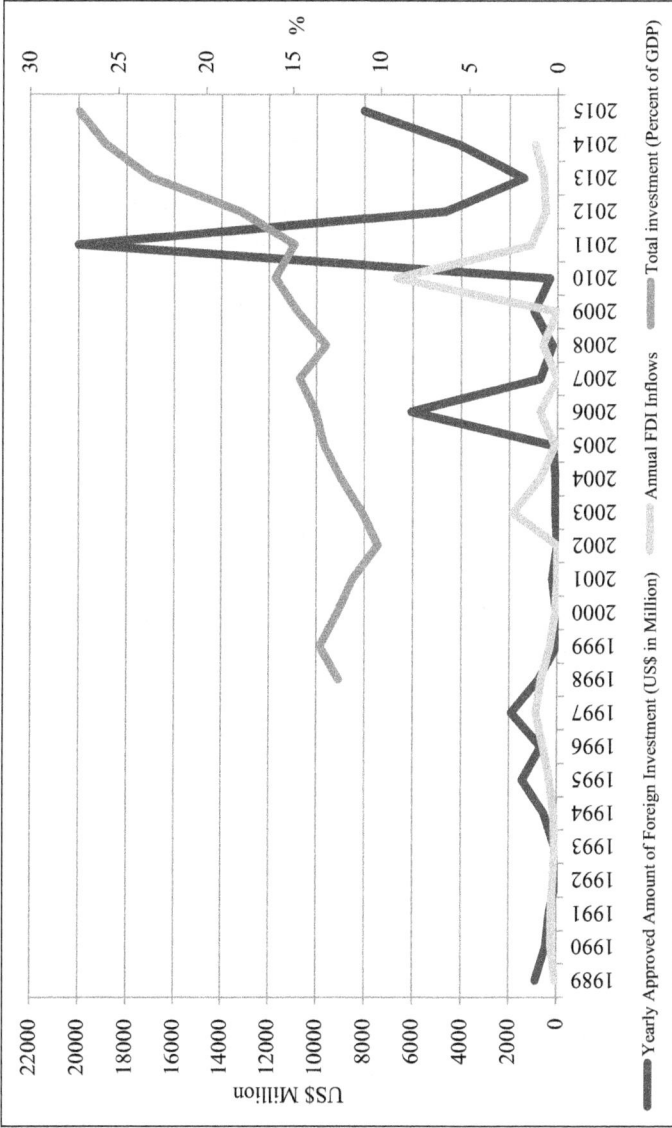

Sources: Approved FDI, Directorate of Investment and Company Administration, Ministry of National Planning and Economic Development, Nay Pyi Taw, Myanmar; Total investment IMF World Economic Outlook database, Available: <http://www.imf.org/external/pubs/ft/weo/2015/01/weodata/weorept.aspx> (accessed August 2015); GDP in current US dollars World Economic Outlook database, Available: <http://www.imf.org/external/pubs/ft/weo/2015/01/weodata/weorept.aspx> (accessed August 2015); Annual Foreign Direct Investment Inflows, United Nations Conference on Trade and Development (UNCTAD Stat), Available: <http://unctadstat.unctad.org/wds/TableViewer/tableView.aspx> (accessed August 2015).

investment projects in power plants including large dams, and investments in oil and natural gas exploration and in mining. While agreements were signed, construction of some of these large foreign financed projects was never started. For instance, FDI approval of US$6 billion in 2005 mainly relates to a hydropower dam — Tasang hydropower project on the Than Lwin river — to be financed by Thailand. That investment alone represented 70 per cent of all FDI committed between 1988 and 2005. The project has been dormant since signing. Similarly FDI of nearly US$20 billion approved in 2010 partly reflects Chinese intended investments in two hydropower projects, in the dual oil and gas pipeline connecting Kyaupyu port to the Yunnan province of China and investment in the large Letpadaung copper mine. It also includes a proposed Thai investment in a 4,000 MW coal-fired power plant in the Dawei SEZ. The project was cancelled in 2012, and a much smaller plant for 400MW is now planned.

As a result of the trade and economic sanctions, hardly any FDI went to manufacturing and other sectors of the economy. The huge differential between the official exchange rate — 6 kyat to the U.S. dollar — and the market rate — between 850 and 1,000 kyat to the U.S. dollar — which prevailed up to April 2012 as well as the underdeveloped financial system where all foreign financial transactions were highly controlled until 2012, are also main factors which negatively impacted FDI. Overall, inconsistent economic policies and regulations, weak governance, poor infrastructure including the lack of electricity, and uncertainties relating to the economic sanctions made Myanmar until 2012 a very risky investment destination.

Until very recently, data on FDI approvals for Myanmar must also be taken with caution. The data shows FDI projects approved by the Myanmar Investment Commission (MIC). As mentioned above, some of these approvals were never realized. Long lags might happen between approvals and actual disbursements particularly for large projects such as in hydropower and mining. In the case of Myanmar, joint venture projects with military enterprises such as Myanmar Economic Holdings are mostly not recorded. Finally, investments by local joint venture partners are included in MIC approval data. For instance, in 2005 and 2010, actual FDI inflows based on balance of payments data and measured by UNCTAD amounted to US$235 million and US$1,285 million respectively or 1.7 per cent and 2.6 per cent of GDP, much smaller than the amounts approved. The OECD in a recent Myanmar investment policy review (OECD 2014a) noted that Myanmar FDI approvals until recently did not reflect actual

TABLE 9.1
Cumulative Foreign Direct Investment in Myanmar by Sector (up to 31 March 2011)
(US$ million)

Sr. No.	Sector	Permitted Enterprises		
		No.	Approved Amount (US$)	%
1	Power	4	14,529.742	40.30
2	Oil and Gas	104	13,815.375	38.80
3	Manufacturing	159	1,728.447	4.79
4	Mining	64	2,794.463	7.75
5	Real Estate	19	1,056.453	2.93
6	Hotel and Tourism	45	1,064.811	2.95
7	Livestock and Fisheries	25	324.358	0.90
8	Transport and Communication	16	313.272	0.87
9	Industrial Estate	3	193.113	0.54
10	Construction	2	37.767	0.10
11	Agriculture	7	173.101	0.49
12	Other Services	6	23.686	0.07
Total		454	36,054.588	100.00

Source: Directorate of Investment and Company Administration, Ministry of National Planning and Economic Development, Myanmar.

inflows. After the start of the economic reforms in 2012, with diversification of foreign investments in manufacturing, hotel and tourism, real estate and telecommunications, actual inflows appear to be more in line with approvals.

By the end of 2010, 80 per cent of FDI had cumulatively been in power and oil and gas. Mining accounted for 7.75 per cent, manufacturing 4.8 per cent, and hotel and tourism and real estate 3 per cent respectively. All other sectors accounted for a total of only 3 per cent. As shown in Table 9.1, although the approval data overestimates actual inflows of FDI in power, both the manufacturing and services sector still hardly benefitted from FDI in Myanmar until 2012.

Experience with FDI in Myanmar is in sharp contrast with that of Vietnam which opened its economy and introduced a market economic system at about the same time as Myanmar at the end of the 1980s. Before the 1997 Asian financial crisis, on an actual inflow basis, FDI in Vietnam amounted annually to about US$2 billion while in Myanmar it averaged US$401 million per year from 1993 to 1997. From 2000 to 2010, average annual FDI flows to Vietnam reached US$3.9 billion compared to US$468 million to Myanmar. Importantly in Vietnam, most FDI went to manufacturing, contributing to a rapid shift in the economy from agriculture to industry (Masima 2006; McKinsey 2013). While initially FDI targeted manufacturing for the domestic market, both for consumer goods and industrial goods, very rapidly much FDI contributed to the development of export-oriented industries. FDI flowed mostly to sectors with strong economic linkages to other sectors in the economy including services. In contrast, until recently most FDI in Myanmar concentrated in power and extractive industries with few linkages to the rest of the economy or to employment.

A significant proportion of FDI to Vietnam also originated in East Asia and ASEAN, as more labour-intensive lower value-added manufacturing in these countries relocated to Vietnam following the well-known flying geese partner of development (Radelet and Sachs 1997; Ozawa 2010). Besides Japan, South Korea, Taiwan, Singapore, Malaysia and Thailand were early on important sources of FDI in Vietnam. Before the 1997 Asian financial crisis, 60 per cent of FDI in Vietnam originated in East Asia (Masima 2006). In one decade from 1990 to 2000, Vietnam transformed from a closed economy to an economy with trade turnover of more than GDP (Van Arkadie and Mallon 2003). For different reasons, essentially the impact of Western economic sanctions, in the 1990s and the years 2000, FDI to Myanmar also originated mainly in East Asian countries and in ASEAN. But the major difference with Vietnam is FDI in Myanmar was narrowly targeted at extractive industries with hardly any FDI in other sectors, particularly manufacturing. As a result, the impact on Myanmar's economy was minimal except as a much needed source of foreign currency. As shown in Table 9.2, by 2010 about 36.6 per cent of FDI came from other ASEAN countries, particularly from Thailand with a share of 26.9 per cent. FDI from China and Hong Kong accounted for 26.6 per cent and 17.5 per cent respectively while investment from South Korea has also been significant at 8.1 per cent.

After the formation of a new government in March 2011, a remarkable programme of economic and political reforms was started and Western economic sanctions were progressively lifted. The most important economic reforms were however introduced from 2012 onwards including a new Foreign Investment Law (FIL) in November 2012, an Export and Import Law in September 2012 and the unification of the exchange rate in April 2012. The enactment of the new FIL and its accompanying implementation regulations mark a milestone towards a more open and secure legal environment for investment but it is only a first step in a long process.

TABLE 9.2
Cumulative Foreign Direct Investment in Myanmar by Country
(up to 31 March 2011)
(ASEAN and East Asia, US$ million)

Sr. No.	Country	Permitted Enterprises		
		No.	Approved Amount (US$)	%
1	Indonesia	12	241.497	0.67
2	Malaysia	38	975.097	2.70
3	Philippine	2	146.667	0.41
4	Singapore	74	1,818.603	5.04
5	Thailand	61	9,568.093	26.87
6	Vietnam	2	23.649	0.07
ASEAN Total		189	12,773.606	35.76
7	China	32	9,603.168	26.64
8	Hong Kong	38	6,308.495	17.50
9	Japan	22	204.762	0.58
10	Republic of Korea	47	2,915.717	8.09
East Asia Total		139	19,032.142	52.81
ASEAN and East Asia Total		328	31,805.748	88.57

Source: Directorate of Investment and Company Administration, Ministry of National Planning and Economic Development, Myanmar.

In January 2013, the government adopted a "Framework for Economic and Social Reforms" (FESR) which outlines its policy priorities for 2012–15 (Ministry of National Planning and Economic Development 2013). The FESR outlines main reforms in order to achieve "quick wins" while also defining the broad parameters for the long-term goals of a national comprehensive development plan. Among others, the FESR emphasizes the importance of private sector development and FDI. To make the investment environment more transparent, the government is currently finalizing the consolidation of the FIL with the Myanmar Citizens Investment Law — a law defining the investment areas reserved for Myanmar citizens. The consolidated new law which will apply to both domestic and foreign investors is likely to be approved in 2016. The MIC is also being reformed and made independent and licensing practices made more transparent. Finally, the government has joined the International Finance Corporation's (IFC) Doing Business Indicators in 2013 in an effort to improve consistently the country's business environment. The FDI regime is thus clearly given the highest priority in the government's reform plans.

Another area highlighted in the FESR is the creation of Special Economic Zones (SEZ) and the promulgation of an SEZ Law which was enacted in January 2014. The SEZs are to be set up to overcome infrastructure bottlenecks and attract FDI, mainly for exports. Three SEZs are to be set up in the country — Thilawa, Kyaukpyu and Dawei. The Thilawa SEZ, located southeast of Yangon, is a joint venture with Japanese companies and will be the first one becoming operational by the end of 2015. Some parts of the Kyaukpyu SEZ, mainly the Chinese oil and gas terminal connected to the Yunnan province of China by a dual oil and gas pipeline, have been built while the export zone is in the detailed design stage. Some infrastructure investment has been made in the Dawei SEZ which is mainly promoted by Thailand. The Dawei SEZ will however take much longer to develop due to financial issues and the lack of connectivity to nearby Thailand. Also several industrial parks and zones have been in existence in Myanmar but they are weakly regulated and infrastructure often remains basic. Some industrial zones close to Yangon have however seen significant investments over the past two years mainly in garment manufacturing. In 2014, one garment manufacturing facility opened on average each week in Myanmar. Land access even in the industrial zones remains however a major issue. To open more opportunities for investors, both domestic and foreign, and providing the supporting infrastructure, the government is developing an industrial zones' law which will regulate and guide the setting up and operations of industrial zones. Similar zones have been successfully set up in many Asian countries, including China, Thailand and Vietnam.

The FESR also intends to reposition Myanmar in the international community. Working with other ASEAN countries to achieve the ASEAN Economic Community (AEC) by 2015 is highlighted as it enhanced participation in other regional cooperation programmes such as the GMS. The government has clearly indicated that it will fully meet its commitments under the AEC, develop the GMS transport and economic corridors and cooperated with other ASEAN countries in sectors such as energy, telecommunications, tourism, agriculture, environment, human development and the joint use of non-renewable resources.

The commitments by the Myanmar government to integrate and cooperate with regional countries and normalize relations with the international community provided a clear signal for investors. Not surprisingly FDI inflows started to rise significantly in the past few years (Table 9.3). Approved FDI also became more diverse both in terms of sector distribution and countries of origin (Table 9.4). However, total inflows continued to show some fluctuations year on year depending on investments in the power and oil and gas sectors which tend to be bulky.

Of total approved inflows of US$4.6 billion in 2011, US$4.3 billion was Chinese investment in the power sector. FDI in 2012 fell to US$1.4 billion but became more diversified sector wise. For instance, approved FDI in manufacturing was US$400.7 million in 2012, up from US$32.2 million in 2011 — an increase of more than ten times. Similarly hotel and tourism attracted FDI of US$300 million, the first investment since 2009 when it amounted to a mere US$15 million. This trend continued in 2013 and in 2014 with FDI totalling US$4.1 and US$8.0 billion respectively, spread over a wide range of sectors including agriculture, livestock and fisheries, mining, manufacturing, transport and communications, hotel and tourism, and real estate, in addition to power and oil and gas. FDI in manufacturing rose to a record US$1.8 billion in 2013, nearly the same amount as cumulative FDI approvals in manufacturing from 1988 to 2012. In 2014, FDI in the

TABLE 9.3
Yearly Approved Foreign Investment by Sector (US$ million)

Sr. No.	Sector	2010	2011	2012	2013	2014
1	Agriculture	138.750	—	9.650	20.269	39.666
2	Livestock & Fisheries	—	—	5.600	96.016	26.861
3	Mining	1,396.077	19.897	15.334	32.730	6.259
4	Manufacturing	66.321	32.254	400.720	1,826.980	1,502.013
5	Power	8,218.520	4,343.978	364.201	46.511	40.110
6	Oil and Gas	10,179.297	247.697	309.200	—	3,220.306
7	Construction	—	—	—	—	—
8	Transport & Communication	—	0.634	—	1,190.232	1,679.304
9	Hotel and Tourism	—	—	300.000	435.210	357.949
10	Real Estate	—	—	—	440.573	780.745
11	Industrial Estate	—	—	—	—	—
12	Other Services	—	—	14.766	18.534	357.320
	Total	19,998.97	4,644.460	1,419.470	4,107.060	8,010.533

Source: Directorate of Investment and Company Administration, Ministry of National Planning and Economic Development, Myanmar.

TABLE 9.4
Yearly Approved Foreign Investment by Country
(ASEAN and East Asia, US$ million)

Sr. No.	Country	2010	2011	2012	2013	2014
1	Brunei Darussalam	—	—	1.000	2.273	43.873
2	Indonesia	—	—	—	—	—
3	Laos	—	—	—	0.883	—
4	Malaysia	76.750	51.864	4.324	616.108	6.724
5	Philippine	—	—	—	—	0.506
6	Singapore	226.170	—	418.233	2,300.121	4,297.185
7	Thailand	2,146.000	—	1.300	529.072	165.679
8	Vietnam	—	18.147	329.390	142.000	175.400
	ASEAN Total	2,448.920	70.011	754.247	3,590.457	4,689.367
9	China	8,269.229	4,345.728	231.773	56.920	511.415
10	Hong Kong	5,798.277	—	84.839	107.102	625.556
11	Japan	7.140	4.318	51.063	55.711	85.740
12	Republic of Korea	2,676.399	25.572	37.942	81.205	299.586
	East Asia Total	16,751.045	4,375.618	405.617	300.938	1,522.297
	ASEAN and East Asia Total	19,199.965	4,445.629	1,159.864	3,891.395	6,211.664

Source: Directorate of Investment and Company Administration, Ministry of National Planning and Economic Development, Myanmar.

sector rose by a further US$1.5 billion for 141 projects. For 2015, the target for total FDI approvals is US$6 billion. In the first four months of fiscal year 2015, US$2.6 billion FDI for 64 projects was approved. A number of projects were approved in the oil and gas sector as large foreign companies finalized their production sharing agreements for the offshore exploration tenders they won in the previous year (*Myanmar Times* 2015).

As FDI became more diversified, the number of projects also increased substantially. Project approvals rose from 13 in 2011 to 94 and 81 in 2012 and 2013 respectively while in 2014, 211 projects got approved. The biggest changes came in manufacturing. For instance, the number of foreign investments in the garment industry has risen exponentially in 2013 and 2014 as the industry benefitted from the lowest labour costs in Asia and duty free access to the European Union market. Other main manufacturing projects included automobile, medicine, tobacco, and food and beverages (DICA 2014).

As a result of the lifting of trade sanctions, the 2012 new FDI law and other reforms aiming at opening the economy (ADB 2014), FDI from a larger number of countries started to flow into Myanmar from 2013 onwards (Table 9.4). All ASEAN countries except for Cambodia invested into Myanmar, and together accounted for about 70 per cent of total approved FDI in 2013 and 2014. Singapore, Thailand and Malaysia were the largest investors, but Vietnam has also become a sizeable investor starting in 2012 in real estate. In 2014, 43 Singaporean projects were approved and 11 projects by Thai investors.

In the changing pattern of FDI since 2013, the most remarkable feature is the sizeable reduction in FDI from China from US$4.3 billion in 2011 to an average of about US$270 million over the past three years. This apparent decline in Chinese FDI can be explained by a number of reasons. First, the suspension by the Myanmar President's office of the construction on the large US$3.6 billion Chinese financed Myitsone dam in September 2011 has deeply affected Chinese confidence in financing large projects, particularly hydropower projects. Several of these projects, some quite controversial from a cultural and environmental point of view, are however still under consideration. Second, the Chinese investment in the large Letpadaung copper mine in the Sagaing region has faced major protests by local residents and has raised suspicions against Chinese investments. Finally, because of Chinese dominance of FDI in the past decades, the government has been pursuing a policy of greater diversification of sources of FDI since the reforms. China will no doubt remain a major foreign investor in energy and natural resources in Myanmar in the future but might take a lower profile than in the past.

It is evident from Table 9.3 that as the political and economic reforms started in 2011 deepened, Western economic and trade sanctions were lifted and confidence in the directions of the reforms grew, FDI approvals into Myanmar increased rapidly, representing about 12.7 per cent of GDP in 2014 and 49 per cent of gross capital formation. Sectors of activity targeted and countries of origin also diversified greatly. While the surge in approvals clearly reflects the interest of investors, only a fraction of approvals can be expected to translate into actual investments, and with some lag. Balance of payments data on foreign direct investment inflows shows more modest levels of inflows though on an upward trend since 2011. Actual FDI inflows based on UNCTAD data have increased from US$2.2 billion in 2012 to US$2.6 billion in 2013, and an estimate US$3.35 billion in 2014.

In the early years of trade and investment reforms, a surge in FDI approvals and realized FDI is not unusual. For instance, actual FDI in Vietnam rose to 49 per cent of total investment by 1994, only four years after the start of its main reforms (OECD 2014a) and reached US$1.945 billion. However maintaining high levels of FDI inflows proved more difficult, and by 2004, FDI felt to 11 per cent of investment — US$1.6 billion — before picking up again in the late years 2000 — amounting to an average of US$7–8 billion.

4. ASEAN AND MYANMAR'S FDI POTENTIAL

As the data shows, Myanmar offers major opportunities for foreign investors and in particular for investors from ASEAN countries. While the country benefits from unique features such as geographical location, land size, a large population and rich and diverse natural resources, to maintain and enhance its attractiveness for foreign investors, Myanmar needs to continue deepening its economic reform process and address the many impediments still negatively affecting FDI in the country. As a latecomer, the country can learn much from the experiences of others ASEAN countries while also catching new opportunities offered by digital technologies.

The institutional and policy issues affecting the investment climate in Myanmar are extensively discussed in two recent OECD reports (OECD 2014a and OECD 2014b). Not surprising after many years of isolation, the legal, regulatory and institutional environment for foreign investment often remains opaque and uncertain. The new Foreign Investment Law (FIL) enacted in 2012 together with its implementing regulations has contributed much to make foreign investment legally more secure. However, investment protection, criteria for approving investments, contracts enforcement and dispute settlements remain important areas where clarification and greater transparency is needed. The legal context for FDI remains very complex, partly because another law, the Myanmar Citizens Investment Law, defines the investment rights and privileges of Myanmar citizens. Many sectors are restricted or prohibited for foreign investment. In some cases, foreign investment approvals have to be secured both from line ministries as well as the Myanmar Investment Commission (MIC) which administers the FIL. The MIC itself exercises a lot of discretion in its approval of projects and on the conditions attached to individual projects. The OECD review notes that "flexibility comes at a cost" (OECD 2014*a*, p. 33). Overlapping administrative responsibilities are further complicated by a complex taxation system. The underdeveloped state of the financial system is also a serious obstacle to investment both domestic and foreign, and needs to be addressed. The limited opening of the banking system to foreign institutions in 2015 is however a positive step forward, but much remains to be done.

Land acquisition and use, and property rights are also major issues which negatively impact many potential investments. The availability of infrastructure, in particular power and transport, remains a major problem. While there has been much improvement over the past few years, particularly in telecommunications with the provision of operating licences to two major foreign providers, huge investment in physical and social infrastructure is needed to improve the business environment in Myanmar. Some of these investments such as in power generation can be provided in the form of private investment from operators in the region. To remedy the lack of infrastructure and jumpstart export-led industrialization, the government is developing three special economic zones (SEZs) — Thilawa, Dawei and Kyaukpyu — which will be administered under a new SEZ Law enacted in January 2014. It has also been reviewing the operation and administration of a number of former and new industrial parks spread across the country. The Thilawa SEZ is scheduled to become operational by the end of 2015.

As Myanmar expands and deepens its economic reforms over the next few years, it can learn much from the development experience of other ASEAN countries. In terms of size of the country and the economy, population and natural resources endowment, the experience of Vietnam appears however the most directly relevant. Vietnam at the beginning of its open-door policy and market-oriented transition in the early 1990s was in a situation similar to Myanmar today. Its industrial structure, mainly state-owned, was outdated, its economic policy-making institutions were very weak and its legal system hardly existing. Moreover the country was deeply indebted. Yet the country very rapidly managed to attract substantial amounts of FDI mainly in the manufacturing sector. In terms of GDP, FDI amounted to 9.6 per cent annually from 1994 to 1997. FDI slowed considerably after the 1997 Asian financial crisis but revived in the mid-2000s to 8–9 per cent of GDP and remained at 5–6 per cent of GDP in the past five years. As a result, Vietnam GDP expanded at an average rate of about 7.5 per cent over the past two decades.

For Myanmar, a few key factors in Vietnam's early development experience are worth highlighting. First, very early on, the government managed a major transformation in agriculture which rapidly raised rural income. This was done by ensuring secure land ownership and use for farming and rural households, allowing functioning markets in agriculture, and providing basic infrastructure and support services (Van Arkadie and Mallon 2003). The importance of secure access to land and its use must be emphasized. In the case of Myanmar, the availability of vast areas of unused land opens also the possibility of foreign investment in commercial land farming e.g. for sugarcane production. Second, from 1993 onwards, the Vietnamese government ensured a predictable and stable macroeconomic policy environment, with moderate inflation and a stable exchange rate. Third, the government enacted several new laws governing business entities. The Enterprise Law enacted in January 2000 was, for instance, one of the main laws guiding the incorporation of all enterprises including state-owned enterprise. Finally, while the Law on Foreign Investment was adopted in 1986, it was amended many times over subsequent years to improve "registration procedures, tax policies, rights to transfer abroad capital and foreign exchange, and access to land" (OECD 2014*a*). Eventually, by 2005, discrimination between domestic and foreign investment was eliminated and put under the same legal umbrella. Within ASEAN, Myanmar is the only country with separate laws governing domestic and foreign investment. The government is however finalizing the merger of the two laws. Vietnam's experience — as that of other Asian countries — shows that reforming the investment environment must a continuous process. The management of FDI approvals in Vietnam also entails many lessons for Myanmar. Currently, all FDI approvals in Myanmar are managed by the MIC which is composed of senior officials, including several Union ministers. The MIC has considerable discretionary powers. In Vietnam in the mid-1990s, the central government became overwhelmed by the large number of FDI requests to approve. Because of this, in many cases, greater attention was given to larger projects, discriminating against sometimes better smaller ones. Concrete approval criteria together with the decentralization of procedures were progressively introduced to improve and accelerate approval decisions.

As Myanmar is presently seeking to do, Vietnam in the 1990s also developed many industrial parks and special economic zones to attract mainly regional investors initially in low-cost labour-intensive export industries (Van Arkadie and Mallon 2003). In some cases, parks were created mainly to produce goods for the domestic market by companies such as Daewoo. The government committed resources to provide supporting infrastructure. While the development of many industrial parks and economic zones in Vietnam was highly successful and together account for a sizeable share of industry and exports, many parks also showed mixed results and some are almost empty (GRIPS Development Forum 2003). There is much experience in this area both inside and outside of Asia which Myanmar can look at. Rather than having a proliferation of industrial zones, international experience shows that attracting foreign investors into strategically located urban industrial zones with favourable conditions for clustering, innovation and integration into global value chains has the best chance of success (Yusuf and Kudo 2015). Proximity to large urban centres favours agglomeration economies. The success of SEZs and industrial parks also depends on the capacity of the government to design an effective policy framework to clearly define their specific role and to implemented complementary policies. The successful industrial parks and economic zones in Vietnam are mostly located in the large urban areas around Ho Chi Minh City and Hanoi.

Vietnam's FDI-supported industrialization experience clearly holds valuable lessons for Myanmar as the country continues with its reforms. As shown by the Vietnamese experience, maintaining high levels of foreign direct investments requires however constant improvements in the investment environment, protection of investors and equal treatment of foreign and domestic investors. By doing so, Myanmar can expect to benefit from a twenty-first century form of the Asian "flying geese" model, and benefit from the huge potential for structural change and technological catch-up to accelerate growth (ADB 2014). Compared to Vietnam two and a half decades ago, huge advances in information and communications technologies will also allow Myanmar to leapfrog stages of development (McKinsey 2013). At the same time, much deeper regional integration within Asia in general and ASEAN in particular as well as rising labour and production costs across Asia, and mainly in China, should also work in Myanmar's advantage.

In the past few years, a number of studies have been undertaken on the long-term growth prospects of Myanmar (ADBI 2014; McKinsey 2013; IMF 2014; ADB 2014. Most studies estimate GDP growth to average around

8 per cent between 2010 and 2030, and GDP per capita to quadruple by 2030. Comparing the growth performance of a number of Asian countries in the period following major economic reforms, the IMF projects average GDP growth up to 2033 at 7 per cent. Cambodia (1993–2012), Vietnam (1988–2007) and Thailand (1980–96) respectively sustained average growth of 7.7 per cent, 7.2 per cent and 8.0 per cent during their economic transformation periods. China's economy expanded by 10 per cent between 1982 and 2002. Given Myanmar's low population growth, a more rapid shift in employment to sectors with high productivity growth will be required, thus also leading to more rapid urbanization as typically larger urban centers favour agglomeration of industries and the creation of industry clusters, and create the best conditions for attracting foreign invested firms with links to global value chains (GVCs) (Yusuf and Kudo 2015).

The McKinsey study also highlights rapid urbanization and estimates that Myanmar's labour productivity needs to grow at an annual rate of at least 7 per cent, similar to that achieved by China from 1994 to 2006 or Thailand from 1982 to 1995. The investment to GDP ratio should to rise to an average of 30 per cent, amounting by 2030 to a total of US$650 billion of which, given the projected savings rate, at least US$100 billion would be in the form of FDI. Provided the regulatory framework for investment is much improved as discussed above, Myanmar should be able to easily mobilize such amount of FDI.

A recent study by the Asian Development Bank confirms the above results and highlights the importance of FDI over the next few decades (ADB 2014). Using a single-country computable general equilibrium (CGE) model (ADB 2014, Appendix 2), the ADB study tests a scenario where FDI inflows increase to 6 per cent of GDP by 2020 and stay at that level up to 2030. Such high FDI scenario would result in average growth of 9.5 per cent from 2010 to 2030.

Looking at the development experience of some of the other ASEAN countries and the many advantages of Myanmar, FDI reaching 6 per cent of GDP is quite achievable. Although there were substantial fluctuations due to financial crises such as the 1997 Asian financial crisis and the 2007–08 global financial crisis, FDI to ASEAN amounted to about 4–6 per cent of GDP over the past two decades (World Bank 2014). Already since 2012, actual FDI inflows into Myanmar accounted for 4–5 per cent of GDP. Currently, IMF projections to 2018 estimate FDI reaching somewhat over 5 per cent of GDP starting in 2014 (IMF 2014). Such high FDI scenario would amount to total FDI of about US$165 billion between 2010 and 2030, somewhat higher than the McKinsey study estimate.

To attract such large FDI, Myanmar needs to position itself to benefit from a third wave of industry relocations where many industries which relocated over the past two and a half decades from the NIEs and Japan to China, Vietnam and other ASEAN countries relocate again to Myanmar due to rising labour and other operating costs in their current location. In addition to lower labour costs, these industries can also tap the growing relatively large Myanmar domestic market as they did in Vietnam for instance over two decades ago. They can also benefit from Myanmar's location advantages for exports and from its vast natural resources.

5. ASEAN FDI AND MYANMAR: SECTOR POTENTIAL

The changes that are happening in Myanmar since the political and economic reforms started in 2011 will have a profound impact on how ASEAN evolves over the next few decades (ADBI 2014). The main impact will no doubt be on a new frontier opening for ASEAN FDI within its own borders. For ASEAN firms, besides providing an expanded market, the opening of Myanmar will offer major FDI opportunities enabling them to strengthen their value chains, achieve significant productivity gains and enhance their competitiveness. Recent FDI data from ASEAN shows the beginning of these changes, for instance with significant investments by Singapore and Thai firms in the manufacturing, hotels, tourism and real estate and by Vietnamese firms in real estate. Banks from Singapore, Malaysia and Thailand have also been given limited licences to operate. Looking forward, most sectors of the economy will be attractive to ASEAN investors (Oxford Business Group 2014; OECD 2014b).

Energy and Mining: Given the large unexplored offshore and onshore areas, exploration and production facilities for oil and natural gas will continue to provide major FDI opportunities. Already a number of ASEAN companies have been allocated exploration blocks in recent rounds of auctioning. In the energy sector also, the development of thermal and hydropower projects will be very attractive for ASEAN investors, particularly from Thailand. Finally, in spite of strong competition from China, the mining sector offers good prospects for FDI although foreign investors need special authorization to be involved in mining.

Agriculture and fisheries: While there are major opportunities for contract farming from ASEAN firms, in particular from Thailand, the FDI opportunities in agriculture and in fisheries reside mainly in the downstream high value-added agro-industries and processing (Wong 2015). Myanmar offers huge potential in agriculture. Importantly, being a least developed country (LDC), Myanmar has preferential access to large markets such as the EU for its agricultural and fisheries products.

Manufacturing: With relatively low labour costs, the country has a comparative advantage in labour-intensive manufacturing sectors. This opens a unique opportunity for ASEAN firms to invest and relocate some of their more labour-intensive industries in a country close to home and as part of the AEC "single market and production base". In some ways the changes in Myanmar can be compared to the earlier EU expansion in Eastern European countries. In the first phase, industries targeted at the fast-growing domestic market together with export potential will see significant ASEAN investment. These include sectors such as food and beverages, garments and textiles, leather, footwear, furniture, wood products, toys and rubber and plastic products (McKinsey 2013). Given Myanmar's natural resources, several other manufacturing areas are also very attractive to ASEAN FDI such as the jewellery industry. As happened in other ASEAN countries, Myanmar will progressively move to higher value-added manufacturing industries, probably faster than other ASEAN countries earlier in their stage of development, partly as a result of the AEC which gives the country a better opportunity to enter regional and global value chains. The development of large SEZs such as Thilawa, Kyaukpyu and Dawei, as well as several border area industrial zones along the Thai-Myanmar border will also attract progressively higher value-added industries. Already several investments in automotive assembly plants have been realized or are planned. These will be linked to the automobile industry in Thailand. FDI from other ASEAN countries in machinery, electrical and communications equipment and the petrochemical industry are envisaged. As the more advanced ASEAN countries move up the value chain and focus more on innovation and research, Myanmar will benefit from the relocation of some of their more mature industries (DICA 2014). Finally, Myanmar is keen to pursue an industrialization strategy based on the development of its SMEs. This will provide ASEAN SMEs with major opportunities to partner with Myanmar SMEs.

Infrastructure: To support a high growth and industrialization strategy, Myanmar needs to vastly improve its infrastructure in all areas including road, rail, air and maritime transport, power, telecommunications, and water and sanitation. As high growth will also lead to rapid urbanization, urban infrastructure needs to be substantially improved. While most of the infrastructure will be developed by the government with the support of development partners, the opportunities for the private sector including FDI financing will be huge. In the transport area, ports and airports can be developed or upgraded through BOTs or similar arrangements. A recent example is the development of the new Yangon airport at Hanthawaddy which was awarded in 2014 to a Singapore-Japanese consortium under a thirty-year concession. The total investment is estimate at US$1.5 billion. In the telecommunications sector, already two international mobile operators, Telenor and Oredoo, have been awarded concessions in 2014. The area where FDI opportunities in infrastructure are probably the greatest is in power generation. Currently installed capacity is only about 3,735 MW, comparable to Thailand in 1981. Only about 30 per cent of the population has access to power. It is estimated that for the economy to grow by about 8 per cent over the next 15 years, total power generation for the domestic market has to reach 24,000 MW by 2030 (Verbiest 2014). In hydropower alone, Myanmar has identified 44 large projects for development with a total capacity of 41,276 MW. As in the case of Laos, electricity exports could become a major export sector for Myanmar.

Social Infrastructure: Given the low level of human resources development and the lack of investments over the past five decades in education and health, substantial financing is needed in these sectors, with the public sector playing an important role. Even though public expenditures have already been increased substantially over the past two years, the required investments to improve the level of education and the state of the health sector are huge. FDI and partnering with renowned foreign providers offer an opportunity to catch up in these key areas. In both cases, ASEAN countries can bring financing and the expertise needed. Already several Thai health providers have opened facilities in Myanmar.

Services: The liberalization of the services sector has been relatively slow under the AEC. Nevertheless manufacturing and financial services attracted 32 and 21 per cent respectively of all FDI in ASEAN since

2000 (World Bank 2014). There are however wide variations among the countries. The opening of the services sectors to FDI is at an initial stage in Myanmar. Besides trade services, much of Myanmar's services sector is highly underdeveloped, including financial services. Progressive opening of some of the services sectors is happening. As mentioned, the telecommunication sector has already attracted major FDI. Nine international banks including four ASEAN banks were provided a limited operating licence in September 2014, and this is most likely a first step in further opening the sector, possibly through joint ventures with local banks. Finally, the insurance sector is expected to be opened soon to foreign investors.

Tourism and Real Estate: As FDI inflows increase and the country opens, the number of expatriates living in Myanmar is fast rising and the demand for quality accommodation and office space has been growing rapidly and is expected to remain strong over the next two decades. At the same time, tourist arrivals have also been growing very fast. Forecasts are for well over 7 million arrivals by 2020 and double that by 2030, up from 3 million in 2014 (ADB 2014; Ministry of Hotels and Tourism 2014). Myanmar's tourism potential is indeed huge. The fast rise in tourism is severely stretching the country's hotel capacity and other tourist facilities, and will continue to do so over the years to come. Myanmar thus offers major FDI opportunities for ASEAN property and hotel development and management firms.

6. CONCLUSION

The political and economic reforms in Myanmar and the opening of the country to trade and investment is a major landmark in the economic development of Southeast Asia and indeed of Asia as a whole. Myanmar until 2011 was the "missing link" in the economy of Asia. For ASEAN, the return of Myanmar to the international community is a major historical event, coming just as the AEC is entering into effect. The reforms in Myanmar will allow the AEC to be fully realized and provide an opportunity for the ASEAN economy as a whole to sustain a higher growth path. In this process, FDI from ASEAN countries in the agriculture, manufacturing, services sectors of Myanmar will play a key role over the next two decades. At the same time, Myanmar's energy resources including natural gas and hydropower will contribute significantly to ASEAN's energy security.

While the potential for a major expansion of ASEAN FDI flows to the country are real, they cannot be taken for granted. On the part of the Myanmar government, reforms will have to continue and be vigorously pursued in the administrative, legal, taxation, institutional and governance areas. The rule of law, developing a level playing field for foreign businesses, addressing the high costs of doing business and combating corruption are all important factors to attract responsible quality foreign investment. Several recent studies have highlighted the main reform areas (ADB 2014; OECD 2014; OECD 2013; McKinsey 2013). While the government has put in place broad development objectives under the FESR and the National Comprehensive Development Plan, it needs to complement these policy documents with clearly articulated sector growth objectives and a corresponding investment strategy. An investment master plan could set the investment priorities and objectives over a certain time horizon — as done for instance in the 1980s with Eastern Seaboard plan of the Thai Government. At the same time, domestic regional priorities — at state and division levels — should be identified. Finally, there is a need to set clear rules on environmental and social impact assessments needed for projects.

Finally, on the part of ASEAN foreign investors, to be successful in Myanmar, it will be important to pursue responsible investment where labour rights, land use and the environmental impact of projects are carefully evaluated. Myanmar has strong civil society organizations which monitor investments closely. Responsible business conduct is particularly important in Myanmar, partly also because regulating public sector institutions often lack implementation capacity. So it is important for ASEAN businesses to follow a strict code of conduct (OECD 2014a).

References

Asian Development Bank. *Myanmar in transition: Opportunities and Challenges.* Mandaluyong City: Philippines: Asian Development Bank, 2012 <http://www.adb.org/publications/myanmar-transition-opportunities-and-challenges> (accessed 30 October 2014).
———. *Myanmar: Unlocking the Potential.* Mandaluyong City, Philippines: Asian Development Bank, 2014 <http://www.adb.org/publications/myanmar-unlocking-potential> (accessed 30 October 2014).

Asian Development Bank Institute. *ASEAN 2030: Towards a Borderless Economic Community*. Tokyo: Asian Development Bank Institute, 2014 <http://www.adb.org/publications/asean-2030-toward-borderless-economic-community-0> (accessed 29 October 2014).

Directorate of Investment and Company Administration (DICA). *The study on Long-Term Foreign Direct Investment Promotion Plan in Myanmar*. Mimeographed. DICA, Nay Pyi Taw, 2014.

Findlay, Ronald, Cyn-Young Park, and Jean-Pierre A. Verbiest. *Myanmar: Unlocking the Potential, A Strategy For High, Sustained, and Inclusive Growth*. Mandaluyong City, Philippines, ADB Economics Working Paper Series, No. 437, 2015 <http://www.adb.org/sites/default/files/publications/161904/ewp-437.pdf> (accessed 10 August 2015).

Ginsburg, Norton. *Atlas of Economic Development*. Chicago: University of Chicago Press, 1961.

International Monetary Fund. Myanmar: 2014 Article IV consultation- Staff Report. Washington, D.C.: IMF Country Report No. 14/307, 2014 <http://www.imf.org> (accessed 10 August 2015).

Jamieson, W. and S. Schipani. "Tourism Development Potential and Challenges in Myanmar". Mandaluyong City, Philippines: Asian Development Bank, Forthcoming, ADB Economics Working Paper Series, 2015.

Lim, H. and Yasuhiro Yamada. *Economic Reforms in Myanmar: Pathways and Prospects*. Bangkok: IDE-JETRO, Bangkok Research Center, 2013.

Masima, Pietro P. *Vietnam's Development Strategies*. Routledge, London and New York, 2006 <https://www.academia.edu/1476665/vietnams_development_strategies> (accessed 10 August 2015).

McKinsey Global Institute. *Myanmar's Moment: Unique Opportunities, Major Challenges*. New York: McKinsey & Company, 2013 <http://www.mckinsey.com/insights/asia-pacific/myanmars_moment> (accessed 10 October 2014).

Ministry of Hotels and Tourism. *Myanmar: Tourism Master Plan 2013–2020*. Nay Pyi Taw, 2013.

Ministry of National Planning and Economic Development. *Framework for Economic and Social Reforms 2012–2015*. Nay Pyi Taw, 2013.

Myanmar Times. "Offshore block winners announced". 26 March 2014.

National Graduate Institute of Policy Studies (GRIPS). Vietnam's Industrialization Strategy in the Age of Globalization. GRIPS Development Forum, Tokyo, 2003 <http://www.grips.ac.jp/forum/module/vietnam/main_en.pdf> (accessed 15 August 2015).

Organisation for Economic Co-operation and Development (OECD). *Multidimensional Review of Myanmar: Volume 1. Initial Assessment, OECD Development Pathways*. Paris, OECD Publishing, 2013 <http://dx.doi.org?10.1787/9789264202085-en> (accessed 10 October 2014).

———. *OECD Investment Policy Reviews: Myanmar 2014*. Paris: OECD Publishing,

2014a <http://dx.doi.org/10.1787/9789264206441-en> (accessed 10 October 2014).

———. *Multi-dimensional Review of Myanmar: Volume 2. In-Depth Analysis and Recommendations, OECD Development Pathways*. Paris, OECD Publishing, 2014b <http://dx.doi.org?10.1787/9789264220577-en> (accessed 10 August 2015).

Oxford Business Group. *The Report Myanmar 2014*. London, 2014.

Ozawa, T. *The (Japan-Born) "Flying-Geese" Theory of Economic Development Revisited-and Reformulated from a Structuralist Perspective*. New York: Columbia Business School, Center on Japanese Economy and Business, Working Paper Series No. 291, 2010 <http://academiccommons.columbia.edu/download/fedora_content/download/ac:129254/CONTENT/WP_291.pdf> (accessed 20 December 2014).

Radelet, S. and J. Sachs. "Asia's Reemergence". *Foreign Affairs* 76, no. 6 (1997): 44–59 <http://earthinstitute.columbia.edu/sitefiles/file/about/director/documents/ar97.pdf> (accessed 20 December 2014).

Thein, M. *Economic Development of Myanmar*. Singapore: Institute of Southeast Asian Studies, 2004.

Van Arkadie, B. and Ray Mallon. *Vietnam — a transition tiger?* Canberra: Australian National University, Asia Pacific Press, 2003.

Verbiest, Jean-Pierre A. "Myanmar: An Emerging ASEAN Energy Giant?". Paper presented at the SciencesPo-CERI Colloque on "ASEAN's Energy Security Challenges", Paris, 2014 <http://www.sciencespo.fr/ceri/fr/content/dossiersduceri/asean-s-energy-security-challenges> (accessed 10 August 2015).

Wong, Larry. "Myanmar: Agriculture and Rural Development". Background paper for study "Myanmar: Unlocking the Potential". Mandaluyong City, Philippines. Forthcoming ADB Economics Working Paper Series, Manila, 2015.

World Bank. *East Asia Pacific Economic Update: Preserving Stability and Promoting Growth*. Washington, D.C., April 2014 <http://www.worldbank.org/content/dam/worldbank/document/region/eap-update-april-2014-full-report-pdf> (accessed 10 October 2014).

Yusuf, S. and T. Kudo. "SME Cluster Based Development in Myanmar". Background paper for study "Myanmar: Unlocking the Potential". Mandaluyong City, Philippines. Forthcoming ADB Economics Working Paper Series, 2015.

INDEX

Note: Page number followed by "n" refer to endnotes

www.ingramcontent.com/pod-product-compliance
Lightning Source LLC
Chambersburg PA
CBHW060359220326
41598CB00023B/2964